ISSUES IN THE JEWISH-CHRISTIAN DIALOGUE: JEWISH PERSPECTIVES ON COVENANT, MISSION AND WITNESS

Studies in Judaism and Christianity

Exploration of issues in the contemporary dialogue between Christians and Jews.

Editors

Lawrence Boadt, C.S.P.
Helga Croner
Leon Klenicki
Kevin A. Lynch, C.S.P.

ISSUES IN THE
JEWISH-CHRISTIAN DIALOGUE:

Jewish Perspectives on Covenant, Mission and Witness

Edited by

**Helga Croner
and
Leon Klenicki**

A Stimulus Book

Paulist Press • New York • Ramsey

Acknowledgments

Selections from THE TIGER BENEATH THE SKIN by Zvi Kolitz, copyright 1947 by Creative Age Press, Inc. (now a division of Farrar, Straus & Giroux, Inc.), copyright renewed 1975 by Zvi Kolitz, are reprinted with the permission of Farrar, Straus & Giroux, Inc.

A selection from NIGHT by Elie Wiesel, translated from the French by Stella Rodway, © Les Editions De Minuit, 1958, English translation © Mac Gibbon & Kee, 1960, is reprinted with the permission of Hill and Wang (now a division of Farrar, Straus & Giroux, Inc.).

A selection from JUDAISM AS A CIVILIZATION by Mordecai M. Kaplan is reprinted by permission of the Jewish Reconstructionist Foundation.

A selection reprinted from THE GUIDE TO THE PERPLEXED by Moses Maimonides, translated by Shlomo Pines is reprinted by permission of The University of Chicago Press, copyright © 1963.

Library of Congress
Catalog Card Number: 79-88933

ISBN: 0-8091-2238-3

BM
612.5
J85 | 30,913

Published by Paulist Press
Editorial Office: 1865 Broadway, New York, N.Y. 10023
Business Office: 545 Island Road, Ramsey, N.J. 07446

Printed and bound in the
United States of America

Contents

Abbreviations

CCAR   Central Conference of American Rabbis
HUC-JIR   Hebrew Union College-Jewish Institute of Religion
JTSA   Jewish Theological Seminary of America
TB   Babylonian Talmud
TJ   Talmud of Jerusalem (Palestinian)

Hebrew Terms

akedah Yitzchak	binding of Isaac
berit	circumcision, covenant, agreement
ed	witness
El, Elohim	God
haggadah	narration
hakham	wiseman
halakha	(*halakh* = to go) a way to go; a way of being, translated into customs, ritual and prayer
hasid	pious one
hohmat	knowledge
kavanah	single-mindedness (toward *halakha* and prayer)
kiyyum ha-mitzvah	internalization of the precept
lishma	right intention (toward *halakha)*
malkhut	kingdom (of God)
middot	the thirteen qualities of God
mitzvah	precept
ol malkhut Shamayim	yoke of the kingdom of Heaven
olam	world
peulat ha-mitzvah	performance of the precept
shoah	devastation, the Holocaust
Tanakh	Hebrew Scriptures
Yamim Noraim	Days of Awe
zadik	righteous one
zelem	image
zerizut	eagerness (toward *halakha)*

Foreword

This volume of STIMULUS BOOKS addresses itself to some of the basic issues of the Jewish-Christian dialogue, raised by the various statements of Christian churches that have been published over the last several years. More than that: This book presents the reaction of some Jewish scholars to problems of our day that move and impel them to speak their mind. The Editors hope to offer with this volume a representative picture of contemporary Jewish thought as well as to indicate new dimensions for the interreligious dialogue.

The essays in this volume are original, copyrighted material that has not been published elsewhere. An overlapping of topics and of some of the literature adduced was not only unavoidable but actually welcomed by the Editors. With the help of the index provided, the reader will be able to attain an insight into the subject matter as it is treated by Jewish scholars of the various branches of Judaism.

The relevant Christian documents are collected in volume I of this Series, under the title *Stepping Stones to Further Jewish-Christian Relations:* An Unabridged Collection of Christian Documents.

Helga Croner

Introduction:
The Language We Speak

Leon Klenicki

> Once man becomes aware of his epistemological nakedness, God Himself must help him to fashion a conceptual garment.[1]

The religious Jewish experience is a vital, unique process-phenomenon involving the very essence of being, the very meaning of existence. It implicates God—creator, liberator, partner of a sacred alliance—and a people of individuals committed to witness the covenantal relationship. The awareness of God's word and action denote a transformation of the self. To the moment when God is present, the Jewish person responds with a specific conduct, a way of being, a *halakha* that translates into action the encounter with God. That constitutes praxis: the individual's and community's committed actualization of God's word and religious experience into prayer, ritual, customs, and ethical action. Praxis is the living experience of God.

Israel—individuals and the community at large—has answered to the signs of revelation in different ways that have shaped Jews and Judaism for centuries. The response to God is always the beginning of a way of life, for which there are different times.

There are times of silence.

In the very beginning there was a call: God addressed and summoned Abraham. The call changed the patriarch's life; he would leave the daily framework of his life-style, his country, his birthplace, his father's house, for an unknown place, a yet unknown spiritual commitment. The divine command implied a certain way of searching for ultimate reality. It started at the periphery and ended at the heart of Jewish being. A classical biblical commentary, *Haketav Ve Hakkabalah*,[2] suggests that Genesis 12 refers to a spiritual rather than physical withdrawal entailing stages, as in a mystical experience, each one preparing for a deeper understanding at the next stage.

The laconic biblical text does not give any intimate detail of the inner life of Abraham. The verses hint at a deep transformation reflected in the change of name, from Abram to Abraham, and the setting up of an altar to offer sacrifices. In that society, the change of name meant a true break with reality, the state, the family, a giving up of the comforts and security linked to the identification by name that was and is even today so important a part of Middle East culture.

Abraham responded not by word but by an active, committed silence. He does not suspend language, his is a creative, silent response:

> Silence is an autonomous phenomenon. It is therefore not identical with the suspension of language. It is not merely the negative condition that sets in when the positive is removed; it is rather an independent whole, subsisting in and through itself. It is creative, as language is creative; and it is formative of human beings as language is formative, but not in the same degree. Silence belongs to the basic structure of man.[3]

There are times of rebellion.

This is best exemplified in the figure of the prophet Jonah. He is called to action, to save a people of destruction, to witness in a foreign land. God's command is not answered by action but by a denial. Jonah abandons his place, his milieu, to avoid his destiny, a call to vocation. He finally realizes his obligation, the need to respond to revelation, and he goes to Niniveh.

There are times of exile and return.

The Babylonian exile was a shattering event. The community felt lost, without hope, without future. The people tried to understand the reasons for the disaster, the possible meaning of their punishment. Their questioning was deeply touched by the inquiry about God, His presence in exile. Was it possible to worship God outside the familiar skies, outside of Jerusalem? National life was in crisis, at a turning point, not in decadence, which would become a constant feature in Jewish history through the centuries. It is a moment of doubt, of reflection, which is followed by an answer to the historical challenge. The crisis crushes the foundations but does not stall the process of responding creatively. Exile and the challenge of return to the Promised Land brought about a response and a praxis that were to be expounded for nearly eight centuries. It was the rabbinic response of explication and commentary of the Written Law, the biblical text as it related to daily life and community endeavor. The word of God became, once again, a form of practice, individual and community action.

Simon Rawidowicz refers to this special, unique dimension of Jewish spirituality:

> Interpretation lives by crisis, in various degrees. The crisis that stimulates it will become its criterion. Interpretation can be characterized by a particular attitude of the interpreter who struggles between preserving and rejecting some forms or content of the world at his interpretative "mercy"; by a tension between continuation and rebellion, tradition and innovation. It derives its strength both from a deep attachment to the "text" and from an "alienation" from it, a certain distance, a gap which has to be bridged. Interpretation is the "way out" when man is compelled to "take it" or "break it." Many a battle was fought and lost in the battle for interpretation. And the battle goes on and will go on as long as *homo* is *interpres.*[4]

The biblical text is the ground of being that requires an expansion, a way of relating it to the life perspectives of the individual. The encounter with God imposes a re-living of the revelatory situation and the total fulfillment of the commandments. The community is asked "to observe and keep the Shabbath" (Ex 17:12-17), with no specific details of how to follow the biblical injunction.

The biblical text requires an explanation, a detailed explanation. God gave Israel a text to expound, to make it and its explanation a reality in practice and commitment. Time and space become a sacred experience through the power of the textual interpretation:

> Explication and commentary follow the text step by step, "uncover" and explain it from the aspect of its form and content, language and historical background. Interpretation is centered on the "soul" of the text, its leitmotif, its main purpose, its essence, its particular character. Interpretation assumes that there is a hidden layer both in the "form" and the "content" of the document to be interpreted; this "hidden" needs uncovering. There is mystery between the words and between the lines, that which the document ought to have said and did not say, either because it could not say (for various reasons) or it did not want to say— this is it which intrigues the interpreter, who will naturally dig in the

hidden layers of the "text." He wants to make the implicit in the text explicit, to "spell out" that which is implied. . . .

Modern man is often surprised at and makes fun of the older, classical or medieval interpretations—in religious, visual arts and literature. He does not realize how much his own system of understanding, research, evaluation, appreciation of arts, all his creativity is interpretation. When in an adequately critical frame of mind, he avoids the pitfalls of older interpretation, only to fall into new ones, made by him and his time. . . . Interpretation worthy of its name—when reaching some measure of perfection—is a revolution from within, planned and executed by insiders with the purpose of reshaping their "home," without any pressure (or any decisive pressure) from outside, disregarding adjustment to the outside.[5]

The actualization of the Written Law is the creative realm of the Oral Law, the expounded text of the biblical word. The rabbis expressed this "revolution from within"[6] in a literature compiled through centuries of interpretation and adaptation, in the Mishnah, Midrash, the Jerusalem Talmud and Babylonian Talmud.

The thinking of the rabbis reflected two levels of religious existence. One is *halakha* or the domain of commandment, ritual, and custom. It is represented in the Mishnah and the Talmud, pure examples of praxis, of religiosity in action, of living experience. The other level is the existential dimension of the God-person-community relationship, the midrashic and aggadic explanations that attempt to expound the literary sections of the Bible in all their paradoxes, difficulties of expression and nuances. It is an existential explanation of very human events and projections of the Bible.

*There are times of an inner thirst for God
in the search for a meaning of words.*

The rabbinic method of interpretation, rabbinic halakhic ideology, was the way in which Judaism for many centuries found expression. It was practically the only expression of Jewish religious life up to modern times. The Industrial Revolution, along with a change in social structures, brought about a new understanding of life that challenged religion in all its forms and manifestations. The strict rule of religion, theology as the queen of sciences, broke down under the impact of social change which considered science and culture a way of life. Salvation was seen, and still is quite often in our day, as a part of social transformation and a scientific miracle.

Judaism was not immune to the challenge and change of modern times. Their impact was felt in the division and growth of the three religious branches, Orthodoxy, Conservatism, and Reform, and the manner each of them considered *halakha* and its relationship to society and change. The religious being, once again, was replying to history.

Judaism as spiritual expression in all its religious forms, suffered an either-or confrontation in the 20th century. The crisis, still a visible reality in Jewish life, is part of the crisis situation that all religious people are experiencing, at a time that has witnessed total destruction—the Holocaust—and the renewal of hope—the creation of the state of Israel.

Judaism has suffered the loneliness of total exile. The experience of Auschwitz has caused a questioning in fear and trembling: Why the silence of God in the midst of horror and destruction? Why the eclipse of God's mercy toward His people? The inquiry touches both Christians and Jews. It is part of a reckoning of the soul and, especially after the Second Vatican Council, has generated questions about the impact of two thousand years of a moral and ethical commitment in the heart of a Europe that invented gas chambers and mass killings. Have we Jews and Christians been totally faithful to our ethical commitment? Have we witnessed Sinai and Golgotha in the midst of horror? The questions are still to be answered. In Judaism the response is an attempt to face and cope with the confrontation of destruction and renewal. Tradition forms the ground, the roots of existence, but the search is open to new perspectives, to a theological inquiry sensitive to the spiritual achievements of contemporary man.

The very word "theology" requires an analytical clarification in order to avoid the prejudice of centuries past. Theological exercise has not been a traditional discipline in Judaism. The term itself meets with suspicion, for historical connotations were not necessarily related to the science of God. Medieval disputations, the sad reality of the Inquisition, and the typological imperialism of Christianity in confronting Judaism have left distrust, a sad experience for Jews.

But theological inquiry has not been foreign to Jewish thinkers. Theological *summae* have generally appeared at times of crisis. Examples of this reality are Maimonides' (1135-1204), *The Guide of the Perplexed*, facing the impact on Judaism of Greek and Arabic thinking; the *Sepher Ikkarim* (Book of Principles) by Joseph Albo (d. 1140), responding to the Disputations; or Hermann Cohen's *summa* on the influence of idealism and Kantian thought.[7]

Theology is a response, a reflection, a sounding out of ideas in close relation to life and its requirements. Shubert Spero has pointed out the question quite clearly:

> One is doing theology as soon as one becomes reflective about one's religious beliefs and puts into words either for one's own benefit or in order to communicate to others what it is that one believes in or why one is engaged in certain religious practices.[8]

Theology is a demand for justification at a time of doubt but, essentially, a thinking process analyzing the "implications of the Jewish religion."[9] Jewish theology has a vocation of its own:

> The (Jewish) theologian is embarked on the more difficult task of discovering what it is that a Jew can believe in the present.[10]

The present collection of essays represents the reflective response of a group of religious persons deeply concerned about Jewish faith and commitment in our time. This preoccupation is mirrored in the search for new meanings, new interpretations that will give to Jewish life the dimension of a living faith. The authors look into our tradition and at the spiritual tools of our time, in search of meaning and of a language to express that meaning.

This book deals with two aspects of Jewish theological thought, "Covenant" and the question of "Witness and Mission." In the first section, Leonard Kravitz examines the meaning and dimensions of the term covenant. He clarifies the very terminology he uses, the idea of covenant, and the different kinds of covenant in the Bible. Particular attention is paid to the philosophical approach through the centuries, from the medieval period to the search of Martin Buber and Franz Rosenzweig. Kravitz finally considers the contemporary historical experience, especially the American pluralistic impact, the formulation of a covenant theology as a response to the "rationalistic approach of much of Reform Judaism in America and partly in response to the horrors of the Holocaust."

Elliot Dorff conveys an understanding of the meaning of covenant to two contemporary Jewish thinkers. He distinguishes between the objectivist point of view, that of Mordecai M. Kaplan; and the existentialist approach, the philosophy of Hermann Cohen. The 20th century has witnessed a return to empiricism, "adding new formulations such as pragmatism, naturalism, and linguistic analysis." The concept of God is a search for new levels of understanding beyond the classical theism of the

century

Bible and rabbinic theology. As defined by Kaplan, God is "the power that makes for salvation," expressed in a covenantal experience that is to work towards an ethical commitment, reflected in the community and national endeavor of Judaism. Hermann Cohen, explains Dorff, emphasizes the experience of the individual, specifically his ethical experience of religion. This existentialist approach was initiated by the German philosopher, a neo-Kantian and leader of the so-called Marburg school.

The covenant in its Sinaitic, biblical, and halakhic-rabbinic dimensions is treated by Manfred Vogel in relation to other faith commitments, Christianity in particular. The author studies the relationship of Tanakh and New Testament, the question of universalism versus particularism, as well as the "abrogation" idea. He expounds on Judaism and Christianity as covenants directed to specific groups, pointing out that the "only difference between the two covenants is with regard to the question of who is being addressed by the covenant. While the old covenant addresses the people of Israel, the new covenant addresses the gentile nations of the world—but the content of the address is the same in both covenants."

The second part of this volume is devoted to an analysis of "Witness and Mission" in our time, after the death experience of the Holocaust and the experience of resurrection expressed in American Jewish life and the realization of a messianic dream, the creation of the state of Israel. A definition of witness in terms of Jewish classical sources is made by Ben Zion Bokser. He defines these terms in biblical and rabbinic dimensions. His comments on Rav Kook will contribute to making known the ideas of the former chief rabbi of Palestine, before the creation of the state of Israel.

Leon Stitskin, of blessed memory, was a brilliant mind whose contributions to the knowledge of medieval Jewish philosophical sources have helped Jews and Christians to become acquainted with writers and schools crucial to the understanding of the philosopical development of Judaism. But Stitskin's major contribution was the idea of personalism to which he devoted his last published book, *Jewish Philosophy, A Study in Personalism*. Stitskin expounds in the present study on the personalistic meaning of witness as "the existential stance of each individual in his relationship with God,"that derives "from one's experimental reality and existential condition."

The religious experience is seen phenomenologically by Stitskin, in its various nuances of personal life—particularly, the ethical and spiritual—and expressing the fulfillment of the *mitzvot* as a means to an end: the testimony of witness to God in the personal dimension of existence. Stitskin maintains that we will bear witness to God when we respond to

His challenge for self-authentication. This challenge was never so vivid and anguishing as in our days, especially after the Holocaust. The experience of evil, total and endless, is a mystery of Israel. Its significance will be a concern for generations, a concern also for any committed religious person. Auschwitz is the constant reminder of human failure after millennia of ethical commitment and religious testimony, both Jewish and Christian. It is also a beginning, the first stage of soul-reckoning.

Both Daniel Polish and Martin A. Cohen reckon in their studies with the significance of witnessing and mission after the Holocaust. Polish defines the concept of witness in regard to the *shoah* and asks if we dare make witness at all. The consideration of the *shoah* itself is a reckoning with past ideas, at times mere illusions that framed Jewish integration to western society, an apparently perfect state that was shattered by the German experience. Yet the Holocaust has not dried up Jewish experience; the image of the dry bones, Ez 37:1-14, once again becomes a reality. Polish emphasizes the Jewish witness after the Holocaust as a "recognition of the darker side of the world and human nature and the commitment to the life of the Jewish people." This commitment involves a recognition of God, despite the theological temptation of total denial or the search for new dimensions, new concepts of God, a spiritual operation that postpones the basic, difficult, anguishing fact of the encounter God-Jewish person beyond ideologies and dialectical games.

It is in a state of total desolation that Israel is asking about its mission, if any, after Auschwitz. Martin A. Cohen attempts to respond, after examining the thought of contemporary Jewish theologians concerned with the meaning of God and the *shoah*. Auschwitz has brought the "realization of the moral primitiveness of human civilization and the miraculous unassimilability of the Jew." The Holocaust meant the end of one time and the beginning of another. For the Jewish individual and community it is a renewal of mission, of witnessing God in a world with very special problems. That mission, rooted in the Wilderness Ethic, is directed to a universe agonizing over terracide, hunger, discrimination, and the dehumanization of civilization. This mission to the world is related to the inner mission of the Jewish people, to the existence and development of the state of Israel, to the Jews in Soviet countries, and to the search for meaningful theological thinking that makes tradition a way of life. Cohen points out that "in the face of Auschwitz, it is the mature mission of Israel to address the garden of life as did Akiba, to retain idealism, reject despair, and serve as a light and inspiration. In this way, above all, the people Israel can witness that God lives, and that where God lives, hope resides."

The contributors to this volume do not desire to look for, or create, a language to satisfy the fashionable whims of the moment, nor a vocabulary with mysterious, obscure meanings that hide the sincere search for God. This search reflects an open-hearted, totally committed, dramatic thirst for God. It is a process entailing a reckoning with the terms that have shaped Judaism for centuries. It is a trend to actualize God's commands towards a new *halakha* as well as an historical search that started because "traditions have no longer kept pace with the present and are no longer expressed as being unquestionably obvious."[11]

Jewish Perspectives on Covenant, Mission and Witness is a response in word and praxis, in the spirit of Rabbi Hiyya, a man of the last generation of Tannaim (3rd cent. CE):

> May it be Thy will
> oh Lord, our God
> that the study of Thy Torah be our proficiency,
> that our heart be not sorrowful
> nor our eyes be darkened.[12]

Notes

1. Shubert Spero, "Is There an Indigenous Jewish Theology?", in *Tradition*, vol. 9, nos. 1-2, Spring-Summer 1967, p. 49.

2. Cited in Nehama Leibowitz, *Studies in Bereshit (Genesis)*, (Jerusalem: World Zionist Organization, 1974), p. 113.

3. Max Picard, *The World of Silence* (South Bend: Gateway Editions, 1952) p. 15.

4. Simon Rawidowicz, "On Interpretation," in *American Academy for Jewish Research Proceedings*, vol. 26, 1957, p. 85.

5. *Ibid.*, pp. 86f.

6. *Ibid.*; cf. especially Ellis Rivkin, *A Hidden Revolution* (Nashville: Abingdon, 1978).

7. Hermann Cohen, *Religion of Reason out of the Sources of Judaism* (New York: Fredk. Ungar, 1972).

8. Shubert Spero, *op.cit.*, p. 53.

9. Louis Jacobs, *A Jewish Theology* (New York: Behrman House, 1973), p. 1.

10. *Ibid.*

11. Juergen Moltmann, *Hope and Planning* (New York: Harper & Row, 1971), p. 101.

12. TB *Berakhoth* 16b, cited in Meyer J. Perath, *Rabbinical Devotion, Prayers of the Jewish Sages* (Assen: Van Gorcum, 1964).

I. COVENANT

1.

The Covenant in Jewish Tradition:
Historical Considerations

Leonard Kravitz

To speak of the covenant under historical considerations, is to raise questions some of which are not easily answered. What do we mean by "considerations"? What do we mean by "historical"? What do we mean by "covenant"? Are we interested in the linguistic analysis of a word presented by a specific literature, are we interested in this word as it is related to other words in this literature, are we interested in this word as it is related to other literatures, are we studying the institutions generated by this word, are we concerned with the symbolic structures embodied by it, are we making a judgment as to the truth claim of relationships which the particular word and the specific literature proclaim? To raise these questions is not to answer them; it is to put the reader on notice that there is a difference in our "consideration," whether we approach our task as partisans or neutrals.

To approach our consideration "historically" is to face the double meaning of history: that which happened in the past and the record of that which happened in the past. The past and its record, alas, are not the same. Hence the question will be raised whether the claim embodied in "covenant" presents an historical datum or is merely an element in a literary tradition developed by a particular people which reflects what they thought happened.

Do we relate to that tradition "historically"? Do we accept the manner in which it presents itself as a source, accepting its own chronology? Or do we view it, as historical critics might, finding that which presents itself as chronologically first, in point of literary development may be chronologically last?

Is there an implicit assumption of development in our historical considerations? Do we expect that covenant and its related ideas, symbols, and institutions will undergo changes with the passage of time? Are we prepared to see the effect of a particular *Sitz im Leben* on a pattern of thinking? If so, what safeguards do we have against our own *Tendenz*, lest that which we anticipate be automatically that which we see?

For what purposes do we undertake this study? Are we looking for similarities among different religious traditions or are we attempting to explicate the unique quality of one particular tradition? Are we viewing religious traditions neutrally? Is such a neutrality possible?

Our reflection upon and our attempts to answer these and other questions will be the elements of any consideration which can truly be called "historical." It begins with methodological questions. A study of the covenant will begin with analytical questions as well.

1. The Idea of Covenant

However conceived, the term covenant contains an entailment of ideas which requires explication. Whether as covenant, part, treaty, or agreement[1], the arrangement assumes mutuality; both parties are aware of what it is that they are doing. So stated, it follows that the idea of God related to the idea of covenant is that of God as person, i.e., one who is conscious, who wills, and who communicates. Upon further reflection, it might be argued *pari passu* that the idea of God as person entails the idea of covenant; a God who could speak would be impotent without a people to listen, a God who could command would be less than God were there no one to obey His commands. Indeed, even the imposition of a covenant upon a recalcitrant people, suggested in the rabbinic midrash that God suspended Mount Sinai over the heads of the children of Israel to compel their acquiescence to the Law[2], is entailed in the idea of a personal God, a God mighty enough to impose His will. It would seem then that the personhood of God and covenant are correlative ideas.

From a more human point of view, the idea of covenant contains other entailments. Reports of divine-human covenants are to be found in specific religious literatures. It comes as no surprise that those who maintain, teach, and learn these literatures believe themselves to be the descendants of those with whom those covenants were made. Being a specific agreement at a particular time with a particular people, covenant carries with it the notion that God did not make a similar agreement with another people in the same manner nor at the same time as He made it with the forefathers of those maintaining the literature. If other literatures contain such a covenant, it is either rejected as false or, if partially accepted, held to be superseded by the covenant reported in the particular literature.

Hence particularity is an entailment of the idea of covenant; indeed, one might argue that they are correlative ideas, along with the idea of God as person. A God who makes a covenant makes it with a particular people at a particular time. Such a God may have a relationship with the cosmos and with all mankind; yet the very importance of the covenant is that the God of all has deigned to make it with this particular people, thus proclaiming their particular significance. This is the meaning of the midrash that suggests, had Israel at Sinai not accepted the Law, the world and all that is in it would have been returned to nothingness and void.[3] Conversely, even that covenant made with mankind, symbolized by the rainbow, that never again will there be a flood of destruction upon the earth is reported in the literature of a specific people (Gn 8:21f).

There is yet another human entailment in the idea of covenant; it is suggested in the phrase *mipnai hataeynu* or *peccatis nullis*. If a covenant is felt to have been made with God with the implied condition of providential care and if that care is not apparent, then the failure in performance cannot be ascribed to the divine partner, but rather to the human one. The people by their actions of commission or omission have sinned and because of their sins have suffered.

Thus the divine-human covenant in its relation to the good-and-evil phenomena of the world must have the provision that non-performance can only be one-sided. God to be God must perform. The refrain *mipnai hataeynu* is, paradoxically enough, the attempt to affirm the covenant—it is our failings, not His failure, that have caused our pain.

Even when the human failing is not manifest as in periods of persecution, it must be assumed. Hence, when in the liturgical poem *Eleh Ezkara*—which depicts the suffering of the sages and symbolically that of the Jewish people—the question is raised as to the untoward result of the observance of the Law, "Is this Torah and is such its reward?"[4], the answer is given that further questioning will bring the world back to its state of nothingness and void. The possibility of a moral order implicit in the divine-human covenant is preferable to the certainty of none.

We have then the interplay between the internal logic of an idea and the historical circumstances in which that idea develops. The covenant once made by an eternal, unchanging God will be felt to remain in force, no matter the vicissitudes of the people with whom that covenant was made. Once made with the "fathers," it is now incumbent upon the "sons"; they, in subsequent generations, are bound to the best of their abilities to do that which was intended by their "fathers" and by their fathers' God.

Thus covenant as an idea contains within it a "locking in" of the future. It is a past commitment whose reality is felt in the present and whose fulfillment touches generations yet unborn. As long as those generations see themselves related to their past, they are related to the covenant.

The Bible is the result of a people relating itself to its past. It is a selection of a larger, no longer extant literature. That which we have in the Hebrew Bible gives a particular view of the history of the Hebrew people. That which we read is more than history; it is sacred history, the story of the linkage of the human to the divine. Out of the records of the events surrounding the life of the Jewish people, the writers and redactors of the Bible created a drama; the *dramatis personae* are God and man, individuals and peoples. There is a scenario of divine and human interaction; the action moves now on a cosmic stage, now is expressed in an individual soliloquy, the focus of attention is now upon a people, now upon a family.

2. A Succession of Covenants

Once we understand the biblical narrative as reflecting divine and human interaction, we have assumed a covenantal relationship whether such is explicitly stated or not. In this manner, we may understand the story of the first man and the first woman: The creator God having molded a man and having built a woman sets the two within the garden which He had planted. The divine part of the covenant had been fulfilled; the needs of the primal pair had been met. Their responsibility to the relationship was to observe the simple prohibition of not eating of the tree of the knowledge of good and evil. In this they failed and were cast out of the garden of delight, going out to form through their children the beginning of the chain of human history.

The story of Noah focuses attention upon a family. God having given mankind a world to live in finds that world filled with violence. Man has lived not as man but as animal; men have not fulfilled the responsibility implicit in being created in the image of God. Their destruction by the flood is the necessary consequence. By preserving Noah and his family, God makes possible the continuation of the human story. An explicit covenant is made with these few upon whom all subsequent life will depend: Never again will there be a flood to destroy the earth and that which lives upon it.

The next covenant presented by the Bible is made with Abraham: Its form is both implicit and explicit. Abraham is told to leave kith and kin and go out into the wilderness. In consequence he is promised that he will become a great nation; through him shall all the nations of the earth be blessed. In the explicit covenant between the "pieces," Abraham is promised the land of Israel while being informed of what will happen to his descendants in the future. In yet another explicit covenant, Abraham is promised perfection and is commanded to undergo circumcision. That rite will be for Abraham's descendants, so that for them the word *berit* will suggest circumcision as much as covenant.

Berit as a mere agreement among men will be found in the report of Isaac's making a *berit* with Abimelech. Even so, there will be a divine aspect to that covenant: Isaac's dwelling in Abimelech's domain is linked to the fulfillment of a divine promise of progeny as numerous as the stars—through his seed too would all the nations of the world be blessed.

When Jacob, Isaac's son, left his home to escape from the wrath of his brother Esau, he (or the biblical writer) presented a divine-human covenant. Said Jacob, if God would provide him with food to eat and raiment to wear and if He would watch him in the way that he was going, then "the Lord would be his God" (Gn 28:21). On Jacob's part, were the conditions met, he would give a tithe of all that he possessed.

To act out the divine scenario, Jacob's sons sell one of their number, Joseph, into Egyptian captivity. As the plot unfolds, Joseph moves from prison house to palace, from slave to second to Pharaoh. Moved by famine, Joseph's brothers and then his father go down to Egypt, that they may play their part in the divine plan: Their children and their children's children are to increase in number in the four hundred years of the Egyptian sojourn foretold to Abraham, so that from the sons of Jacob may emerge the sixty myriads of the children of Israel who will be enslaved.

To fulfill the covenant made with Abraham, a new leader, Moses, is called. Like Abraham, he is called to his task in the wilderness. Like Abraham, he is a shepherd; later legend might embellish that fact to suggest that it was his kind qualities as shepherd that made Moses worthy of being the leader of the children of Israel. A burning bush that was not consumed was the symbol of the continuation of the covenant amidst the flames of suffering. A further sign is given: When God will bring forth the people from their bondage, they will come to worship Him upon the very spot where He had made Himself known to Moses their deliverer. And so the story proceeds with Moses' pleading and Pharaoh's obduracy, with plagues, pursuits, and the splitting of the Red Sea.

a. The Sinaitic Covenant

We come then to the quintessential covenant experience of the Bible, the scene at Sinai. Amid thunder and lightning, the mountain trembling, the cloud of smoke rising, the Shofar's ever louder raucous cry, Moses having gone up on high, the people having encamped below, the children of Israel take it upon themselves to become the people of God. The conditions of the covenant incumbent upon the divine partner have already been met: "I am the Lord your God who took you out of the land of Egypt out of the house of bondage (Ex 20:1). The conditions incumbent upon the human partner are those commitments which immediately follow in the Decalogue and those which the ongoing tradition will add.

It may be noted that as with the covenants made by God with Abraham and Moses, so the covenant made at Sinai: As shepherds in the wilderness do the children of Israel make their covenant with God.

No sooner had the children of Israel made the covenant than they betrayed it with the worship of the golden calf. Affirmation and betrayal of the covenant would be a cyclical element of much of biblical history. Indeed, if one views the first section of the Hebrew Bible, the Torah, as the book of the making of the covenant, one may see the second section, the Prophets (encompassing the prophetic literature and the historical books), as the book of the breaking of the covenant. Against the people's faithlessness to the covenant, the prophets preached; about the impending punishment for such unfaithfulness, the prophets warned; for the ultimate reconciliation of the Jewish people with their God, the prophets hoped.

The sections differ by more than ascribed title. The Torah is the book of the wilderness, the wilderness to which Abraham was called, in which Moses received his charge, and through which the children of Israel wandered after receiving their Law. *Prophets* is the book of the land, the land to which shepherds came, in which they were transformed into farmers, and toward which their descendants would turn in prayer. Wilderness and land would have their impact upon the people and their relation to the covenant. The remembrances of the former and the temptations of the latter would be constant elements in the prophetic writings. In the wilderness the people had been isolated from contaminating contact with the surrounding peoples. In the land they would be pressed up against its inhabitants and their ways. In the wilderness there had been few foreign gods to beguile them; even so, the children of Israel had succumbed to the golden calf. In the land, the lure of new gods would swell as every sacred grove beckoned.

Not only were foreign gods tempting, but so were different political structures. As shepherds, the children of Israel had had chieftains, not kings; the patriarchs, Moses and Joshua, did not pass automatically their leadership roles to their first born sons. Each leader was felt to have been selected by God. The tribal chiefs who entered the land under Joshua were unable to achieve a centralized leadership upon his death. Lacking leadership and beguiled by the gods of the land, the tribes lost their sense of national cohesion. Only in the face of an external threat did they achieve a sense of unity and only for the period of the threat. In such periods temporary leaders, called judges, took control, only to pass into oblivion with the passing of the threat. As the children of Israel proceeded with their transformation into farmers, becoming more like their neighbors, they began to desire that which their neighbors had, i.e., a king. Feeling this to be a rejection of God, the prophet Samuel was to warn the people in the name of God that a king would press their sons and daughters into his service, despoil their lands, and decimate their flocks. Still, they wanted a king.

A king they got in the person of Saul. The last of the judges, the first of the kings, Saul is depicted as a tragic figure. Unsure of his own leadership, unable to fulfill the commandments of the Lord, insanely jealous of the rising star of David, Saul falls by his own hand at the battle in which his sons are slain. No dynasty proceeds from him.

It is with David that the kingdom develops. He becomes in the Bible and in the later tradition the ideal king. With him and with his household, God has made an eternal covenant. From him would come the messiah who in ushering in the end of days would finally fulfill the terms of the covenant and bring to the people of the covenant their ultimate deliverance. Though one biblical tradition made of David a singer of psalms, another suggested that in his role of king with its attendant violence, he was not worthy of building the Temple, the sanctuary for God. To Solomon, his son, was given this task.

In the dedicatory prayer which he offered, Solomon spoke of the Temple as the place to which the children of Israel might come to offer prayer and to seek atonement; within its walls the God of the Heavens would hear the people on earth. Should enemies attack because the people had sinned or should rain not fall because of their transgressions, the people might repair to the sanctuary to seek God's favor and to be delivered from their difficulties. So stated, it becomes clear that in the biblical mind, the Temple became the mechanism for the maintenance of the covenant.

Yet the Temple was not proof against the temptations of its surroundings. Even its builder, Solomon, built a high place for Kemosh the god of Moab. His punishment, carried out during the feckless reign of his son Rehoboam, was the division of his realm into a northern kingdom of Israel and a southern kingdom of Judah.

King followed king in each kingdom. The blandishments of that which was near were overshadowed by the dangers of that which was further off. Both kingdoms were trapped in the net of power as they were affected by the emerging imperia of Assyria and Babylonia. The northern kingdom was destroyed by the Assyrians in 722 and the southern kingdom was invaded by Babylonia in 586. The Babylonians occupied the land, carried off its elite into captivity, and destroyed the Temple. Jerusalem, ". . . she that had been a princess among the provinces, became now a tributary" (Lam 1:1).

The brutal events of history now raised questions with regard to the covenant. "God had destroyed and had not pitied" (Lam 2:2). In one regard, paradoxically enough, the destruction so long foretold, the warnings of the prophets so long unheeded, proved the existence of the covenant. The prophetic words had been fulfilled:

If ye are obedient and do good, ye shall consume the good of the land. But if ye refuse and are disobedient, the sword shall consume you (Is 1:18f).

They had been consumed. If God's ability to vindicate the covenant brought such destruction—human frailty remaining a constant and that which happened in the past might well happen in the future, cleaving to the covenant bringing with it linkage to peril—of what benefit, then, was the covenant to Israel?

b. The Covenant of the Heart

Jeremiah, who had lived through the invasion he had predicted and who had been carried into the Babylonian exile, provided an answer. A new and different covenant would be established with the Jewish people; God would write that covenant upon the tablets of their hearts (Jer 31:33). It would be so internalized, so much part of their being that they would not be able to break it. Of necessity, that new covenant would be fulfilled.

The prophet we call Deutero-Isaiah came to a similar conclusion. Returning from the Babylonian exile, he taught that the covenant would be maintained, if need be, on God's part alone. The suffering people had suffered enough; their sins were requited, indeed, in double measure for all their iniquities. As God had created the world by His will, so by His will had He chosen His people Israel. By that will had He made His covenant with them, to fulfill His purposes; they were to restore the ravaged land and they were to be a light unto all nations.

The prophet whose words we read in the last ten chapters of the Book of Isaiah speaks in a similar vein. God has established an eternal covenant with His people. He has poured out His spirit upon them and He has placed His word in their mouths and in the mouths of their children to all eternity. It would seem that we are to understand from this that that which God commands His people is not that which has to be learned and which then can be forgotten. It is part of their being and cannot be controverted. It is the legacy of each generation of the Jewish people.

As with Jeremiah, so with Deutero- and Trito-Isaiah: We have the idea of a covenant so established on the divine side that it cannot be broken on the human side. The God of Israel is inextricably linked to the people of Israel in a covenant which is eternal and unbreakable.

3. The Covenant in Succeeding History

Even so, the events of history did not cease, the vicissitudes of life did not end, and the Jewish people, then and now, did not achieve a period without problems. The tiny kingdom of Judah remained but a cockleshell upon the stormy seas of competing imperial powers. As the Assyrians had been superseded by the Babylonians, so they in turn were superseded by the Persians. Cyrus the Mede brought about the glorious period of restoration foretold by Deutero-Isaiah. At Cyrus' command, some of the Jews exiled to Babylonia returned to the land of Judah, led by Nehemiah and Ezra. Nehemiah directed the rebuilding of the city and its Temple. Gathering the people together, Ezra had them hear and re-accept the words of the Torah. He rehearsed with them their history and reminded them of the covenant which God had made with their fathers (Neh, chaps. 8, 9).

Whatever may be the historical problems in determining which precise part of the Pentateuch was read by Ezra, it is clear that later Jewish tradition saw in Ezra the Scribe, the man of the Book, one so worthy that he might have brought down the Law had not Moses already done so. It would seem that from Ezra's time on, the book of the Torah would become the symbol of the covenant which God had made with the Jewish people.

For a time, tranquillity surrounded the rescued people. Alas, they could not escape the changes of imperia. That empire founded by Cyrus would fall before the one founded by Alexander. The latter's relations with the Jewish community in Judah were apparently viewed as positive, a circumstance that may be deduced from the fact that certain rabbinic documents were dated from his period and that Alexander became a popular name among Jews.

What might have been a positive relationship would change when Alexander died. His empire was divided among his generals. Two groups emerged, the Ptolemies in Egypt and the Seleucids in Syria. The Jewish community found itself caught between the competing groups. An attempt by the Seleucid king Antiochus Epiphanes to be worshipped as embodiment of the state caused the Maccabean revolt of 168-165 BCE.

That revolt was a battle for the covenant, for the Law felt to be its elaboration, and for circumcision as its symbol. It was a battle fought without and within. The Maccabees resisted further increments of Seleucid control, by which Antiochus sought to keep the Jewish community from the observance of the Law. They opposed as well the attempts of some Jews, called Hellenizers, to emulate the style of Greek life. Circumcision served as a focus for both aspects of the battle. In his attack on the Law, Antiochus had proscribed the rite of circumcision. In their aping of the modes of the arena, some of the Hellenizers had gone as far as exercizing in the nude, and in their eagerness to appear like other athletes had sought to remove the mark of the covenant from their flesh. The rallying cry of, "the law and the covenant" (e.g. 1 Macc 2:28) suggests the Maccabean defense of the terms of and the specificity implied in, the covenant.

With the success of the Maccabean revolt and the re-dedication of the Temple, the Jewish people in Palestine moved into a period of quasi-independence. The Temple served as the center of restored religious life and the descendants of the Maccabees took political control. Yet all the while, great societal and religious changes were in the offing. Within one hundred years, a new imperial power would be on the scene and a new system of religious life and leadership would appear.

Rome succeeded the Seleucids in the control of Palestine. Ostensibly to decide on the proper candidate for the office of high priest, Rome in the person of Pompey entered the land in 63 BCE. The period of Roman control which ensued lasted for some five hundred years, affecting profoundly subsequent Jewish history. The interactions between Roman power and the Jewish polity had their effects on the intimately linked religious and political realms. The institutions of modern Judaism, the synagogue, the rabbinate, the vast rabbinic literature, the Bible in its present form, and the prayerbook, all derive from that period. The diaspora as idea, i.e. the ongoing existence of Jewish communities outside the Land, with the attendant separation of political and religious status, has its origin in Roman times.

The fluctuations of Roman power would make for changing and even contradictory relations with the Jewish people. In the beginning, Rome supported the house of Herod; later, it relentlessly crushed any sign of independence. The Romans destroyed the Temple in 70 CE but allowed the Torah to be taught in Yavneh. Later, the teaching of the Torah was prohibited, which prohibition was one of the sources of the Bar Kokhba revolt of 132-135 CE. Seventy years later, however, Roman power would allow and even support the promulgation of the Mishnah, the first codification of the Oral Law. Even while Roman might ground down the Jews in Palestine, Roman society in Rome itself accepted the existence of thriving Jewish communities.

The fluctuations were interpreted by the Jews in terms of the covenant. The loss of political independence and particularly the destruction of the Temple were understood as punishment for the sins of the people. The abortive Bar Kokhba revolt seen at first in a messianic manner as the divine fulfillment of the covenant, was in its failure once again seen as punishment for sin. The more favored times of Judah the Prince, the codifier of the Mishnah, were seen as due in part to his exemplary nature. Later Jewish tradition was to call him *rabbenu hakadosh*, our holy rabbi.

4. The Institution of Synagogues

Though the Temple was destroyed in 70 CE, Judaism was not. A new institution, the synagogue, had already come upon the scene. Coherent with the urbanization which had further developed in the Roman period, the synagogue presented a new mode of worship and a new form of leadership. Prayer and study, not sacrifice, were the means by which the Jew could approach his God and relate himself to the covenant. Study was the means by which any Jew could achieve leadership; the role of rabbi was dependent on learning not lineage. That which was studied was Scripture and its interpretation; the rabbis had developed the notion that divine revelation had occurred in two forms. At Sinai, there had been given not only a Written Law but an Oral Law to interpret and expand the former. Indeed, in one rabbinic opinion, the very basis of the covenant was the Oral Law. The Sabbath lights may serve as an example of its power. Nowhere ordained in the Torah, apparently contravening its plain sense, the Sabbath lights by the force of the Oral Law and through the teaching of rabbis became a commandment incumbent upon every Jew and worthy of the formula of benediction, "Who has sanctified us through His commandments and has commanded us to light the Sabbath Lights."[15]

The Oral Law expanded the commandments and elaborated the terms of the covenant. In the rabbinic mind, the multiplication of God's demands was the means by which Israel might become more and more a holy people, more and more a people set apart.

The *mitzvoth* were techniques to affirm the special linkage between God and Israel. This elaboration of the perceived terms of the covenant may be seen as a defense in the face of the challenge by the nascent Christian community and its claim that the old covenant had been superseded by the new. The stress on Jewish texts, whether biblical or liturgical, was the rabbinic means of denying the claim that Christian texts were divine and a method to isolate those Judeo-Christians who might have accepted the idea of two covenants, old and new. For the rabbis and Jewish community the "old" covenant, particularly with its rabbinic elaboration, still stood, precluding for them any other.

5. The Symbols of the Covenant

The old covenant was affirmed in yet another way. As in Maccabean times, so in Roman, particularly in the face of the emerging church, circumcision stood as a symbol of the covenant. As the Apostolic Church debated the necessity of the rite in the acceptance of converts and raised thereby the question of its relation to the old covenant (Acts, chap. 15), the teachers of the synagogue stressed circumcision all the more. It had stood for a perfection that transcended nature, as seen in the injunction to Abraham, "Walk before Me and be perfect" (Gn 17:1). Now it stood for a perfection that transcended this life: The same Abraham was said to stand before the gates of Gehinnom keeping from entrance all who were circumcised.

Circumcision was not the only symbol of the covenant or indicator of Jewish specificity. We read of a rabbinic debate as to the meaning of the verse, "And ye shall keep My covenant that ye may be My treasure from among all peoples" (Ex 19:5). What is meant by "My covenant"? According to one rabbi, the phrase referred to the Sabbath. To still another, it referred to the prohibition against idolatry.[6] The debate was possible because in the rabbinic mind all three were specific to the Jewish people and any of the three could serve as symbol of the covenant.

As they understood the covenant, it was the task of the rabbis to increase the specificity of its terms, to make of the Jewish people a holy people, a people distinguished by their actions, a people devoted to God and His Law. To that end, the rabbis made Judaism the religion of law. As Roman power faltered and the new imperium of Byzantium flourished, the process of law formation continued. The Mishnah was expanded by discussion, collected in the Gemarah. Mishnah and Gemarah became the Talmud, the prime text of the Judaism that would follow. Academies were established in Palestine and Babylonia to teach it; authority was based on its knowledge. Abstracts and codes were prepared from its contents that it might better serve as an immediate source of jurisprudence.

And serve it did, in the Land and in those communities that had sprung up outside it, in the old settlement in Babylonia and in the newer settlements in Roman Europe, and serve it would in those new settlements which would occur when, into the arena of history vacated by the city-states of Rome and Byzantium, there would come a new movement out of the wilderness, with its new prophet, Mohammed, and its new scriptures, the Koran.

Jewish law was the carapace of the Jewish community wherever it was found, brought in by the Jew wherever he settled, whether in the Fertile Crescent or in Europe, whether under Christian or Moslem domination. Individuals and communities were governed by that Law. Prayer and business, the Sabbath and sexual relations were dealt with by a system of law believed to have been given at Sinai, interpreted by the rabbis, and transmitted to that particular time and place. Governing all of life, Jewish Law served to insulate the Jew from the effects of his surroundings.

Not only was the Jewish community separated from its host society by its own restrictions, it was separated as well by the restrictions of the legal systems of its hosts, whether religious or secular. In Christian or Moslem law as in royal or ducal law, the Jews were viewed as a separate and distinct entity. In addition, the social role of the Jewish community, whether as merchants, money lenders, or technicians of government made for a sense of separation from the law and lives of the host society. Indeed, the medieval Jewish community fulfilled in its being the verse, ". . . a people that dwells alone" (Nm 23:9).

6. Judaism and Philosophy

That sense of aloneness would be somewhat mitigated when in the Moslem period philosophy entered Jewish life. Explicitly or implicitly, this old/new way of thinking would raise questions regarding the covenant and its embodiment in the Law. How to relate the covenant to the God of the philosophers, how to relate the commandments to the philosophers' quest, how to relate the Torah to the philosophers' teaching?

In some regard, these questions tormented but few. When philosophy entered the medieval world, penetrating first the Islamic, then the Jewish, and then the Christian communities, it affected the elites of each faith group without affecting their realities. For Islam, Judaism, and Christianity, religious law was law; whatever new ideas might enter, they could not affect that law without shaking the societal structures based thereupon and toppling those elites. Hence the law remained the law, and philosophy was held to be impossible of ever becoming popular, i.e. available to the non-elite.[7] In reality and in theory, philosophy remained the ideology of the elite.

Philosophy moreover presented problems with regard to that specificity which had been at the heart of each faith group's relation with its God and with its particular religious law. Philosophy is and was universal, i.e. open to truth pursued by those within and without a particular religious group. We read of Jew quoting Christian and Moslem,[8] and Christian quoting Jew,[9] not as members of disparate religious communities but as philosophers quoting or disputing other philosophers. Philosophy by creating a universe of discourse which transcended specific creedal concerns (cf. Averroës' statement that a philosopher should explain his own tradition in the fairest possible way[10]) tended to suggest that religious law of whatever kind, emanating from whichever faith community, was a technique of social control, something necessary to rule the rude masses.[11] Such a view could hardly sustain a covenant situation.

More than that, the philosopher's goal of truth was at some distance from the religionist's goal of obedience. This is not to say that the philosopher disobeyed the Law—such disobedience would have affected negatively the societal structure within which he operated and upon which his status depended. It is to say that the philosopher aimed at a different target. His was the category of true-and-false rather than good-and-evil.[12]

The religious tradition "properly interpreted" might yield or approximate the truth which the philosopher sought, yet that interpretation could only be in universal terms, understood but by a small elite. The covenant seen in the biblical and rabbinic tradition had been a group enterprise (cf. the midrash that if one Israelite had been missing at Sinai, the Law would not have been given[13]). Philosophy by its nature was an individual undertaking. The would-be philosopher proceeded through a regimen of studies[14] none of which required the perusal of those "religious" texts upon which the belief in the covenant was based. What was required was mathematics, physics, and metaphysics, available to all men regardless of their relation to the covenant. By those studies, the individual activated his own intellect that he might make connection with divine active intellect. That connection was the source of providence in this world and of immortality in the next[15], not the particular linkage to the God of the covenant presented in those religious texts which structured his day-to-day life in particular and his society in general.

We have here a paradox: The literature of the covenant dealt with a particular people, but dealt with that people as as whole; the literature of the philosopher related to the individual but was presented in universal terms.

Universal ideas bespoke a certain societal ambiance. Persecution would destroy that ambiance and shrink the universe of discourse of the philosopher. In the classic *Kuzari* by Judah Halevi (1080-1142), a philosophical novella purporting to explain the actual conversion of a Khazar kingdom to Judaism, we find philosophy turned in upon itself. It cannot produce certainty nor can it lead to the knowledge of God. Only the Torah can. The Torah was the product of revelation attested to by the sixty myriads of Israelites who, standing at Sinai, experienced the giving of the Law.

The Israelites, in Halevi's view, were able to experience the events at Sinai because of their specific nature; they alone of all people were open to prophecy. To wonder why prophecy was not available to other people is for him akin to wondering why all animals are not rational.[16] Prophecy is for Halevi a genetic endowment passed only through the descendants of Abraham, enabling them to come into contact with the divine influence. The latter, *inyan elohi*, operates in Halevi's thinking in a manner similar to the divine active intellect in the thinking of the philosophers, bestowing on the individual Jew "a higher form."[17]

There are further parallels. Both the philosophers and Halevi had accepted the notion of genetic elites. In the philosophers' view it was an elite of intellect, in Halevi's an elite of descent. For both, a native capacity had to be brought to actuality by the study of texts; for the philosophers they were philosophical texts, for Halevi Jewish ones. The philosophers held that some places were amenable to philosophy;[18] Halevi held that the land of Israel was most amenable to revelation. They contended that certain languages enhanced thinking; Halevi held that prophecy could occur only in the Hebrew language. As with the philosophers so with Halevi, one may see a kind of automatic process in his thinking about revelation: When there is a concatenation of people, land, and language, prophecy—it would seem—must occur.

For Halevi the events at Sinai became the proof for the existence of

God, not we might notice, the God of the philosophers who is, but the God of the Torah who reveals. Such a God revealed an aspect of His unique nature and His special relationship to the Jewish people by making known to them His specific name YHWE. That name cannot be understood by philosophical speculation[19] but is in some unfathomable manner directly involved in the creation of the world.[20]

Abraham, according to Halevi, was the first to understand the true meaning of this divine name; that understanding brought him to make a covenant with his Creator. That covenant was made with Abraham's hands and his feet, with his speech, and with the rite of circumcision.

Circumcision as that which is commanded and that which is obeyed gives evidence of the difference between divine action and human reason. Human reason can attain to the meaning of those social and rational laws which are the province of all mankind. It cannot attain to the meaning of those divine actions which are related to the people of God as part of His plan and purpose for them.[21]

Abraham's obedience to the commandment of circumcision established the covenant with God and confirmed the linkage of the divine influence to his descendants.[22] Not only circumcision but the Sabbath and the holy days specific to the Jewish people maintain that linkage.[23]

The stress on the particular, the centrality of Israel, land and people, the emphasis on circumcision, the Sabbath, and the holy days may well be related to that societal situation suggested by the second title of Halevi's *Kuzari*: A defense of a despised faith. Within medieval Jewish history, Halevi's approach would remain a symbol of particularity.

Halevi would be followed by Maimonides (1135-1204) and Gersonides (1288-1344) who would proceed in a more "philosophical" manner. For both of them, the intellect was all. Their conceptual relation to the covenant, at least as is apparent from their philosophical works, is problematic.

Jewish history would provide another thinker whose approach would be akin to that of Halevi. The massacres of 1391 signalled the beginning of the end of the proud Spanish Jewish civilization. Among the victims was the son of Hasdai Crescas (1340-1410), adviser to King Juan. Crescas' response was to write *Or Hashem*, the Light of the Lord.

Or Hashem reflects and even advances many of the approaches of Halevi. As with Halevi, so for Crescas philosophy is powerless to bring the Jew closer to his God. Only love can do that, the love that is manifested by the Jew's observance of the commandments of the Torah given in love by God. So love begets love, the Law is the vehicle of the divine love, its observance that of loving human response.

For Crescas who attacked the Aristotelian structure upon which much of medieval Jewish (and non-Jewish) philosophy rested,[24] philosophical investigation could not even prove the basic question on the unity of God; only the scriptural statement, "Hear O Israel, the Lord our God, the Lord is One" could.[25] It should be noted that this statement, this declaration of faith, was and is the basic element of Jewish liturgy, structuring the evening and morning services and serving as that confession to be recited at the moment of death, whether by natural means or in the face of martyrdom. The implication of Crescas' statement is that only the Jewish people by its Scriptures and with its liturgy can attain that which the philosophers seek: the true knowledge of God.

For the more "philosophical" philosophers such as Gersonides, God's knowledge of the transitory particular was problematic. How could the unchanging God be related to the changing particular? Hence God could not know the individual person. For Crescas, God knows. He can then call to His service whomsoever He wishes and extend His providence to those who respond to His call. The Jewish people who responded at Sinai have by right an added measure of providence.

As God chose whomsoever He wished to respond to His will, so God chose as prophets those who loved Him and performed His commandments.[26] Crescas here has moved far from the view of Maimonides that philosophical preparation is a prerequisite for prophecy.

In the face of God's choice, the choice of man—in Crescas' thinking—is limited. God's foreknowledge limits man's freedom. Yet even here, one may be rewarded for the exertion expended or punished for the exertion misdirected. That exertion is in relation to the observance of the commandments of the Torah. The reward for exertion and observance is eternal bliss in the life to come and resurrection in the future yet to be.[27]

We have in Crescas' thinking with its view of God as source of law and love and its view of the Jew as the one who responds in love to achieve eternal bliss, a kind of philosophical midrash on the covenant. Only the kind of God of whom Crescas speaks can make a covenant; only the kind of Jew interested in observing the commandments can keep a covenant. Hasdai Crescas was one of the last of the Jewish medieval philosophers; he was the one to stress most vigorously the idea of a personal God.

7. Judaism in the 19th Century

The modern period of Jewish history is marked by the dissolution of the shell of separate status, a shell, as we have seen, formed by an outer layer of the law of the society in which Jews were domiciled and an inner layer of Jewish community. In France, the actions of the Napoleonic

Sanhedrin of 1806/7 which offered the Jew the possibility of being that which he had never been before, a citizen, changed the perception of the Jew and Judaism. As one of Napoleon's commissioners at the Sanhedrin put it, "The Jews ceased to be a people and remained only a religion."[28]

Judaism as "only a religion" would confront problems it had never faced before. Jewish law now would be that which the individual voluntarily assumed not that which could be imposed upon him. That sense of separateness which law, external and internal, had imposed in the past was now to be dissipated by the heady sense of belonging to the nation-state. A Jew now no longer was a Jew *in* France or *in* Germany; he was (in theory at least) a Jew *of* France or *of* Germany. He now identified himself (again, at least in theory) as a Frenchman or German. Chosenness which had been a group status was affected by citizenship which was an individual status.

A tension, not always perceived, existed between that sense of belonging, by which the Jew felt part of the nation-state, and that of being different, which had in some measure motivated the feeling of a covenantal relationship. It was difficult to feel that God had caused a specific relationship with the religious group to which an individual belonged, all the while he saw himself more related to others of the nation. Yet a modicum of difference had to be maintained in order to justify the continuance of the particular religious tradition. For some of the early Reform Jewish thinkers, i.e., those who were among the first to confront the new problems of modernity, the solution was to see in the Jewish people a particular, a divine gift worth preserving.

Abraham Geiger (1810-1874) may serve as an example. For him, the Jewish people *qua* people have a particular gift for religion, the concept of the One and Universal God is their gift to the world. Though the daughter religions of Judaism—Christianity and Islam—have carried the idea of God to the ends of the earth, in their contact with the world they have been somewhat tainted by traces of paganism. Judaism and the Jewish people must persist that pure ethical monotheism be presented to the world and that the daughter religions may receive correction.[29]

While it is clear that the idea of the Jewish people having a genius for religion is the analogue of the Romantic idea that certain nations have certain gifts, e.g., the Greeks for beauty and the Romans for law, it is not evident how the Jewish people as a collectivity could use that genius while living individually as citizens. Yet one would hear of the mission of Israel and its task of converting the world to ethical monotheism. Once again, the Jews were to be, "A kingdom of priests and a holy people" (Ex 19:6). That became problematic, at least in terms of a people set apart, as Jews jettisoned those patterns of life which tended to make them different from their fellow citizens. It is indeed difficult to be a priest without the accoutrements of priesthood.

Within the philosophical and theological categories in which this new religious thinking was framed, the idea of a personal God who could command and choose and thus make a covenant with a particular people was problematical. As for the medieval philosophers, so for the early Reform thinkers, God was more idea than commanding presence, more the absolute than He who in love had given the Torah to His people Israel. For such thinkers, the idea of covenant would remain a very abstract concept, if it existed at all.[30]

8. Some Jewish Thinkers of the 20th Century

Franz Rosenzweig (1886-1929) has had a lasting effect on modern Jewish theology, particularly by his magnum opus, *The Star of Redemption*. For Rosenzweig, God, the world, and man were not to be captured in any system of thought but were to be confronted by a new pattern of thinking based on the characteristics of speech.[31] Thought, abstract and timeless, suggested that the thinker could somehow remain uninvolved with these realities. Speech, concrete and timebound, suggested that the thinker could not.

Speech suggested further that the three entities of God, the world, and man could not be collapsed the one into the other, as philosophical systems of the past had done. Speech, as a theoretical approach, is to remind us that the three are to be addressed but never fully to be expressed.

God's existence was known to Rosenzweig by religious experience.[32] *The Star of Redemption* was an attempt to explicate that experience. God does speak to man. As speech is conscious and personal, so is the relation of God to man, of God to the world, of man to God, and of man to the world. The terms revelation and creation describe God's relation to man and the world; man's relation to the world is described as redemption. God relates to the world and to man in terms of speech. Man relates to God and the world in terms of love and deed. The three realities of God, world, and man form the triangle of relation: creation, revelation, and redemption. The two triangles form the star of redemption, which is the schema of religious relationships.

The Jewish people are they who have taken within their being the star of redemption. Their religious calendar reflects the three-fold relationships of creation, revelation, and redemption. They are for that reason an eternal people[33] set, ". . . between the temporal and the holy."[34] They are a blood community with its own language of Hebrew and its own religious law that is able to stand apart from the world and so be committed to its own God who is the God of all nations.[35]

Because of their ability to look inwardly through their own history to their relation with God and outwardly through world history to God's relation with the world, the Jewish people may be seen as a beacon-fire capable of illuminating the darkness of the world. The daughter religion of Christianity may be seen as the rays sent out from the fire to the world.

This view of Judaism as the eternal fire and Christianity as the eternal rays has been taken by some[36] to embody, as it were, two covenantal relationships, one with Jewry, the other with Christendom.

Yet one may wonder, for in *The Star of Redemption* there are clear parallels to and a particularly significant quotation from the *Kuzari* by Judah Halevi. For both Halevi and Rosenzweig, experience rather than ratiocination validated Judaism.[37] For both, the Jewish people formed a blood community ultimately set apart from others.[38] For both, the Hebrew language is a holy tongue reflecting that special status.[39] The Jewish calendar for both of them mirrors the unique relationship between God and His people; indeed, the notion that the Sabbath and the festivals presented the ideas of creation, revelation, and redemption is already anticipated in the *Kuzari*.[40] With all this in mind, Rosenzweig's quoting of the *Kuzari's* statement dealing with the messiah that,

> ... the nations are the readying and the preparation of the Messiah whom we await. He will be the fruit, and all will become his fruit and acknowledge him, and the tree will be one. Then they will praise and glorify the root which once they despised, of which Isaiah spoke,[41]

suggests not two covenants but rather the fairly standard idea that Christianity is but the preparation for the ultimate messianic advent.[42]

Relationship and speech were to be aspects of the thought of Martin Buber (1878-1965), Rosenzweig's contemporary and fellow Bible translator. Approaching life from a mystical direction, Buber was to write his classic, *I and Thou*,[43] which delineated two different attitudes to the world. The first, I-and-It, suggested the use of people or things as tools. The second, I-and-Thou, suggested a total relationship to be expressed with words and/or with one's total being. In such a context, man is always open to the possibility of dialogue with God; illumination may be afforded by the relationship.[44]

Influenced in part by the joyous mystical Hasidic sect within Judaism and in part by his education at the Universities of Vienna and Berlin, Buber was to see manifest in the Jewish people a particular development: The movement toward the ever more perfect realization of the interrelated ideas of unity, deed, and future.[45]

In his book *The Prophetic Faith*, Buber sought to investigate the origins of the feelings of linkage between the Jewish people and their God. He sought to use the Bible not only to explicate a literary development. It reflects to him real occurrences, particularly those events by which the Jewish people feel addressed by God. Scripture mirrors the interaction between the people and their God and that of the leaders and the led. The idea of covenant flows out of those interactions. As Buber explained it:

> Berith, covenant, between YHWE and Israel denotes an expansion of the leadership and the following to cover every department of the people's life . . . (T)he people feel . . . that a covenant with such a deity as this means no legal agreement, but a surrender to the divine power and grace.[46]

In a sense, Buber's view of the covenant is but a special case of the I-thou relationship. That relationship with God is always available, as Buber was wont to quote the Hasidic statement, "Where is God to be found? Wherever you let Him in." For Buber however there is a particular people with a particular genius for religion (shades of Halevi and Geiger!) and, as the Bible indicates, that people has been ever prepared to respond to God's direction. Covenant, then, becomes not only a there-and-then situation but a here-and-now possibility for Jews and, indeed, for all men.

A contemporary of Rosenzweig and Buber was Leo Baeck (1873-1956). In 1905, in response to Harnack's book *The Essence of Christianity*, Baeck had published *The Essence of Judaism*.[47] In that book he presented his view of a "classic" Judaism over against a "romantic" Christianity, a Judaism whose essence it was to conquer time and to respond to the divine "Thou shalt," in every generation.

The mood of Baeck's book *This People Israel*, published some forty years later, is much different. The book came into being, not out of a theoretical attack on Judaism but out of a physical attack on Jews. It was composed not in a study but in a concentration camp. It focused not on Judaism as a system of ideas whose essence might be presented but on the Jewish people as an unique historical entity whose existence might be instructive.

That people was formed by a *berit*, a covenant. In Baeck's thinking, the idea of covenant was all encompassing:

In the world of nature it confronts us as the cosmos which is simply there; in the human world it confronts us as a cosmos which, ever again, ought to come into being. Law, creation, revelation, they are all the same, they are God's covenant. . . . Above, below, before, and after, all that comes and goes is that which is and remains, the covenant of the One.[48]

The Jewish people seeing in its own history its link to humanity in the future, is the people which carries the sense of the covenant with God, the Creator of all men and the ultimate Unifier of all men. It is, therefore, a people with a task: To keep alive its memory of God's covenant with them and to teach to the world God's covenant with all humankind.[49]

9. Covenant Theology in Our Day

Partly in response to the rationalistic approach of much of Reform Judaism in America and partly in response to the horrors of the Holocaust, a small but influential group of Reform Jewish thinkers, known as covenant theologians, has emerged. Operating in the main out of existentialist presuppositions, these theologians have affirmed, in the words of Emil Fackenheim, that

He, the God of Israel, still lives, and the liberal Jew, son of the Covenant, still stands at Mt. Sinai, as did his fathers.[50]

The covenant theologian, then, looks backward and forward. As Jakob Petuchowski put it, he accepts,

. . . the reality of God's covenant with Israel and the obligation which rests upon every individual Jew to strain his ear for the Word of God addressed to him personally.[51]

The stress is not only on the individual but on the group. That which the individual Jew must observe is for Eugene B. Borowitz,

. . . living discipline which flows from the consciousness of standing in direct personal relationship with God, not merely as a private self, but as one of the community with whom He has convenanted.[52]

There is a tension, then, between the principle of autonomy affirmed by these theologians (who after all are representatives of Liberal or Reform Judaism) and the needs of the community. Petuchowski wrote that,

... an undue amount of subjectivism would be checked by the requirements of the "holy community"; yet the "holy community" itself in its modern form will become possible only because of the personal commitments of Jewish *individuals,* who have learned to "observe" God's commandments to *them.*[53]

As is apparent, the idea of covenant has carried with it the reciprocal entailment of a personal God. As Borowitz has written:

If God is real, if He is truly God, men should speak to Him, seek Him, commune with Him regularly—anything less can only be considered folly. And as there is no time when He is not God, when the universe is free of His rule or when men are released from His commandments, so there is not a time when men may ignore Him with impunity.[54]

10. Summary

What may we glean from this brief survey of "covenant"? It tells us as much of the Jewish situation as of the ways that Jews have viewed the idea of covenant. When Jews see themselves as part of a greater society, so much so that they take on the thought patterns of that society, then the idea of covenant loses its specific dimensions and, as it were, the call of Sinai is muted.

The more general thought patterns tend to negate the idea of a personal God with whom alone a covenant might be made. The word may be maintained, though the specificity of its meaning is lost. The covenant, historically considered, reflects the oscillations of Jewish history.

Notes

1. Cf. D. J. McCarthy, *Old Testament Covenant* (Oxford: Blackwell, 1972) *idem, Treaty and Covenant; A Study of Form in the Ancient Oriental Documents and in the Old Testament,* Analecta Biblica (Rome: Pontifical Biblical Institute, 1963), p. 21. Cf. also George Mendenhall, *The Tenth Generation* (Baltimore: Johns Hopkins Press, 1973); on p. 14 he states that, "for . . . the synthesis of faith, action, and the experience that constitute what we call religion, there is no known symbol in the entire Bible that brings these three together in any satisfactory form, than the covenant as it has been isolated on the basis of contemporary political forms."

2. TB *Abodah Zarah* 3a.

3. TB *Shabbat* 88a; *Tanhuma Noach* 3; and elsewhere.

4. "Eleh Ezkara," in *High Holiday Prayer Book,* Philip Birnbaum, transl. (New York: Hebrew Publ. Co., 1951), pp. 841f.

5. *Daily Prayer Book*, Philip Birnbaum, transl. (New York: Hebrew Publ. Co., 1948), p. 222.

6. *Mekilta de Rabbi Ishmael*, Bahodesh, II, 202.

7. Moses Maimonides, *The Guide of the Perplexed*, Shlomo Pines, transl. and annot. (Chicago: University of Chicago Press, 1962), I, 33 and 34. Henceforth cited as *Guide*.

8. *Ibid.*, I, 71.

9. E.g. Thomas Aquinas, *Summa Theologica* I, 13, 2. Cf. Anton C. Pegis, ed. and annot. (New York: Random House, 1945), where in the index of authors mentioned by St. Thomas, Pegis gives all the citations of Maimonides (Rabbi Moyses).

10. Averroes, *Tahafut al Tahafut* (The Incoherence of the Incoherence), Simon van den Bergh, transl. and annot. (London: Luzac, 1954), "About the Natural Sciences" 4th Discussion, p. 360.

11. Alfarabi, *Philosophy of Plato and Aristotle*, Muhsin Madi, transl. (Glencoe, Ill.: Free Press, 1962), I, 44-48. Judah Halevi, *Book of Kuzari*, Hartwig Hirschfeld, transl. and annot. (London: M. L. Cailingold, 1931; republished New York: Pardes, 1946), I, 1. Henceforth cited as *Kuzari*. Maimonides, *Guide* CXI, 27f.

12. Maimonides, *Guide*, I, 2.

13. *Deuteronomy Rabbah* 7, 8.

14. Maimonides, *Guide* I, 34.

15. *Ibid.*, XI, 11.

16. Halevi, *Kuzari* I, 103.

17. *Ibid.*, V, 10.

18 .Cf. Alexander Altman, "Torat Ha-aklimim l'Rabbi Judah Halevi" ("The Climatological Factor in Judah Halevi's Theory of Prophecy"), in *Melilah* (Manchester: Manchester Univ. Press 1944), pp. 1-17.

19. Halevi, *Kuzari* IV, 15.

20. *Ibid.*, IV, 25.

21. *Ibid.*, CXI, 7.10.

22. *Ibid.*, 7.

23. *Ibid.*, XI, 35.50.

24. Cf. Meyer Waxman, *The Philosophy of Don Hasdai Crescas* (New York: Columbia University Press, 1920); H. A. Wolfson, *Crescas' Critique of Aristotle* (Cambridge: Harvard University Press, 1971).

25. Hasdai Crescas, *Or Hashem* (Vienna: Adalb. della Torre, 1860), First Treatise, III, 4.

26. *Ibid.*, Second Treatise, IV, 4.

27. *Ibid.*, Third Treatise, IV.

28. Pertalis fils, quoted in, Howard Sachar, *The Course of Modern Jewish History* (New York: Delta, 1967), p. 63.

29. Cf. Jacob Agus, *Modern Philosophies of Judaism* (New York: Behrman House, 1941), pp. 5-11. Henceforth cited as *Philosophies.*

30. Cf. Jakob J. Petuchowski, "Revelation in Reform Judaism," in CCAR Yearbook, 1959, pp. 212-239.

31. Franz Rosenzweig, *The Star of Redemption*, William W. Hallo, transl. (New York: Holt, Rinehart & Winston, 1972). Henceforth cited as *Star*.

32. Agus, *Philosophies* p. 158.

33. Rosenzweig, *Star* p. 328.

34. *Ibid.*, p. 304.

35. *Ibid.*, p. 329.

36. Agus, *Philosophies* p. 193; and Will Herberg, *Faith Enacted as History: Essays in Biblical Theology*, Bernhard W. Anderson, ed. (Philadelphia: Westminster Press, 1976), pp. 18-20 and 58-62.

37. Halevi's proof of the 600,000 witnesses to the events at Sinai, *Kuzari* I, 83 is alluded to by Rosenzweig, *Star* pp. 96f. One might say that Rosenzweig's religious development was a re-tracing of the Khazar king's passage from philosophy to Judaism, touching Christianity while skipping Islam; cf. *Kuzari*, I, 1-10.

38 Rosenzweig, *Star* p. 299; Halevi, *Kuzari* I, 27; also I, 47.49.95f.

39. Rosenzweig, *Star* p. 304; Halevi, *Kuzari* II, 66.68.

40. Rosenzweig, *Star* pp. 309ff; Halevi, *Kuzari* CXI, 10.

41. Rosenzweig, *Star* p. 379; Halevi, *Kuzari* IV, 23.

42. Cf. "Christianity," in *Jewish Encyclopedia*, Isadore Singer, ed. (New York: Funk & Wagnalls, 1910).

43. Martin Buber, *I and Thou*, Ronald G. Smith, transl. (New York: Scribner, 1958).

44. Agus, *Philosophies*, p. 229.

45. Maurice Friedman, *Martin Buber, The Life of Dialogue* (Chicago: University of Chicago Press, 1955), p. 32.

46. Martin Buber, *The Prophetic Faith*, Carlyle Wilton-Davies, transl. (New York: Macmillan, 1949). p. 51

47. Leo Baeck, *The Essence of Judaism*, Victor Grubenwieser and Leonard Perl, transl., rendered by Irving Howe (New York: Schocken, 1948).

48. Leo Baeck, *This People Israel: The Meaning of Jewish Existence,* Albert H. Friedlander, transl. (New York: Holt, Rinehart & Winston, 1964), p. 13.

49. *Ibid.*, p. 396.

50. Emil Fackenheim, *Quest for Past and Future* (Bloomington: Indiana University Press, 1968), p. 48; also quoted in Larry Kushner, "In Search of a Modern Presence of the Ancient God: Covenant Theology," Master's Thesis, HUC-JIR, 1969, p. 19. Henceforth cited as CT.

51. Jakob J. Petuchowski, "The Limits of 'People-Centered' Judaism," in *Commentary* XXVII (May 1959), pp. 387-394; also quoted in CT, p. 46.

52. Eugene B. Borowitz, "On Celebrating Sinai," in CCAR Yearbook, June 1966; also quoted in CT, p. 47.

53. Jakob J. Petuchowski, *Ever Since Sinai: A Modern View of the Torah* (New York: Scribe, 1961), p. 114; also quoted in CT, p. 54.

54. Eugene B. Borowitz, *A New Jewish Theology in the Making* (Philadelphia: Westminster Press, 1958); also quoted in CT, p. 31.

2.
The Meaning of Covenant:
A Contemporary Understanding

Elliot Dorff

1. The Concept of Covenant in Modern Times

The word "covenant" is not part of the normal vocabulary of modern man. Those who use it at all generally restrict its application to religious contexts, and to ancient ones at that. Moderns are uncomfortable with the word, as they are uncomfortable with religion generally.

For modern Jews the discomfort with "covenant" goes even deeper than that. To the extent that they reflect on the concept that the word denotes—and almost as soon as they do—they find it troubling. The rabbis of the Talmud and Middle Ages substituted other terms to express their commitment to the Jewish tradition because Christians had adopted it in claiming that there was a new covenant (*habrit hahadashah* which is usually translated "The New Testament" but literally means "The New Covenant") which superseded the old one. Jewish leaders therefore avoided using the term lest it evoke Christian associations and questions about Christian claims.

Modern Jews have had the opposite problem with the term. The Enlightenment engendered the desire on the part of Jews to form relationships with Christians and to be seen as citizens of the world rather than narrowly as Jews. Consequently, while Jews of rabbinic and medieval times avoided the term covenant for fear that it would encourage assimilation with Christians, modern Jews avoided it because of the exclusivity involved in the concept. As a result, for many years now Jews have been unaccustomed to using the term.

In recent times, however, that situation has changed rather dramatically and there is a renewed interest in the concept of covenant. Part of the reason is that Jews are increasingly seeking to renew their ties with the sources of their tradition and the word and concept of covenant appear prominently in the Bible, the text Jews are most likely to study first of all. More importantly, Jews no longer accept the universalist, Enlightenment ideology as unreservedly as they did before. They have come to realize that people must identify in smaller groups before they can have concern for humanity as a whole and that assimilation does not help mankind. In consequence, contract theories of government and society have achieved a new popularity as Jews and non-Jews seek a closer sense of community. Even American Jews, who not so long ago supported the ideal of the American melting pot in both word and deed, have now become disillusioned about the possibility and desirability of that goal. Instead, like other Americans, Jews now seek pluralism rather than homogenization, and pluralism demands a vigorous assertion of one's own ethnicity. As a result of these changes, Jews are no longer immediately embarrassed by the notion of covenant; on the contrary, they seek to explore it as a way of reaffirming their ties to the tradition and a helpful concept in developing a healthy relationship with the non-Jewish world, one which preserves a sense of being distinct and yet related to others.

2. Two Views of Covenant

In the first part of this paper we will analyze the ways in which two modern Jewish philosophers have interpreted the covenant. The purpose of that section is not to present an exhaustive summary of modern Jewish concepts of the covenant but to gain insights into what the covenant might mean to us in our own day, from two thinkers with widely varying views on the subject.

While there are many ways to classify Jewish and non-Jewish philosophers in modern times, for our purposes it will be helpful to distinguish between objectivists and existentialists. The two groups are distinct primarily in their methodology:

Objectivists try to take a detached, dispassionate view of the experiences they seek to analyze. They stress the general, shared aspects of our experience. Objectivists are commonly divided into two sub-groups, rationalists who stress the functioning of reason in our understanding of the world, and empiricists who emphasize the role of sense experiences as the foundation of our knowledge. Although philosophers in one sub-group often seem to ignore the aspect of experience stressed by the other, our knowledge is clearly a product of reason as well as senses.

As philosophers in the twentieth century have increasingly realized, we also learn from our individual, involved experiences. In fact, if we analyze and describe our lives in a detached, objective way only, we often distort the nature of our experience. Philosophers who stress the individual's unique and private experiences with the outside world, are called "existentialists."[1] Objectivists and existentialists often ignore and even ridicule the results produced by the other group, but a truly adequate philosophy will try to take both avenues of knowledge into account because we do, in fact, learn from both.

As representative examples of the two schools, Mordecai M. Kaplan and Hermann Cohen were chosen, Kaplan because of his thoroughgoing and suggestive reinterpretation of the covenant idea, and Cohen because of his relative unfamiliarity to American audiences and his great influence on two well-known and seminal figures, Franz Rosenzweig and Martin Buber. Since the objectivists were on the scene long before the existentialists, we shall begin with Kaplan.

3. An Objectivist Approach: Mordecai M. Kaplan

While the seventeenth century was the age of rationalism, the eighteenth saw the rise of empiricism. Nineteenth century thought returned to rationalism, but in the new mode introduced by the magisterial figures of Immanuel Kant and Georg Friedrich Hegel. Objectivists in the twentieth century have again turned to empiricism, adding new formulations such as pragmatism, naturalism, and linguistic analysis. Jews have not yet explored the potential fruitfulness of linguistic analysis with regard to Judaism but they have produced Jewish theologies in the pragmatist and naturalist veins. The most prolific and creative expositor of this approach is the twentieth century American thinker, Mordecai M. Kaplan (1881-), founder of a theology and a movement which he dubbed "Reconstructionism."

Kaplan is best known for his definition of Judaism as, "an evolving, religious civilization." It is a civilization and not just a religion in that it includes commitment to a land, language, people, history, and culture in addition to specific beliefs and practices. It is nevertheless a religious civilization because religious beliefs and practices are at its core. These affect every other aspect of the Jewish civilization, and one who identifies through one or more of the non-religious elements without adopting some form of the religion has latched on to the periphery rather than the center of what it means to be a Jew. Moreover, Judaism is an evolving religious civilization in that it has changed in many ways over the centuries and must continue to do so in the present.

Kaplan's pragmatism is especially evident in the "evolving" part of the definition. For him the decision as to how Judaism should change in our time is a pragmatic matter, not a metaphysical, revelational, or legal one. The primary consideration in making such decisions is the need of the Jewish people, not the demands of a text considered to be revealed by God. Each individual Jew, moreover, must formulate his own set of beliefs and ritual practices. Legal terminology makes sense only in moral areas, and there only if the Jews succeed in forming cohesive, organized communities which can enforce such laws.

Kaplan's pragmatic approach to Jewish law and thought is grounded in his naturalism, which is most prominent in the "religious" part of his definition of Judaism. He defines God as, "the power that makes for salvation," i.e. the forces in nature that enable us to overcome our limitations and frustrations and push us to be creative and realize our potential for good. The goal, salvation, is thus not a state of eternal bliss in the hereafter introduced by a personal messiah; it is rather "life abundant," a this-worldly state to which God and all human beings can contribute by,

cultivation of basic values, like faith, patience, inner freedom, humility, thankfulness, justice, and love, which enable a man to be and do his best and to bear uncomplainingly the worst that may befall him.[2]

Tradition helps the Jew work toward this naturalistic version of salvation. The tradition, however, was not revealed by God. Since God is a force, He is not personal (although Kaplan refers to God as "He"), hence could not have revealed what we find in sacred Jewish texts. In each generation rather, Jews have attempted as well as they could to achieve the divine in life, in thought (the true) and practice (the good), guided by—but not restricted to—the tradition they inherited from their ancestors.[3]

It is the "civilization" part of Kaplan's definition, however, that has the most implications for his concept of covenant. He denies, for theological and moral reasons, that Jews are in any sense a chosen people. Theologically, if God is "the power that makes for salvation," He does not have a will and cannot choose anybody. Even if God could choose, such an election would be morally repugnant because it leads to arrogant chauvinism and disdain for others in those who consider themselves chosen, and to a corresponding hatred on the part of those who feel excluded from the supposedly chosen group.[4]

On the other hand, Kaplan also denies the validity of a thoroughgoing universalism because that runs counter to human psychology and morality and will ultimately deprive the world of the unique contributions of individual civilizations, Jewish and non-Jewish. Since this point is less understood and accepted, I will reproduce his arguments at some length:

> Everyone yearns to be a member of some people, and deems it a catastrophe to have no people to which to belong. . . . We cannot do without being needed, and without something of which we are proud. This is why we need . . . to embrace a group, inclusive of a sufficient number of generations to render certain that our being desired or needed is not ephemeral and that all of us . . . can recall some person, event or achievement we can be proud of. . . . These considerations prove that the question whether Jews shall retain their nationhood is not a political but a moral question. If what makes them a nation is the Torah and all that it represents as symbol, as content and as process, it is their duty to uphold their nationhood, even as their ancestors had to uphold the unity of God, to the point of martyrdom. . . . It is not so much our duty to our fathers that makes it important for us to maintain the continuity of our tradition as it is our duty to our children. All human progress has been achieved by the fact that each generation begins its career where its predecessors left off, availing itself of the accumulated knowledge and wisdom of past ages.[5]

What is called for, then, is a vigorous, self-respecting nationhood which strives to realize universal moral goals through its distinctive patterns of thought and ritual practice:

> In order that Jews may know who they are, what their place is in the world, and what resources they, as a group, possess with which to serve mankind, they must stress what it is that unites them as Jews.[6]

One can therefore talk about the "vocation" of the Jewish people even though one cannot properly ascribe a unique mission or chosenness to it. While all people are called to the service of God, the concrete content of that duty will vary according to the specific conditions and talents of individuals and nations. Even though Jews are not chosen to serve God over and above any other people of the world, they do have a unique calling to serve God in their own specific circumstances, which include a national homeland, a large, widely dispersed diaspora, and a long history of development.[7] This, then, is the new interpretation of covenant that modern Jews must foster: A partnership of the Jewish people among themselves and with God, to achieve salvation ("life abundant") in their own distinctive way:

> If we regard God as the Life of the universe, the Power that evokes personality in men and nations, then the sense of the nation's responsibility for contributing creatively to human welfare and progress in the light of its own best experience becomes the modern equivalent of the covenant idea. In it is implied that reciprocity between God and the nation that the term covenant denotes.[8]

The Jewish covenant is to be trans-national, consisting of Jews the world over working toward the salvation of all. Kaplan recognizes the importance of establishing a Jewish national homeland in Israel, where the Jewish civilization can be lived to its fullest, but he also claims that it is unrealistic to think that all Jews will migrate there. If we understand nationhood in cultural and ethical terms instead of political and geographic categories however, we can see how Jews in the diaspora can be at once full, loyal citizens of the country in which they live and yet full-fledged members of the Jewish nation.

According to Kaplan, the active participation of Jews in Jewish ethical nationhood is a boon to their native countries and mankind as a whole since it enables the Jew to contribute to both. The existence of diaspora Jewry is also a boon to the Jewish people. Since such Jews constantly come into direct contact with non-Jewish cultures, they provide a conduit through which appropriate elements of those cultures can be assimilated into Judaism. The diaspora experience can thus enrich Judaism tremendously.

> The status of the Jews which emerges from this program is that of an international nation with its home in Palestine.[9]

In sum, we must conceive of "Judaism as a Civilization," with its religion "The Religion of Ethical Nationhood"—as he titled his first and last books.

What are the obligations of such a covenant? In some ways they are narrower than those of the traditional Jewish covenant, and in some ways broader. They are narrower in that fulfillment of Kaplan's version of the covenant does not require obedience to all of the commandments of traditional Judaism.

> Judaism must permit progress to take its course, and must somehow retain its unity without imposing a uniform regimen of conduct upon its adherents. Progress in any phase of life takes place when some individual or group inaugurates a needed change. If that change justifies itself, it wins general acquiescence. It is only when we conceive Judaism as a developing civilization, which can retain its individual character, despite great latitude in belief and practice, that there can be any room for progress. . . . There is no gainsaying the fact that many of the Jewish religious folkways have outlived their usefulness, and no amount of reinterpretation will enable them to exert a spiritualizing influence upon the Jew. A revision of the entire system of Jewish customs is imperative.[10]

The revision of which Kaplan speaks involves adding some laws and dropping or modifying others. Once Jewish ritual practices are viewed as folkways of the Jewish civilization rather than as law, the individual Jew need not feel guilty or sinful for his omissions or modifications. On the contrary, Kaplan says, a distinct advantage of such an approach is that

> Jews will be able to exercise better judgment as to the manner of their observance.[11]

They can determine more accurately which customs continue to be meaningful or not.

The dietary laws, for example, are an important element in Jewish identity and

> should be reinstated in every Jewish home as a means of contributing to the home that atmosphere in which national folkways are subtly combined with folk religion.[12]

But since their main purpose

> is to add Jewish atmosphere to the home, there is no reason for suffering the inconvenience and self-deprivation which result from a rigid adherence outside the home. From the standpoint urged here it would not be amiss for a Jew to eat freely in the house of a Gentile, and to refrain from eating *trefa* in the house of a fellow-Jew.[13]

Since Jewish rituals are folkways and not divine laws for Kaplan and since the individual can choose which folkways to adopt and how, his concept of the covenant is narrower than the traditional covenant, in number of rituals required of the Jew and in the degree of obligation attached to each.

In other ways, however, Kaplan's version of the covenant demands as much of the Jew as Jewish law does, and in some areas even more. He does not diminish the moral obligations of Judaism in any way whatsoever. In ritual areas he gives more latitude to the individual than Jewish law does, as we have seen, but he does require observance of the rituals which a Jew finds meaningful and which he can observe without undue hardship.

Since many Jews observe nothing at all, the net result of his version of the covenant is that more is demanded of most Jews than they observe at present. As he says in regard to the Sabbath, Jews commonly observe either everything or nothing. Under his approach, each Jew would have to exercise careful judgment as to what to observe and what not, and the very process of decision would probably attract more Jews to Jewish observance.[14]

Kaplan's conception of the covenant is more expansive than the traditional notion in that he encourages the conscious creation of new ritual patterns which would accentuate the joy and aesthetic quality of Jewish living. Kaplan wants modern Jews to enhance and invigorate life with new rituals until the positive actually outweighs the negative in Jewish practice.[15]

But it is in regard to the non-religious elements of Jewish civilization that Kaplan's concept of covenant broadens the traditional notion most of all. Since all elements of the Jewish civilization—land, language, art, music, literature, law, dance, food, clothing, folksways, etc.—are part of what it means to be a Jew, no single expression of Jewishness should be sufficient for the Jew.

Kaplan's emphasis on the non-religious, civilizational elements of Jewish identity makes his notion of the covenant considerably more expansive than any before or after it, and that will be an important element to include in any modern version of the covenant. So will be his balanced sense of a strong Jewish identity together with an openness to and appreciation of, other peoples of the world. Similarly, his insistence on the importance of both, Israel as a national homeland as well as diaspora Jewry, must be included, for that is simply a recognition of modern facts. No exclusively Zionist theory can reckon with the facts, neither can a non-Zionist one.

Many people would question, on the other hand, Kaplan's understanding of the nature of God, and even more would challenge his theory of the content and authority of Jewish law. Can the Jewish covenant exist under Kaplan's transformation of Jewish law into folkways? He obviously thinks that that is the only realistic way to talk about the content of the covenant in the voluntaristic and varied contexts in which modern Jews live but this writer, for one, has his doubts, as will become clear later on.

4. An Existentialist Approach: Hermann Cohen

Existentialism emphasizes the experience of the individual rather than the shared experiences of the group as the basis for knowledge, and it pays particular attention to what the individual learns when he is actively involved in life rather than what he reports when he tries to stand back from his experiences to analyze them. A prominent existentialist doctrine, from which the school got its name, is that existence is prior to essence, i.e. our actual, individual experiences in life are chronologically as well as logically prior to our detached, objective consideration of the nature and content of those experiences. Consequently, say the existentialists, it is our individual, involved experiences which must form the basis for our knowledge.[16]

The progenitor of modern Jewish existentialism was Hermann Cohen (1842-1918), a German Jewish philosopher who began as an objectivist philosopher of the purest type. In his early writings he claimed that religion is a primitive form of ethics which will disappear once a rationally based ethic has been popularized, and that God is merely a religious articulation of the concept that nature is not adverse to the realization of ethics.

In those early doctrines, Cohen was largely echoing Kant. In 1915, however, he published *Der Begriff der Religion im System der Philosophie* (The Concept of Religion within the System of Philosophy), in which he pointed out that, since reason generalizes over particulars to produce concepts and rules, an ethics based upon reason can only deal with humanity as a whole, not the individual. The rules of ethics, moreover, are absolute: From the point of view of ethics an immoral act remains so forever. Yet, human experience differs from ethical theory in both respects. People experience life as individuals at least as much as they do as members of groups, and they need to have a way of absolving a moral wrong.

It was especially the individual's sense of sin and guilt that convinced Cohen that philosophy must pay more attention to the experience of the individual. People may feel guilty for transgressions commmitted by their particular group or by humanity as a whole, but they more commonly experience sin, guilt, and repentance as an individual phenomenon rather than a group one. If there is no way of mitigating the severity of the guilt that the individual feels, he may well be immobilized by it and incapable of further moral effort. Practical ethics therefore requires a personal God who can forgive the individual and help him re-shape himself into a moral person. Even such a God can never erase the immoral act but He can give the sinner the confidence to act morally in the future.

Thus, religion is still subservient to ethics in Cohen's later writings as in his earlier ones, but God has been changed from a concept to an existent, personal being and religion assigned an important, continuing role in the moral life of mankind. Both of these changes derived from Cohen's new attention to the individual's experience, hence his tremendous influence on later existentialists like Rosenzweig and Buber.[17]

Even though Cohen's later writings are more sympathetic to religion than his earlier ones, he seems an unlikely source for ideas on the covenant. His emphasis on the individual seems at odds with the whole notion of a group phenomenon like the covenant. Moreover, he interpreted creation, revelation and redemption in non-temporal, general terms embracing all of humanity, largely following the rationalist mode of his youth.[18]

Despite Cohen's individualism and universalism, he claims that the Jewish people have a unique role to play in human history, a role which defines its covenant with God and makes it imperative that they retain their identity as Jews. Jews are unique in two ways. First, their religion is the only thoroughly monotheistic one:

> Monotheism is not the thought of one man, but of the whole Jewish national spirit unfolding in the creation and development of this thought which impregnates the entire thinking of the people.[19]

Early Hebraic religion was polytheistic, mirroring the religion of the Canaanites among whom the Hebrews lived, but that polytheistic stage was only a precondition for the development of the thoroughgoing monotheism that Judaism developed from the Burning Bush on.[20] Since then, Jewish monotheism has been "pure" and "absolute,"[21] in contrast to Christianity which confused it with the concepts of a trinity and of God becoming man in the person of Jesus,[22] and in contrast to pantheism of any degree or form. In fact, pantheism is in Cohen's view a more serious threat to true religion and ethics than polytheism because the former denies the transcendence of God. Pantheism removes much of the authority of ethical principles, implying that they are not rooted in the structure of the world, as they must be if they are to be true and absolute. Only monotheism provides an author, justification, and an enforcer for morality, and only monotheism preserves man's integrity so that he can be moral.[23]

The second way in which Jews are unique is in their role as the Suffering Servant. One of the most important implications of monotheism, according to Cohen, is that guilt and suffering are not commensurate:

> To sever the connection between suffering and guilt—to discard, that is, the notion that suffering is a punishment for guilt—is one of the most far-reaching consequences of monotheistic thinking.[24]

To understand this, we must remember that for Cohen monotheism and morality are intimately connected.[25] Monotheism demands morality of us now and pictures the moral life as the ultimate goal of mankind. Normally, however, we think in eudaemonistic terms in which the good should be rewarded and the evil punished. That however implies that reward and punishment are the ultimate ends rather than morality. A symbol is therefore needed to remind us consistently that we should not strive for materialistic pleasures but for moral conduct. Israel is that symbol:

> This historical suffering of Israel gives it its historical dignity, its tragic mission, which represents its share in the divine education of mankind. What other solution is there for the discrepancy between Israel's historical mission and its historical fate? There is no other solution but the one which the following consideration offers: to suffer for the dissemination of monotheism, as the Jews do, is not a sorrowful fate; the suffering is, rather, its tragic calling, for it proves the heartfelt desire for the conversion of the other peoples, which the faithful people feels.[26]

Cohen is careful to point out that Israel does not take the world's guilt upon itself. That would be unjust of God to demand of Israel, since Israel is not guilty. Only God can remove guilt in His mercy, and Christianity erred in thinking that the Suffering Servant assumed the burden of guilt as well as suffering. The requirements of justice, however, do not preclude Israel from suffering for mankind and thereby teaching the anti-eudaemonistic lesson of monotheism to the world.[27]

Even though Cohen denies any ethnic content to the special covenant between God and Israel,[28] he does not negate the importance of ritual observance. Jews need to remain a distinct people in order to preserve and foster monotheistic beliefs and moral behavior, and ritual law serves to isolate the people Israel for that task. In addition to that negative, preservative function, ritual observance also

> is a positive force that stimulates, inspires, fortifies, and deepens religious ideas and beliefs[29]

and that engenders piety for the past. In fact, in response to Paul's claim that the law is a burden, he points out the moral and aesthetic meaning that ritual observance can have. He says,

> the idea that religion is a personal experience seems to be at no point more convincing than in connection with the question of the law.[30]

Cohen is careful to say that he is only justifying

> the continuation of the law in accordance with its general concept—not the particular laws.[31]

But he sees moral value in most of the laws in that they act as symbols for moral values or theological beliefs. Thus, while the content of the covenant entails monotheism and morality exclusively according to Cohen, its preservation and dissemination require observance of most of the ceremonial laws as well.

Aside from Cohen's attention to the individual, the most innovative parts of his approach to the covenant occur in his discussion of its purposes. As we have seen, monotheism and morality constitute the content of the covenant according to him, but man becomes moral only when his actions are no longer self-serving but goal oriented. Consequently, Cohen emphasizes that the covenant is aimed at the creation of the messianic era, that that indeed is the goal of religion generally:

> We believe that the messianic idea is the culmination as well as the touchstone of religion and that religious conviction means Messianic religiosity.[32]

In messianic times all people will recognize God as king and will acknowledge the rules of morality, just as Israel does now.[33]

In thus stressing the messianic goal-directedness of religion, Cohen illuminates an important aspect of the covenant, one which is often not associated with it but which clearly underlies its prophetic understanding. That, and his concentration on the individual's identification with the covenant and purification through it, constitute two of Cohen's most important insights. In modern times, when there is increased attention to the individual on the one hand and to the need for international cooperation on the other, Cohen's approach has much to offer.

Similarly, in a post-Holocaust age, his distinction between suffering and guilt may prove helpful in motivating continued adherence to the covenant. His denial of the ethnic elements of Judaism will have to be tempered, however, because those have proved to be real and important aspects of Jewish identity. Jews will need to form relationships with others but maintain a vigorous identity of their own at the same time. And finally, a modern Jewish concept of the covenant will need to spell out the mechanism for determining the content of covenant much more specifically than Cohen does. *What* constitutes the moral thing to do, and *which* rituals must be observed? Many will not be happy, moreover, with asserting divine authority for moral laws only, relegating rituals to a symbolic status. One wonders how long rituals can endure if they are merely folkways à la Kaplan or symbols, as according to Cohen.

5. The Covenant as Organizing Concept for Modern Jewish Life

Can the covenant idea function as an organizing concept for modern Jewish life? The criteria that I myself would use in judging the various versions of the covenant idea are simple to state, though not so easy to fulfill or apply. We want an interpretation which is historically authentic, yet compelling to a modern Jew. Modern Jews obviously differ in their outlook, sensitivities, knowledge, and desires; but we are seeking an approach which takes account of the results of modern, critical scholarship into the history and texts of the Jewish tradition, performs the functions and captures the strengths of the traditional concept, and also speaks to the facts, problems, and potential of modern Jewish living. These, then, are the features which we seek in a contemporary interpretation of the covenant.

a. The covenant is a relationship between God and the people Israel.

No interpretation which fails to incorporate this fundamental feature of the traditional concept can claim historical authenticity or even logical similarity to the term covenant, as it is usually employed in Judaism. The exact nature of this relationship, however, is a matter of dispute. In particular, when we speak of the covenant, do we mean to assert a reality or a metaphor? The Torah clearly intended to describe a reality in depicting acts of commitment by God and Israel towards each other. Those acts established legal facts in that they created obligations for both partners. Thus the Pentateuchal covenant is a legal instrument in the fullest sense of the term.

The problem with such a literal understanding of the covenant, however, is that it infringes on God's omnipotence because a legal document can only take effect if there is an already existing sphere of law or morality binding both parties. Otherwise there is no mechanism by which the covenant can be enforced and its obligations carry dubious authority. The existence of such a framework, however, would mean that God is bound by outside constraints. The patriarchal, Mosaic, and some of the prophetic and hagiographic traditions were willing to accept that consequence, claiming that God is bound by His own morality or wisdom. Some of the later sections of the Tanakh, however, assert unreservedly that God can do anything, and thus talk of His contractual obligations is muted. This is clearest in *Job* and *Koheleth*, where God is specifically held to be free of all moral bounds (at least as men understand them) due to His power.

Even some of the prophets use the term covenant in metaphoric rather then literal terms, comparing it to the marriage vows between husband and wife.[34] In so doing, the prophets were already transforming the meaning of the term from a legal act to a metaphor for a close, though non-legal relationship. By the time of the rabbis the term virtually went out of use in Jewish circles, both because of the concern to preserve a completely omnipotent God and because of the Christian use of the term.

It was after secular philosophers in the seventeenth century made social-contract theories popular that Jews began to be interested once again in investigating its adaptability as an explanation and expression of Judaism. Some have interpreted the covenant as a legal act, following the social-contract theorists and the early biblical tradition, and some have merely used it as an expression of an ongoing relationship between God and Israel. In any case, a modern version of the covenant idea must at least assert the latter if it is to be a covenant in any recognizable way.[35] This requirement breaks down into three corollary demands of a modern interpretation of the covenant.

*It must include an understanding of God's nature
such that He can enter into a covenant.*

Many theologies can satisfy this requirement, but those which preserve God's personality can do so with most ease. In Roman law already,
communities of people could form a legal body (later called a corporation)
which could function as if it had an independent existence; but that is an
extension of the primary model of covenant making, in which two real
persons contract with one another. Consequently, even if the covenant is a
legal reality, it is best understood if God has a personality. That is true all
the more if the covenant signifies a broad, ongoing relationship between
God and the Jewish people. These considerations would support an existentialist approach because existentialists are especially adept at capturing
the personal element of the covenant.

Rationalists have more trouble because the generalizing character of
reason often leads to a deistic theology, but some affirm God's direct,
verbal revelation of His part of the covenant anyway, ignoring the apparent inconsistency (e.g. Moses Mendelssohn). Others change the notion of
covenant substantially in order to fit their conceptions of God (e.g.
Kaplan); and still others develop rationalist theologies which specifically
include personal attributes of God.[36] In any case, no approach to Judaism
which denies to God a role in the covenant can count as a reasonable
extension of the traditional covenant idea, and those thinkers who adopt a
personal concept of God are able to produce interpretations of the covenant closest to the traditional notion.

It must include a unique role for the people of Israel.

It may be better for Jews to view themselves as having a special
vocation rather than a mission for which they alone were chosen, as
Kaplan maintains, and people of other religions and nations may be able to
contract other covenants with God. But the traditional covenant is unequivocally between God and the people of Israel. Some explanation of
the unique role of Israel in the covenant must therefore be supplied.

It must include a living, active relationship between God and Israel.

In virtually all forms of Jewish religious thought, God is actively
involved in human affairs on a continuing basis, whether the substance of
the covenant is primarily legal or not. Even deistic theologies (e.g. Mendelssohn, Kaplan) affirm such a continuing interaction, although they of
course describe it differently from more traditional, theistic positions.

b. The covenant imposes obligations on the individual Jew
and on the Jewish community,
(specifically those spelled out by the ongoing rabbinic interpretation
of biblical law in each generation).

Any version of the covenant which denies either its obligatory character or the identification of its obligations with classical Jewish law is not a plausible extension of the traditional covenant idea. Even if the covenant is a metaphor for a relationship with God which is non-legal in its nature, there must be some way in which observing Jewish law is justified. Most modern Jewish philosophers who deny that the Torah is the literal, final law of God nevertheless want to link the authority of Jewish law to God in some way, often using the notion of an ongoing covenantal relationship as the medium, but some prefer to base its obligations on totally human factors, understanding the covenant exclusively as a symbol for the many non-legal relationships which God has with us.[37]

As there are disagreements about the role of the covenant in justifying Jewish law, there are also disagreements about specific laws, as there have always been. Nevertheless I would maintain that any modern interpretation of the covenant must in some way require commitment to observing Jewish law, however it is delineated, and must not leave it to the individual to determine the content of the covenant's obligations and which of them he will voluntarily obey. Jews may choose not to adhere to Jewish law, but then it must be clear to them that they are not fulfilling the obligations of the covenant since Jewish law has always been the way in which Jews have understood and articulated the way in which a Jew is supposed to respond to God's interaction with us. In this, Mendelssohn, Cohen, and Rosenzweig are right while Spinoza, Kaplan, and Buber are wrong.[38]

c. The obligations of the covenant include
both rituals and morals.

The covenant requires observance of Jewish ritual law, as Mendelssohn and Rosenzweig claim, despite the arguments of the classical Reformers (e.g. Geiger) and Buber. It is not restricted to that, however, Spinoza and Mendessohn notwithstanding. It also includes moral norms as they are specifically understood and applied in the Jewish tradition. For Judaism, morals are not the universal property of all rational beings; they derive from the covenant and take their specific form therein.[39]

d. The covenant has an inescapable communal dimension.

The covenant is first and foremost between God and the people of

Israel as a community. It is a relationship between God and the individual
Jew only in an indirect, secondary way. That gives Jewish law universal
authority within the Jewish community, regardless of the individual Jew's
mood or stage of development. Mendelssohn's use of social-contract theory captures this element of the covenant well, and Kaplan's stress on the
civilizational character of Judaism calls attention to other aspects of this
communal factor. On the other hand, the individualism inherent in existentialism makes it difficult for those using that approach to account for
the communal nature of Judaism, however much the individualism is
modified by people like Cohen and Rosenzweig.

e. Nevertheless, the covenant also has an individual dimension.

The communal element is dominant in classical Jewish theology, but
the existentialists are not totally misguided in speaking about the individual's relationship to the covenant in even traditional interpretations of it.
That relationship is manifested physically, historically, theologically, and
legally:

1. Physically each Jewish male is brought into the covenant through
circumcision (and, increasingly in modern times, Jewish females are
brought into the covenant at birth through some form of covenant ceremony).

2. Historically, each Jew must see himself as if he participated in the
crucial events of Jewish history. As the Passover Haggadah phrases it:

> In each and every generation one must look upon himself as if he
> personally had come out from Egypt (cf. Ex 13:8).

Similarly, the "wicked son" of the Haggadah has been, throughout history,
the one who fails to identify with his fellow Jews.

3. Theologically, each individual Jew must form his or her own
relationship with God. That, of course, is the area which the existentialists
stress most. The tradition put much more emphasis on the community's
relationship with God. Thus worship became largely standardized in form
and obligatory at specific times, and even confessional prayers were
phrased in the plural. There was room for individual prayer in the
traditional liturgy, however, and the rabbis recognized that even the
people at Sinai heard God according to their own individual capabilities.[40]
Nevertheless, it must be said that the Jewish tradition assumed that the
individual relates to God best through the community.

4. In the area of Jewish law, the rabbis certainly would not accept the
existentialists' claim that the number and nature of a person's obligations

depend on his particular relationship to God. They were, however, interested in encouraging the individual to have the proper intention (*kavanah*) while he fulfilled the prescribed actions (*keva*), and intention is clearly a private matter.

f. The covenant has an historical dimension.

It articulates the relationship between God and the people of Israel throughout history and this has at least two implications:

1. Some elements in former articulations of the covenant are time-bound. Spinoza took this to an extreme, but he was right in calling attention to the fact that any relationship, including that between God and the Jewish people, takes place in time and that specific expressions of the relationship may reflect the concerns, biases, and state of knowledge at a given time. We must identify the eternal elements in those expressions and have the courage to leave behind the time-bound elements. That is easier said than done but it has effectively been accomplished throughout Jewish history, by reinterpretations of Jewish law and beliefs. The tradition retained continuity despite the changes, by making decisions in such matters a communal responsibility.[41]

2. Much of the authority of the covenant derives from the individual Jew's identification with the covenantal relationship between his people and God, throughout history. The relationship is not a new, untested one but old and familiar. Through the covenant, therefore, the Jew can and does feel a sense of security and rootedness, and his commitment to it grows out of the long-term relationship that, through it, he has had with God. This is the reason why Deuteronomy begins with a review of past relations between God and the Jewish people, before spelling out the terms of the covenant.[42] That also is the thrust of the Passover Seder.

As Rosenzweig saw, norms are effective when they grow out of relationships, especially long term ones, hence Buber's notion of "inner power" can and should be used to explain the authority of Jewish law: The Jew will observe it if he sees himself as part of the ongoing tie between his people and God, and that is a much more powerful stimulus than the abstract, social-contract theories which Mendelssohn employs to give authority to the covenant.

g. The covenant includes non-religious, ethnic elements (including especially ties to the land of Israel and to the Hebrew language).

Up to the nineteenth century, Jews did not distinguish between the religious and ethnic parts of Jewish identity. The ties of Israel and the

Hebrew language were religious ties (hence their designations as "holy land" and "holy tongue"—more precisely, "language of holiness"), and all other aspects of Jewish culture were seen as further developments of the Jewish religion. It was only in modern times that the distinction was made, both by those who wanted to affirm the religion and deny the ethnic elements (e.g. Cohen and the classical Reformers), as by those who wished to affirm the ethnic identity of Jews and deny the importance or truth of the religion (e.g. the secular Zionists). Neither of those denials was historically authentic, neither has proved helpful in understanding modern Jewish identity—as recent Reform theologians and Israeli secularists are increasingly admitting.

Consequently, just as a satisfactory, modern understanding of the covenant must explicitly affirm the religious factors in Jewish identity, so too it must affirm what we might now designate the ethnic components of what it means to be a Jew, including the ties to the people and land of Israel, Hebrew and Jewish art, architecture, literature, dance, music, food, and dress. Kaplan, of course, did the most to illuminate this feature of the covenant, and Cohen's denial of the ethnic part of Jewish identity must be considered simply wrong.[43]

h. The purpose of the covenant is to better the world, ultimately creating the messianic era.

Hermann Cohen is the philosopher who draws our attention to this aspect of the covenant most clearly. The idea is strongly embedded in the thought of the prophets and finds expression also in rabbinic literature and in the liturgy.[44]

i. Affirmation of the covenant involves effort, pain and sacrifice.

It is again Hermann Cohen who most clearly delineates this aspect of the covenant. Jews feel uncomfortable in speaking about the sacrifice entailed in the covenant because they generally think of the commandments as a meaningful, joyful structure for life and because Christianity has emphasized the need for sacrifice and the Suffering Servant theme so extensively. Nevertheless, rabbinic literature does include statements which acknowledge the pain which Israel suffers in adhering to the covenant, for instance:

> God gave Israel three fine gifts, but each was given through suffering: the Torah, the land of Israel, and the world to come.
> When Moses came down from Mount Sinai, . . . a decree was issued

concerning Israel that Israel should learn the commandments through affliction and enslavement, through exile and banishment, through straits and through famine. And on account of that suffering which they have undergone, God will repay their recompense in the days of the Messiah many times over.[45]

The rabbis attempted to explain why it is that Israel suffers so much in adhering to God's commandments, but they ultimately gave up, claiming that God's justice cannot be fathomed and that it is wrong to seek reward for one's good deeds anyway:

Be not as servants who minister to their master for the sake of receiving a reward, but be rather like servants who minister to their master without the condition of receiving a reward. . . . R. Aha said: God has made uncertain the reward of those who perform the commands of the Law so that they may do them in fidelity.[46]

The rabbis also spoke at length about the evil inclination which mitigates against fulfilling the commandments and how one might overcome its debilitating effects. Thus the element of suffering in carrying out the obligations of the covenant is no stranger to the Jewish tradition and should be integrated into a modern interpretation of the covenant idea.

j. Nevertheless, the predominant reaction of the Jew
  to the covenant is one of joy.

The commandments may be difficult to observe and adhering to the covenant may entail suffering but, on balance, being part of the covenant is a meritorious and joyful experience.[47] It is also considered the major manifestation of God's love, as the Jew repeats daily in the traditional liturgy:

Enlighten our eyes in Your Torah,
Open our hearts to Your commandments.
Unite our thoughts with singleness of purpose
To hold You in reverence and love. . . .
Bring us safely from the corners of the earth,
And lead us in dignity to our holy land.
You, O God, are the Source of deliverance;
You have chosen us from all peoples and tongues.
You have drawn us close to You;
We praise You and thank You in truth.
With love do we thankfully proclaim Your unity,
And praise You who chose Your people Israel in love.[48]

A modern rendition of the covenant idea must take that into account, too.

These, then, are the features which are crucial to the concept of covenant. That idea has long been an important conceptual framework in which the people of Israel have understood themselves and a powerful stimulus to observe Jewish law. Consequently, non-Jews who wish to understand Judaism, and Jews who wish to further it, must confront this pivotal concept in ancient and modern Jewish thought, for it articulates the Jew's understanding of his present and his hope for the future:

> "And you shall be holy unto Me, for I, the Lord, am holy, and I have severed you from other peoples so that you should be Mine. As I am holy, so you should be holy. As I am separate, so you should be separate. And I have severed you from the other peoples that you should be Mine."[49]

Notes

1. Mystics also emphasize the experience of the individual but they concern themselves chiefly with what the individual experiences when he turns inward, while existentialists stress the individual's experience with the world outside. The two groups differ in their orientation (inward vs. outward experience), ontology (ultimate unity vs. ultimate plurality of being), use of the Bible (a way to union with God vs. a manual of instruction for relationships with fellow-men), and goal (union with God vs. relationships with others).

2. Mordecai M. Kaplan, *The Future of the American Jew* (New York: Reconstructionist Press, 1948), p. 100; cf. chap. 15. Henceforth cited as *Future*.

3. Kaplan's thinking is expounded in a number of works, including *Judaism as a Civilization* (New York: Schocken, 1934, 1967); *The Meaning of God in Modern Jewish Religion* (New York: Behrman, 1937, 1962); *Questions Jews Ask* (New York: Reconstructionist Press, 1956); *Judaism without Supernaturalism* (New York: Reconstructionist Press, 1958); *The Greater Judaism in the Making* (New York: Reconstructionist Press, 1960); *The Religion of Ethical Nationhood* (New York: MacMillan, 1970). The clearest and most direct expositions of his views are, I think, in *The Future of the American Jew* and *Questions Jews Ask*.

4. *The Meaning of God*, pp. 94f; cf. *Future*, chap. 13. Also, *Judaism without Supernaturalism*, chap. 4, where Kaplan applies this analysis in detail to Christianity as well as Judaism.

5. *Future*, p. 82; *Judaism as a Civilization*, pp. 246f, 259f. Henceforth cited as *Civilization*; also, *The Meaning of God*, p. 96.

6. *Questions Jews Ask*, p. 35, cf. p. 413.

7. *Ibid.*, pp. 501f.

8. *Civilization*, pp. 258f; *The Meaning of God*, pp. 102f.

9. *Civilization*, p. 251; cf. pp. 216, 233f, 241.

10. *Ibid.*, pp. 222, 438.

11. *Ibid.*, p. 441.

12. *Ibid.*, pp. 441f.

13. *Ibid.*

14. *Ibid.*, p. 447.

15. *Ibid.*, pp. 432, 439.

16. Cf. note 1.

17. I have called all three men, Cohen, Rosenzweig, and Buber, existentialists, although none of them was actually affiliated with other philosophers of that school, and all three would probably have objected to that designation, for one reason or another. Yet, their stress on the individual and, especially, the individual's experience of loneliness and despair as the starting point for philosophy, warrants that characterization. Most people would, indeed, describe them as existentialists. There definitely are existentialist elements in their thought, even if some hesitate to call them full-fledged existentialists.

18. Hermann Cohen, *Religion of Reason out of the Sources of Judaism*, Simon Kaplan, transl. (New York: Fredk. Ungar, 1972), chaps. 3, 4, 5, 7, 13. Henceforth cited as *Religion*. Also, *Reason and Hope: Selections from the Jewish Writings of Hermann Cohen*, Eva Jospe, ed. and transl. (New York: W. W. Norton, 1971), pp. 46f, 94-101, 132-153. Henceforth cited as *Reason*.

19. *Religion*, chap. 1, par. 4, p. 36.

20. *Ibid.*, pars. 4, 13, pp. 36ff, 42ff.

21. *Reason*, p. 187.

22. *Ibid.*, pp. 45, 53, 150; cf. *Religion*, chap. 13, par. 43, p. 255.

23. *Reason*, pp. 45, 77-101, 150, 152.

24. *Reason*, p. 70.

25. Cf. note 22.

26. *Religion*, pp. 283f.

27. *Ibid.*, pp. 263ff.

28. *Ibid.*, chap. 13, pars. 35, 38, 40, pp. 252-254; chap. 14, par. 4, p. 271; chap. 16, p. 353; also *Reason*, pp. 46-50, 168ff; chap. 6.

29. *Religion*, chap. 16, esp. pp. 365-370; the quotation is from p. 367.

30. *Ibid.*, p. 357.

31. *Ibid.*, p. 366 and chap. 16, esp. pp. 340-344. Cf. *Reason*, p. 79.

32. *Reason*, pp. 126f; cf. pp. 97, 119.

33. *Ibid.*, p. 47.

34. Cf. Hos 2:18-22; Is 54:4-10; cf. also Is 42:6; 49:8, 59:21; Jer 31:31-34, 32:40; Ez 16:59-63.

35. I am indebted to Prof. Amos Funkenstein for calling my attention to this change in meaning of the term covenant, and the ambiguity it introduces into many modern discussions of the concept.

36. For examples of the last of these, cf. Jacob Agus, *Guideposts in Modern*

Judaism (New York: Bloch, 1954), part 2, sec. 2; Elliot Dorff, "Two Ways to Approach God," in *Conservative Judaism*, vol. 30, no. 2 (Winter, 1976), pp. 58-67.

37. Kaplan and his followers are, of course, the primary example for the latter. For a description of a variety of options in understanding the authority of Jewish law, from the most legal to the least legal, cf. Elliot Dorff, *Conservative Judaism: Our Ancestors to our Descendants* (New York: United Synagogue Youth, 1977), chap. 3, sec. D. My position in that publication calls the classical Reform stance into serious question; but it seems to me that the classical Reformers were simply wrong in their understanding of what Judaism was and should be. I anticipate and welcome objections on that score.

38. So is Eugene Borowitz, who stresses the notion of covenant but then leaves it to the individual to decide its content. Cf. *How can a Jew Speak of Faith Today?* (Philadelphia: Westminster Press, 1969), p. 68. As he says there, a traditional Jew would find that strange.

39. Cf. José Faur, "Understanding the Covenant," in *Tradition*, vol. 9, no. 4 (Spring, 1968), pp. 33-54.

40. *Exodus Rabbah* 5, 9.

41. Cf. my article, "Judaism as a Religious Legal System," soon to appear in *Hastings Law Journal*, for a description of how communal decisions determine Jewish law.

42. This was a common feature of all covenants in the ancient Near East; cf. George Mendenhall, "Ancient Oriental and Biblical Law" and "Covenant Forms in Israelite Tradition," in *The Biblical Archaeologist Reader*, no. 3, Edw. F. Cambell, Jr. and David N. Freedman, eds. (Garden City, N. Y.: Doubleday, 1967), chaps. 1, 2.

43. Cf. note 28. There is one rabbinic comment which expresses a position somewhat similar to Cohen's, specifically: "Rabbi Eliezer said: God scattered Israel among the nations for the sole end that proselytes should wax numerous among them. . . . Rabbi Hoshaiah said: God did Israel a benefit when He scattered them among the nations" (TB *Pesahim* 87b). But those statements were probably *post factum* justifications and consolations for the Jews in exile; they certainly were not articulations of ultimate hopes. Virtually all biblical and rabbinic statements on the messianic age tie it to a return of the exiles to Zion, contra Hermann Cohen, including that very section where, following the remarks of Rabbi Eliezer and Rabbi Hoshaiah, Rabbi Yohanan says: "The ingathering of the exiles (to Israel) is as great as the day on which the heavens and earth were created" (TB *Pesahim* 88a).

44. Cf. especially the *Aleynu* prayer, said three times daily. Cf. also *Genesis Rabbah* 11, 6; 13, 13; 43, 7; *Numbers Rabbah* 1, 3; *Deuteronomy Rabbah* 6, 5; and the laws which the rabbis enacted "for the improvement of the world," in TB *Gittin* 36a; 40b; 41b; 45a; 47b; 53a; and TJ *Baba Bathra* 10d.

45. Salomon Buber, ed. and annot., *Midrash Tanhuma* (Jerusalem: Ortsel, 1963), Shemot, par. 1, f. 81a; M. Friedman, ed., *Tanna deve Eliyahu* (Jerusalem: Wahrmann, 1969), p. 117.

46. *Avot* 1, 3; TJ *Peah* 1, 1, f. 15d; cf. *Deuteronomy Rabbah* 6, 2.

47. Cf. TB *Berakoth* 11b (= the source of the blessing which the Jew pronounces each day for having the Torah); TB *Shabbath* 30b; *Bezah* 15b; *Sifre Deuteronomy*, Ki Tavo, par. 303; *Midrash Psalms* on Pss. 24:3, 119:54; and TB *Makkoth* 3, 16, which is repeated at the end of the synagogue reading of each chapter of *Avot*.

48. *Weekday Prayer Book* (New York: Rabbinical Assembly of America, 1974), pp. 45f (with minor changes in the translation); cf. also TB *Aboth* 3, 18.

49. *Sifra* 93d.

3.
Covenant and the Interreligious Encounter

Manfred Vogel

The topic of this chapter, the examination of the notion of covenant in the context of the Jewish-Christian dialogue, introduces one to the dialogue at its deepest, most profound level. For clearly, one would be pursuing the dialogue here on the theological level and it is only on this level that the dialogue can find its ultimate, true significance. After all, Judaism and Christianity are first and foremost communities of faith and as such the fundamental authentic self-understanding of each is to be found in the theological sphere.

But dealing with the notion of covenant not only introduces us to the dialogue at its deepest level, i.e., the theological level; it introduces to us the most fundamental category at this level. For the covenant is not just one of the various categories constituting the theological discourse. In the theological discourse of Judaism and Christianity it is the fundamental category underlying all other categories. This is so by virtue of the fact that the covenant constitutes the fundamental category in the world-view of the Tanakh (Hebrew Scriptures). Consequently, inasmuch as both Judaism and Christianity ground themselves in the Tanakh, the covenant is likewise the fundamental category in their respective theological discourse. Indeed, the covenant represents on the deepest level the common bond between Judaism and Christianity. At the same time, however, seeing that they apprehend the covenant differently, it also represents on the deepest level the point of difference between them.

1. The Covenant in Biblical Faith

Walter Eichrodt has convincingly shown that the various categories of biblical thought (such categories, for example, as the kingship of God, revelation, liberation from myth, etc.) are derived and receive their rationale from the category of the covenant.[1] As such, the centrality of the covenant is clearly established. But its centrality can be further established in terms of its own signification and implications. The covenant is a relational category—it delineates not individual entities in themselves but the relation between them. In the biblical context it delineates the relation between God and man. As such, it impinges upon that which constitutes the very core and essence of the religious phenomenon. For the thrust of the religious view-point, in contra-distinction to the philosophical, lies not in apprehending God as He is in Himself but rather in grasping the relation that exists between Him and man.

Even more decisively, the covenant necessarily implicates a God who is a personal being, a Thou. For a covenant is a binding which is an agreement rather than a blind, necessary, natural interaction. It is a binding that is based on free decision and election rather than being mechanical and inescapable.[2] This, in turn means, that a covenant necessarily implicates the two parties to the relation as personal beings, as Thous. For only a being-of-consciousness, a Thou, can elect and decide; only in the sphere of the Thou can freedom and spontaneity operate. A covenant cannot arise between two impersonal beings, two Its, or even between a personal being, a Thou, and an impersonal being, an It. A relation, therefore, between man and the divine that is constituted as a covenant will of necessity implicate the divine as a Thou.

It is here that ultimate significance and centrality of the covenant really lies. For the covenant implicates that which is most essential and unique to biblical faith: that the divine, in the sense of that which is ultimate, is a personal being. Indeed, this marks the great qualitative divide between biblical faith and the religions that we might designate as pagan. In the latter, the ultimate that man encounters is a blind, inexorable power which may only become personified in its penultimate manifestations (these being the gods of the Pantheon). As Yehezkel Kaufmann has very perceptively shown, these gods are not ultimate[3]; behind them lurks blind power, a relentless fate, be it called *moira, fatum,* or *maat.* The great break that biblical faith signals in the history of religions is that it encounters not only in the penultimate but in the very ultimate itself a being that is conscious, aware, and concerned about man.

It should, then, not be surprising that the notion of covenant between

God and man is unique to biblical faith[4]; none of the pagan religions perceive that relationship as convenantal. Where the divine is encountered as an It, the relation can be constituted as magic but not as covenantal, indeed, biblical faith excludes the possibility of magic.[5]

True, the pagan cultures of the ancient Near East knew all sorts of covenants between individuals, nations and, of course, suzerain and vassals. Yet all these covenants characterized horizontal relations, that is, relations between man and man, not between man and the divine. Any vertical relationship in these cultures was not covenantal but magical.[6]

The innovative genius of biblical faith lies precisely in its capacity to transform a covenantal relation which is horizontal into a vertical one. Though the notion of a covenantal relation was clearly borrowed from surrounding cultures, biblical faith then applied it to a totally new situation which was not perceived and, indeed, not possible in the pagan context.

There is no denying that the covenantal relation is prominently reflected in the Bible in the Sinaitic covenant, a covenant which is clearly patterned after the suzerain-vassal model. Thus, in the Sinaitic covenant the relationship between God and man is indeed understood in terms of demands and stipulations. In return for God's graciousness and protection man is required to obey the laws given to him. It is a covenant of law. Most significantly, the covenant here is conditional—it is contingent upon Israel's obedience to and observance of the stipulations formulated by God.

It is important to note, however, that the Sinaitic covenant is not the only kind of covenant encountered in the Tanakh. We also find the covenant of promise as exemplified in the Noachide covenant. Here, in contradistinction to the Sinaitic covenant, no demands or stipulations are placed upon man; rather, God makes a promise as reward for man's faithfulness.[7]

The theological structure of the covenant of promise is evidently quite different from that of the Sinaitic covenant. First and foremost, the covenant is not conditional. Its realization and fulfillment do not depend on what man does or does not do; it comes as a reward for what man has already done. The action devolves furthermore not on man but on God. It is God who binds Himself to do certain things, man is merely the recipient, the beneficiary of the divine action. Finally, the covenant is concluded with individuals and not with a collectivity of individuals, i.e. a whole nation, as in the case of the Sinaitic covenant.

It is important to keep in mind these two types of covenant when proceeding beyond the perimeter of the Tanakh to post-biblical Judaism and Christianity. There is no question that rabbinic, talmudic Judaism continues to consider itself a covenantal community of faith. The biblical covenantal relation of Israel to God continues to remain fully in effect, nothing is added and nothing abrogated. No essential change occurs in the transition from biblical Israel to rabbinic Judaism with regard to the covenant. Yet, though there is no change in substance, there may well be a change in emphasis regarding the alternative types of covenant delineated in the Tanakh. In rabbinic Judaism the Sinaitic covenant, the covenant of law, becomes the all-important, central category by which Israel's relationship to God is essentially characterized. Indeed, rabbinic Judaism is appropriately designated as *halakhic* Judaism.

One is almost tempted to say that while in the Tanakh the covenantal aspect apears as an ellipse with two centers—the Sinaitic covenant and the covenant of promise—in rabbinic Judaism if appears as a circle with one, and one center only, namely the Sinaitic covenant. Not that the covenants of promise are consciously or unconsciously abrogated; they continue to be maintained and affirmed but their role is relegated to the domain of edification rather than to the economy of redemption.[8]

The situation is quite different in the case of the Christian community of faith. True, Christianity is also within the covenantal perspective and as such belongs to the same basic structure of faith which characterizes the Tanakh and rabbinic Judaism. With regard to its most essential element, i.e. the kind of being that man encounters as ultimate, Christianity is at one with Judaism: God as the ultimate is a personal being, a Thou. The covenantal aspect, then, is a most important unifying factor between the Tanakh, rabbinic Judaism, and Christianity. The latter is placed within the family of biblical faiths and in contradistinction to pagan religions. The importance of this is not be be minimized.

Yet the covenantal perspective also introduces a divisive factor, leading to a radical break. For Christianity claims to introduce a new covenant or at least a radical transformation of the covenantal relation articulated in the Tanakh. This fact inevitably precipitates the question of what the relation is to be between the new covenant and the old. What is the new situation that Christianity introduces into the covenantal relationship of the Tanakh and its continuation in rabbinic Judaism? In what sense is it new?

A delineation of the new in contradistinction to the old is obviously called for; the onus for this task, however, must fall exclusively on Christianity. After all, it is Christianity which considers itself as something new, therefore it should define its relationship to that which preceded it. Judaism can only respond to the various formulations and rationales advanced by Christianity. The very logic of the situation requires that Christianity take the initiative, while Judaism must perforce assume a defensive posture—it cannot initiate, it can only react.[9]

2. The Relationship between the Old and New Covenant

In the history of Christian thought quite a number of formulations have, indeed, been advanced. It will be helpful to consider some of them within some scheme of classification. Such a scheme is provided by Roy Eckardt; he divides the formulations into those that are continuous and those that are discontinuous with the covenantal stance of Judaism.[10]

This classification may prove helpful, particularly if we keep in mind that the designations "continuous" and "discontinuous" may refer to two different significations of the term "Judaism."

One signification would refer to Judaism in the sense of its bearers, i.e. the Jewish people. The question here is: does the appearance of Christianity signify the end of the role of the Jewish people in the economy of redemption? As against this, the other signification would refer to Judaism in the sense of its very substance, namely the covenant. The question here is: does Christianity introduce a new understanding of the relation between man and God, differing from that of the Tanakh and rabbinic Judaism?

This dual signification of Judaism coupled with the continuous-discontinuous distinction provides us with four major categories by which we can proceed to examine the main formulations in which Christianity has attempted to establish its relation to the covenant of the Tanakh and to the Jewish people.

a. Discontinuous formulations

In the discontinuous models, the relationship is established on the basis of abrogation. This abrogation, however, can be applied either to the status of the people of Israel or to the very substance of its covenant. In the first instance, what is abrogated is not the substance of the covenant but the covenantal status of the people. The covenant is old, not in terms of its signification but because in the disposition prior to the coming of Jesus it belonged exclusively to the people of Israel. It is new in the context of Christianity because Christianity takes it from Israel and gives it to others, namely the gentiles. In the second instance the abrogation is directed towards the very substance of the covenant. The old covenant fails to constitute a salvific relation; it actually constitutes an inauthentic or even punitive relation. As such it is ineffective or even evil. The new covenant of Christianity, by abrogating the old covenant, extricates man from this relationship and places him in an authentic salvific relation to the divine.

b. Continuous formulations

Against these discontinuous formulations based on the notion of abrogation, the continuous models are based on the idea of fulfillment. The old is not extirpated from the covenantal context, rejected, or evacuated to make room for the new. There is no caesura; the new rather receives its signification while retaining the validity of the old.

This linkage of the new covenant to the old expresses itself in two different, indeed, contradictory patterns, thus further subdividing the various formulations into two additional distinct groups. According to the first pattern, the relation is established in a continuous direct line, by claiming more of the same; the distinction lies in the new having more of what the old has. According to the second pattern, the relation is established in contradistinction but the contradistinction remains within the covenantal context. True, the distinction is based on a positive evaluation of the new covenant as against a negative evaluation of the old; in this sense the pattern is quite similar to that in the discontinuous models. Yet, the negative evaluation of the old covenant does not imply its rejection. The covenantal context is here structured dialectically rather than one-dimensionally thus holding both the positive and negative evaluation within its perimeter.

3. The Continuous Model in the Direct Line Pattern

In illustrating the continuous model, i.e. the model of fulfillment, in the direct line pattern, there are two formulations which are of special interest.

a. Fulfillment of the Law

This formulation refers to the law which is seen as remaining unfulfilled in the old covenant, correspondingly perceiving the new covenant as providing its ultimate fulfillment. This formulation can be articulated in two versions. The first attributes the fulfillment of the law to the unfulfillment of man—man is incapable of fulfilling the law. What is required, therefore, is the fulfillment of man—his transformation and

reconstitution into a being capable of fulfilling the law.[11] This is effected by
the new covenant. Jer 31:30-35 is often cited here suggesting that the new
covenant is but the fulfillment of Jeremiah's prophecy.[12]

The second version attributes the unfulfillment of the law to the law
itself, i.e. to its very content. This version maintains that the law in the old
covenant is concerned exclusively with the external and outward behavior
of man thus covering only a part of man's life. This deficiency is overcome
and rounded to completion in the new covenant by its encompassing the
internal sphere of man's life as well. It is now not only the external,
concrete act but equally so the inner intention of consciousness that is
contained in the covenantal relation. The new law, then, fulfills the old,
materialistic law by spiritualizing it.[13]

Alternatively, this version also maintains that the old covenant, in
being materialistic, introduces a calculus of reward and punishment, a
moral bookkeeping, so to speak. Reward and justification are contingent
upon the accumulation of observances of the various injunctions. The
relation to God, therefore, is external and quantified. The new covenant,
commensurately, fulfills the old by radicalizing the relation of man to the
divine, requiring the total submission and obedience of man to the divine
will. It involves the whole man and overcomes the legalism of the old law
by the totality of its demand and response.[14]

b. Universality versus particularity

As against the former formulation which centers on the substance of
the covenant, this formulation centers on its bearers, the people of Israel.
In this view the relation to the divine delineated by the old covenant is
unfulfilled inasmuch as it is confined exclusively to a specific ethnic entity,
to the people of Israel, in contradistinction to its universal significance. As
such, it is still but an expression of ethnic particularism. Salvation being
bound here to the category of peoplehood is inescapably parochial and
nationalistic. It is limited, failing to establish the covenant on a universalistic basis with mankind as a whole.[15]

Correspondingly, the new covenant overcomes this particularism by
making the relationship to God available to the world at large. This it does
not do by substitution but by extension of attachment. The covenant
remains with Israel but is made available to the gentiles by extending its
perimeters to include the world outside or, alternatively, by attaching the
nations to the covenant of Israel. This is what the coming of Jesus and the
introduction of the new covenant effect. By this opening up, the new
covenant fulfills the intent and thrust of the old which, indeed, is univer-

salistic in its essence though this universalism failed to find full expression in the context of the Tanakh and rabbinic Judaism.

4. The Continuous Model in the Pattern of Dialectical Oppostion

This model can be illustrated by the formulation which sees the old covenantal relation as revealing the situation of unredeemed man, i.e. man in sin and rebellion. Sin can arise only within a covenantal relation. If man did not stand in such a relationship to God, it would not make sense to speak of him as in a state of sin. And if there were no sin and rebellion then there would be no point in salvation—the liberation from the state of sin which Jesus brings to the world—being offered. Furthermore, unless man knows the wages of sin, the suffering and predicament they entail, he cannot appreciate the scope of God's grace and glory in offering him salvation.

The role, then, which the people of Israel are given to play within the economy of redemption is to manifest in the context of the old covenant the sin and rebellion which provide the necessary background against which the new covenant of salvation can be appreciated in its full force. The logic operating here is similar to that operating in the ethical theory of Neoplatonism—evil, darkness is necessary in order to appreciate goodness, light. Thus, without the people of the old covenant, manifesting the misery of man when in a state of sin and rebellion, the force of salvation offered by the new covenant could not be fully appreciated. This function is required of the people of Israel for the duration, until the whole of mankind has come to see, appreciate, and accept the salvation offered in the new covenant. Clearly, the relation established here between the old and the new covenant is not one of succession but of continuous contemporaneity which is dialectical and counterpunctual.[16]

A formulation similar in many ways to the one just described is contained in a document by the Dutch Reformed Church.[17] According to this view, the role assigned to the people of Israel is to manifest how compassionate, merciful and long-suffering God is toward sinners. Again, Israel signifies the role of sinning man but now in order to show the constant love of God to man, even when he sins—a love that is independent of man's actions, that is freely given and determined by God alone.

This formulation is quite similar to the immediately preceding one in that both affirm the continued validity of the old covenant, contemporaneous with and parallel to the new; in that the people of Israel remain within the convenantal relation, there to play their part; that part being, however, a negative one. The only difference between the two formulations

70   MANFRED VOGEL

consists in that the former centers on the state of man's sinfulness and
rebellion manifested in his attempt to attain justification on his own, by
"works," while the latter centers on divine love and grace, manifested in
its being extended freely and abundantly to sinning man.

5. Comparison of Formulations

Clearly, the classification presented here is by no means thoroughly
consistent and clear-cut in its applicability. This failure, however, is
perhaps inevitable seeing that the continuous-discontinuous framework is
based on the distinction between abrogation and fulfillment, a distinction
merely of degree but not of kind. For both, abrogation and fulfillment,
imply a negative evaluation of their object, though abrogation certainly
implies a much stronger negative evaluation than does fulfillment. Thus
the difference that can be established is only one of degree. Indeed,
underlying the division of the formulations runs a unifying motif of
negative evaluation of the old covenant or its people. The division is
therefore perforce somewhat arbitrary—at a certain degree of negativity a
formulation would be designated to a discontinuous rather than a continuous model. Still, while not too effective as a scheme of division, the
classification allows us to see more clearly the different emphases and
nuances in the various formulations.

6. Jewish Response to the Notion of Abrogation

There is no denying that according to the testimony of the Tanakh the
people of Israel have, again and again, failed to live up to the demands of
the covenantal relation.[18] Nor can it be denied that the prophets repeatedly
warned the people of severe punishment. It is gratuitous, however, to
conclude from the warnings and, indeed, from the occurrence of punishment that the covenantal relation was abrogated. The burden of the
prophetic position is abundantly clear in that the punishment takes place
within the covenantal relation. It is inflicted as a pedagogical means, to
make Israel improve its ways and return to obedience to God.
Suffering and degradation do not indicate that the covenantal relation
is broken; they are deliberate acts of God which make sense and can be
justified only in the context of an ongoing covenantal relationship. If the
covenant were broken, why should Israel be further pursued with punishment considering that they no longer bear the responsibility of abiding by
its stipulations? Thus, the Tanakh does not in any way support the claim
for an abrogation of the covenant.[19]
Still, we must admit that in theory an abrogation of the covenant is

possible. We cannot accept the often advanced theological argument against the "substitution" claim that an abrogation of the covenant is not feasible because it would violate God's faithfulness to His word. Although this argument is sometimes raised in Jewish theology, it is interestingly enough mainly put forward by Christian theologians. It is based on the theological consideration that God, by His very own constitution, could not change—for example, change His mind or act differently in one instance than another—because such change would undermine His perfection. This view indicates the influence of Greek philosophy in which perfection implies lack of change. That does not apply to the biblical view.

We have many examples in the Tanakh where God changes His mind (for the most poignant passage, cf. Ex 32:7-14). The very essence of the biblical God is, indeed, His freedom which implies the possibility of change. Whenever it is argued on textual-historical grounds that God concluded His covenant with Israel forever, there occurs an illegitimate shift from the covenant of demands and stipulations to that of promise; a transfer of the commitment to eternity associated with the Davidic covenant to that of Sinai. The latter in its essence and structure, however, is a conditional covenant. Thus our reply to the claim of "substitution" must be that, though in principle an abrogation is possible, Israel lives in the trust that it has not taken place. Obviously, Christian theologians defending the "substitution" claim do not live in that trust.

7. Judaism and the Law

Man as he is now constituted is not capable of fulfilling the demands of the law, is the motif underlying most of the Christian formulations addressing themselves to the question of *halakha*. In the Jewish view that claim makes sense only on the assumption that the law places demands on man which correspond not to the human but to the divine.

Judaism rejects the notion that *halakha* on principle cannot be fulfilled. While it readily admits that the law is given by God, Judaism considers the giving an act of grace, expressed by the very fact that *halakha* is tailored not to the divine, but to the human standard. As the Tanakh expresses it, "it (the Torah) is not in heaven" (Dt 30:12), or as the rabbis said, "The Torah spoke in human language."[20] This is not to say that the task is easy or that man has thus far succeeded in fulfilling the law; but on principle it is possible.[21] For the purpose of *halakha* is to delineate the way by which man can authentically realize himself as man.

Similarly, Judaism does not accept the notion that judgment is in accordance with the absolute standard of divine perfection. The rabbis held that God judges not only in accordance with His justice but also His mercy, namely, He mitigates His judgment by considering man's weakness. In contradistinction, then, to the various Christian formulations *halakha* in Judaism does not imply the condemnation of man but is, rather, his most precious possession. It is the vehicle which holds for him the hope of redemption, by which he can fully and authentically realize himself as the man he is intended to be.

8. The Context of the Law

Judaism and Christianity place the law in different contexts. Christianity seems to place it primarily in the context of the vertical relation between man and God. This is in a way quite understandable as the law is taken as articulating a covenantal relation. In Judaism, however, the burden of *halakha* impinges upon the horizontal relation between man and man, but this horizontal relation is constituted as an integral part of the covenantal relation. It is a distinctive feature of Judaism that it refracts the vertical through the horizontal relationship: The relation to the vertically transcendent God traverses through the relation to the horizontally situated fellow man. God addresses man through his fellow man and man, in return, responds through his fellow man. The horizontal relation thereby remains within the covenantal context, ultimately pointing toward and terminating in, the vertical. Still, the burden of the covenantal relation is placed here on the relation to one's fellow man, consequently the applicable standard is human and not divine.

The basic difference between Christianity and Judaism manifests itself most clearly, however, where the law is seen by Christianity to be defective from the religious point of view by virtue of the fact that it impinges on the domain of the concrete, outward action rather than upon the conscious inward intention or, alternatively, that it lends itself to a calculation of merit and demerit rather than to the radical, all-encompassing decision of faith.

In response, one can point to many rabbinic statements stressing the importance of inwardness and intention, that is, *kavanah*. A good case can, indeed, be made that for authentic Judaism the optimal situation is achieved only when the proper intention accompanies the right external conduct.[22] It is not justified, then, to maintain that Judaism centers exclusively on the outward conduct of man, accusing it of being an ossified religion. Still, such a response does not delve into the issue at its deepest level, for it must be admitted that *halakha* does, indeed, impinge primarily upon the realm of conduct and that Judaism greatly emphasizes it. In fact, how could law impinge upon inwardness and intention? Intentions and feelings can hardly be legislated.

Yet, who says that the authentic expression of faith belongs exclusively in the realm of inwardness and intention? It is just such an implication that Judaism must challenge. It is valid only when the expression of faith is relegated exclusively to the vertical relation between man and God. But for Judaism, as we have seen, authentic faith finds its main expression in the relation that is refracted through the horizontal dimension. As such, *halakha* precisely because it impinges primarily on outward behavior is, indeed, the valid vehicle for the expression of that faith. For while in the vertical relation between man and God it is inwardness and intention that count, in the horizontal relation between man and man it is outward conduct and the concrete act that count.

A similar case can be made regarding the charge that in Judaism the law leads to justification by a process of adding up merits and demerits. In authentic faith, it is maintained, justification is to be gained by a radical existential decision encompassing the person in his totality. Again, what is claimed here for authentic faith is valid only if it is understood as operative exclusively in the vertical relation. In the horizontal relation, however, there is no escape from quantification. Thus, what is really at issue is the question where faith is to be authentically located. In Christianity, at least that Christianity reflected in this formulation, faith is placed exclusively in the vertical relation; in Judaism, at least that Judaism represented here, authentic faith is placed in the vertical relation refracted in the horizontal dimension.[23]

9. Applicability of the Covenant

In a good many Christian formulations we hear the old covenant is restricted in its application. There are three aspects to this charge. One aspect emphasizes the limitation of the old covenant exclusively to the people of Israel. Not only is the relation itself limited to them but its signification as well. The covenantal bond has no bearing upon the rest of mankind and is thus particularistic in the sense of being parochial.

The second aspect emphasizes that the human pole of the covenantal relation consists of an ethnic entity rather than individual persons. Ethnicity, being a subdivision of humanity, necessarily implies exclusion—in terms of its signification it perforce includes only part of humanity. The category of the unspecified individual, on the other hand, being the unit the sum total of which constitutes humanity, is unversalistic—in terms of its signification none is excluded. A covenantal relation established with the individual, in contradistinction to the ethnic entity, encompasses therefore every member of humanity. Thus the old covenant, being concluded with a specific ethnic entity, is limited and exclusivistic, hence particularistic. The new covenant, on the other hand, being established with the individual person, is all-inclusive and indiscriminate, that is, universalistic.

The third aspect emphasizes the need of extending the covenantal relation to the gentile world. Thus the new covenant is "new" not because of its content but because of the role and function assigned to it in the economy of redemption. In content the new covenant remains "Jewish," so to speak. It is different only because of its role which is to make the "Jewish" covenantal relation available to the gentiles. In contradistinction to the old covenant which lacks the capacity to extend itself beyond the people of Israel, it creates the mechanism (through the agency of Jesus) whereby the gentile world can become "Jewish" without the ethnic adherence implied in the old covenant.

How exactly this is to be accomplished, is less clear; but it seems that this formulation can work with two alternatives. On the one hand, it suggests that the new covenant makes it possible for gentiles as individuals to be attached to the peoplehood of Israel in its religious vocation, without at the same time adopting its ethnic identity. In this way, the gentile becomes "Jewish" in a special sense.

On the other hand, this formulation also suggests that through the agency of the new covenant the covenantal relation established with the people of Israel can now be transferred to and established with, other ethnic entities. Here again, the gentiles become "Jewish" in the special sense of appropriating the religious vocation of the people of Israel while, at the same time, preserving their own ethnic identity. In either case, the characteristic of this version lies in the intention to extend the covenantal relation established with the people of Israel without abrogating or altering in the process its nature and constitution.

10. A Jewish View of Universalism

The Jewish response would differ greatly depending on which of the three aspects is under consideration. The first aspect would be basically rejected. True, in the earliest stages of its history the faith of biblical Israel may well have been nationalistic and parochial. It is also true that in the course of Jewish history the univeralistic concern was at times greatly minimized. In such instances the covenantal relation was, indeed, perceived as a private affair of the people of Israel (such a view was certainly strengthened by the conditions of disaspora existence). Yet, this stance does not really represent the authentic expression of Judaism.

It is only with regard to the task of striving for redemption, that is for the time being, that the people of Israel have a special role and status in the religious vocation. Even so, the rationale and justification for this provisional ethno-centricity is derived from a vocation which is ultimately universalistic. In the last analysis, the covenantal relation of the people of Israel is not parochial; its implications are universalistic.

Regarding the second aspect, one would have to admit the validity of the logic that ethnicity implies particularism. Yet, as we have argued above, this particularistic aspect is provisional only. The all-important thrust of this aspect, however, lies in the claim that the universalistic stance requires the abrogation of ethnicity altogether and its replacement by the individual. Thus the real issue before us is whether universalism can be established on the basis of the ethnic category or whether it inescapably requires that of the individual.

But why should ethnicism exclude universalism? Certainly the sum total of all the ethnic entities comprising mankind, just as the sum total of all individuals, constitutes a universalistic whole. On principle, therefore, there is no reason why the covenantal relation established with the people of Israel could not be duplicated with every ethnic entity in existence, thus realizing itself universally.

Indeed, this universalistic realization is exactly what Judaism envisions for its messianic era. It is very important to note, however, that Judaism's opting for the ethnic rather than the individualist alternative is not a capricious, arbitrary act. It is determined by the very essence of its covenantal relation—its being refracted through the horizontal dimension, through the relation between man and fellow man. In this context, ethnicity is inextricable because only it can provide the matrix for the *totality* of the relations between man and man—the political, economic, and social relations.

Judaism cannot give up the category of ethnicity and still retain its structure of faith. And if Christianity as reflected in this version opts for individualism and abrogates the category of ethnicity, it may well establish itself on a universalistic basis, but at the same time, it also perforce appropriates to itself quite a different structure of faith.

To dispense with ethnicity would abrogate the very content of the old covenantal relation and its very structure of faith. Basing the covenant on the individual does not merely open it up to the world, it implies a totally different kind of relation from that established by the old covenant. For a covenantal relation based on individualism can be constituted only in the direct, vertical relation, not in the horizontal relation. In terms of individualism, the encounter between man and the divine can take place only directly and immediately; a link mediated through the relation of one's fellow man is not feasible.

In the last analysis, then, this formulation under the guise of merely offering to universalize the old covenant, actually abrogates its very structure of faith, offering in its place a totally different structure. Judaism cannot accept this, particularly since the universal perspective, albeit on a different basis, is already available to it.

These considerations explain to a large extent the Jewish response to the third aspect. As we have seen, it suggests that the gentile as an individual can participate, through the agency of Jesus, in the covenantal relation of Israel without himself adopting the ethnic identity of Israel. This aspect is of course much more congenial to Judaism as it does not abrogate its ethnicity. But how is this to be realized? Does not this formulation wind up with a situation in which the covenantal relation of Israel is made available to the gentiles as individuals? Since the relation established by the old covenant necessarily implices the ethnic category, how can this very same relation include individuals who do not belong to the covenantal ethnic entity? Does not this formulation really end up with an understanding of the role of the new covenant that is quite similar to that of the second aspect, namely that the new covenant offers Israel's covenantal relation on the basis of individualism?[24]

The alternative formulation of this aspect avoids that problem. It sees the covenantal relation functioning exclusively in conjunction with the ethnic category. Indeed, this formulation is identical with the Jewish vision of the messianic era when all the nations of the world, each maintaining its ethnic identity, will share in a covenant with God. In this formulation, Judaism and Christianity come closest to one another. The difference consists in that for Judaism it is a vision of the future, an expectation, while for Christianity it is a task or a reality in the present.

11. Striking a Balance

On the basis of the above analysis, can we formulate a viable relationship between Judaism and Christianity? Two possibilities suggest themselves. According to the first, Christianity is seen to introduce through the new covenant a new structure of faith. The relation is established here on the basis that Judaism and Christianity differ in their very content of faith. Still, the fact that the two communities share the notion of covenant indicates that, this difference notwithstanding, they share the belief in God as a Thou.[25]

Thus, the difference lies here not with regard to God but with regard to the perception of man's predicament and commensurately his redemption. Resorting to Buber's terminology, we would say that both Judaism and Christianity view man here as an It-Thou being. For Judaism, however, the predicament lies in man's imbalanced expression of his It and Thou dimensions. It is not the presence of the It as such but its exaggerated dominance which causes the predicament. Commensurately, redemption means the establishing of the proper balance.

For Christianity, the predicament lies in the very constitution of man, that is, the very presence of the It. Salvation therefore means the total extirpation of the It. In contrast to Judaism where redeemed man continues to be an It-Thou being—though now the dimensions are properly balanced—for Christianity redeemed man is an ontologically transformed being, a pure Thou.

This fundamental difference in the perception of the predicament and the formulation of the expected redemption or salvation will explain many of the differences between Judaism and Christianity. To give only a few examples, it will explain the characterization of Judaism as a this-worldly faith in contrast to Christianity as an other-worldly religion; the formulation of the structure of faith in the ethical domain in the case of Judaism, as against its formulation in the ontological domain in Christianity; the expression of faith exclusively in the direct, vertical relation in Christianity as against its expression in the horizontal relation through which the vertical is refracted, in the case of Judaism; the ethnic collectivity of Judaism versus the individual in Christianity as the primary human category; the formulation of the covenant in terms of demands and stipulations in Judaism as against *agape* in Christianity; redemption through works in Judaism over against salvation through grace alone, in Christianity.

Our claim is that all these instances find their ultimate rationale in the basic dissimilarity between Judaism and Christianity regarding the perception of man's ultimate predicament and, correspondingly, his redemption. While Judaism and Christianity relate to the same God, God as Thou (over against the pagan faiths which relate to God as an It) they nonetheless represent two different structures of faith. The covenant in Judaism impinges upon the ethical task of attaining the proper balance between the Thou and the It while in Christianity it signifies the ontological transformation of man to a pure Thou.

The other viable possibility of linking the two covenants centers on the question of the availability of the covenantal relation to humanity as a whole. As argued above, the covenant in Judaism always carried universalistic implications. Though for the time being, in the work towards redemption, it is confined to the people of Israel, in the context of redemption itself it applies to all men. Judaism also provides the means by which the covenant can be extended prior to the end of time to anyone wishing to join it. Any gentile may convert to Judaism and become a member of the people of Israel, thus allowing him to share in the work toward redemption. It is not true, then, to maintain that humanity apart from the people of Israel is neglected and left in disregard by the covenant of Israel. The covenant certainly applies to one and all in the context of redemption, while in the here and now it can become available to anyone who wishes to join Israel.

Yet, we must admit that there are certain aspects of the Jewish covenant which are problematic and indeed unsatisfactory regarding the rest of humanity. Thus it is questionable how at the end of time the covenant is to apply to all humanity. It would seem Judaism takes the position that when the people of Israel by their work bring about redemptive time, the covenant will automatically become available to all men. Humanity, even at that time, remains a passive recipient of the fruits resulting from the labor and striving of the people of Israel. But how can this be, seeing that the very content of the covenant consists of demands and stipulations, thus necessarily demanding an active role of man? How can there be passive acceptance when the very essence of the covenant demands man's active contribution? And if we were to say that in redemptive time the covenant becomes available to humanity not in its completed, realized form but only as a potential, as a challenge; if we were to say that in redemptive time, when Israel has finally succeeded in meeting the stipulations and demands, the covenant is made available to the nations of the world for them to try their hand in fulfilling them; the question arises, why has one to wait until Israel succeeds before offering the challenge to the rest of humanity?[26]

Indeed, not only is the world outside of Judaism not given an opportunity to share in the work toward redemption but it is left without knowledge of or, even more significantly, without relation to, the God who is a Thou. This is clearly a very unsatisfactory situation.[27] The only mitigation that Judaism has to offer is the provision of conversion to its ranks, a solution that has not proven very effective.

Aside from a number of contingent factors, such as the circumstances of exiled existence which militated against conversion, the crux of the problem seems to lie in Judaism's insistence that conversion to its religious community required the adoption of its ethnic identity. Entrance to the covenantal relation is made contingent on an "ethnic conversion."[28] Judaism did not and indeed, given the content of its covenantal relation, could not give up this requirement although it certainly proved a serious block to conversion. Many a gentile who was yearning for the Thou-God of Israel was not ready or willing to give up his own ethnic identity and adopt that of Israel, particularly when the earthly fortunes of the latter were never very impressive.

Aside from such historical considerations, the question arises why, on principle, the gentile should be required to give up his own ethnic identity in order to have access to Israel's covenantal relation? Why should the gentile not be enabled to share and participate in the context of his own ethnic identity? Judaism, in our judgment, does not provide a satisfactory answer to this problem and we have to admit that on this point Christianity can provide better for the gentile world. In fact, there is no reason why Judaism should not accept and welcome Christianity and its new covenant, provided that its role is clearly confined to this function.

Christianity's task is actually two-fold, depending on the extent to which the covenantal faith of Israel is to be made available to the gentile world. In a minimal role Christianity, through the new covenant, would be offering the gentiles entry into the relationship with the God of Israel, the Thou-God. It would offer them the vertical relation with God without imposing upon them the demands and stipulations of the old covenant. The role of Christianity would be to draw away the gentile world from its pagan It-God to the Thou-God of Israel. In this role the ethnic category does not enter the picture and the covenantal relation can be based on the individual. That is perhaps the meaning and intention of the formulation described above whereby Christianity is to extend the covenant of Israel by providing the means of attaching individual gentiles to the old covenant who would become, as it were, Jews in a special sense. They would be Jews minimally, that is, the demands and stipulations regarding the horizontal relationship would not apply to them.[29]

In a maximal role, Christianity through the new covenant gives the gentile world not only the Thou-God of Israel but the covenantal relation in the fullness of its content, thereby asking them to accept the demands and stipulations relating to the horizontal dimension as well. The role of Christianity here would be to transform the nations of the gentile world, each retaining its own ethnic identity, into covenantal nations which fully possess the covenantal relation established with the people of Israel.

In this last version, the new covenant introduces no deviation from, no newness in the content of, the old covenant of Judaism. The covenantal relation impinges on the horizontal relation between man and his fellow-man in its social, economic and political dimensions. The content of faith remains this-worldly—redemption, far from signifying the ontological transformation of man from an It-Thou being to a pure Thou being, signifies here the this-worldly ethical striving of man to establish the proper balance between the It and the Thou dimension of his being.

In this context, the only difference between the two covenants is with regard to the question of who is being addressed by the covenant. While the old covenant addresses the people of Israel, the new covenant addresses the gentile nations of the world—but the content of the address is the same in both covenants.[30] Indeed as regards the content, the new covenant according to this formulation expresses nothing else but the messianic vision of Judaism. The new covenant here merely claims to provide the mechanism by which to strive towards the realization in the present of the messianic vision which in Judaism has been relegated to the future and the mechanism for its execution been left vague.

12. Conclusions

In conclusion we would argue that from the viewpoint of Judaism both formulations are acceptable, the first which sees the two covenants as differing in their very content—the Jewish covenant centering on the ethical striving to establish the proper balance between the It and the Thou dimensions of man's being; the Christian covenant centering on the onto-logical transformation of man to a pure Thou—and the second formulation which sees the two covenants as identical in content, differing only in the clientele they address—the old covenant addressing the people of Israel, the new one addressing the nations of the gentile world.

Yet, it would seem that judging by its structure—its ritual, symbolism, liturgy and, indeed, its theological expression—Christianity is more adequately represented in the first formulation. Its ritual and symbolism lend themselves more readily to being interpreted in the ontological rather than in the ethical domain. Certainly, the burden of Christian self-understanding, historically speaking, would seem to support this formulation.

In more recent times, however, various trends may be detected within Christianity (for example, the various expressions of political and liberation theology) apprehending Christianity in terms that are rather congenial to the second formulation. The essential significance of Christianity is seen here to center on man's ethical striving rather than on his ontological transformation. The role of Christianity is perceived as impinging upon the horizontal relation between man and his fellow-man, in its various social, economic and political manifestations, rather than impinging exclusively on the direct vertical relation between God and the individual person. The essential concern of Christianity is seen to lie in a this-worldly rather than in an other-worldly context. These aspects and many others characterizing such recent trends within Christian theology must of necessity bring Judaism and Christianity very close to one another, and such a rapprochement can only be welcomed by Judaism.

Thus, there are two viable alternative schemes by which the relation between the two covenants, between Judaism and Christianity, can be formulated.[31] Each has its advantages. In the first formulation the spectrum of religious possibilities is greatly enriched by the addition of a most suggestive and profound alternative, i.e. the alternative structure of faith whereby man's salvation is to lie in his ontological transformation to a pure Thou. In the second formulation the thrust of faith of the old covenant is greatly strengthened by its completion with regard to the gentile world. In either case, the life of faith, indeed, of biblical faith is greatly advanced by the presence of both, the Jewish and the Christian covenant.

Notes

1. Cf. Walter Eichrodt, *Theology of the Old Testament*, J. A. Baker, transl. (London: SCM, 1967), vol. I. Eichrodt's contribution in this respect is generally acknowledged and accepted. See for example the acknowledgment by M. Weinfeld, "Covenant," in *Encyclopedia Judaica*; cf. also J. Jocz, *The Covenant* (Grand Rapids: Eerdmans Publ., 1968), p. 10.

2. The Hebrew word *berit* apparently comes from the Akkadian "biritu" which signifies a fetter, i.e. a binding (see M. Weinfeld, *op. cit.*). In the original primitive signification the binding can of course also be mechanical, a binding that involves the parties or at least one of them as an It. This original meaning may still be reflected in a very few places in the Tanakh. See e.g. the reference to covenants with animals in Job 5:23, 40:28, or with death in Is 28:15.18. But the overwhelming burden of the biblical usage of the notion of covenant clearly understands it as implicating decision and election, consequently limits its reference to the relation between parties that are Thous, i.e. to the relation between man and God or between man and man. This point is rightly emphasized by J. Jocz, *(op. cit.)* and even

more emphatically by Roy Eckardt, *Elder and Younger Brothers* (New York: Scribner, 1967), p. 40, where he says, "the very idea of 'covenant' presupposes decision-making on both sides." This is, indeed, so prevalent and characteristic of the biblical view that M. Weinfeld, *op. cit.*, who brings the few instances of the use of covenant with animals or death sees them as but a metaphorical use of the notion of covenant.

3. Cf. Yehezkel Kaufmann, *Toldot Ha Emuna Ha Israelit* (Tel Aviv: Dvir, 1953), vol. II, esp. chaps. 9, 10. For a somewhat more elaborate argumentation of the view presented here, cf. also Manfred Vogel, "Monotheism," in *Encyclopedia Judaica*.

4. Cf. M. Weinfeld, *op. cit.*, where this claim is clearly asserted.

5. Cf. Max Weber, *Ancient Judaism*, H. H. Gerth and D. Martindale, eds. (Glencoe, Ill.: Free Press, 1952), for his understanding of the covenant as antimagical.

6. It has been suggested by M. Weinfeld, *op.cit.*, that this all-important distinction between biblical faith and pagan religion is due to the fact that the covenantal relation—specifically the suzerain-vassal relation which is the model applicable to the divine-human covenantal relation—necessarily implies the exclusivity of the relation. By its very inner logic it dictates that the vassal can have only one suzerain. Biblical faith, by virtue of its monotheistic structure, can offer this exclusivity. There is certainly validity in this explanation but it seems to us that the more basic explanation is the one given above that beneath the distinction between the monotheistic and polytheistic structure lies the more fundamental and important distinction of encountering the ultimate as a personal versus an impersonal being.

7. In the case of Noah, God promises not to bring the deluge again (Gn 9:11); in Abraham's case, He promises to multiply greatly Abraham's descendants and make them into a great nation (Gn 17:4); and in the case of David, He promises that his house will reign forever (2 Sam 7:16).

8. The Noachide covenant of promise, while continuously effective, is relegated to the background; the covenant of promise given to Abraham is seen fulfilled in the creation of the Jewish people and their receiving the Sinaitic covenant or, alternatively, its fulfillment is relegated to messianic times; and the covenant of promise given to David is quite clearly relegated to the future. As such, the covenant of promise is not operative in the here and now. Indeed, by its very logic the covenant of promise can be effective only if the here and now constitutes a fulfillment of the promise. In rabbinic Judaism, however, the here and now does not constitute the messianic era. In that context, the covenant of promise is relegated to the periphery while the Sinaitic covenant becomes the dominant factor in the economy of redemption.

9. For a further analysis of the respective postures in the dialogue of Judaism and Christianity, cf. Manfred Vogel, "The Problem of Dialogue between Judaism and Christianity," in *Journal of Ecumenical Studies*, vol. 4, no. 4, 1967.

10. Cf. Roy Eckardt, *op. cit.*, chaps. 4, 5.

11. This formulation shares an important similarity with the pedagogic or propaedeutic formulation. In both of them, man as he is at present constituted, is unable to fulfill the law. Still, an important difference exists. It lies in the way this predicament is overcome. In the latter formulation, man is liberated, in one way or another, from the yoke of the law. As against this, in the formulation under consideration man is transformed, thus enabling him to fulfill the law.

12. It should be clear that this celebrated passage in Jeremiah does not signify the abrogation of the old covenant substituting in its place a new covenant. What is envisioned is a change in man as regards his ability to fulfill the covenant. The content of the covenant remains the same. Thus, references to this passage in support of the claim that the new covenant is to abrogate and replace the old one regarding its very content are not legitimate. Cf. *Israel en de kerk*, transl. into German by H. Stoevesandt (Zurich: EVZ, 1961), a document of the Dutch Reformed Church. Cf. also Bernard W. Anderson, "The New Covenant and the Old," in *The Old Testament and Christain Faith,* Bernard W. Anderson, ed. (New York: Harper & Row, 1963), for clear statements on this point. The same point is made, and with particular cogency and forcefulness, by Roy Eckardt, *op. cit.*, p. 72, where the preceding references are quoted.

13. Cf. e.g. Rudolf Bultmann, *Primitive Christianity*, R. H. Fuller, transl. (New York: Meridian Books, 1957), pp. 72ff.

14. *Ibid.*, pp. 68, 75ff, 90ff.

15. *Ibid.*, pp. 36, 87. Tillich also faults Judaism, that is the old covenant, for still being particularistic. Cf. *Systematic Theology* (Chicago: University of Chicago Press, 1951), vol. I, pp. 143ff, 227; vol. III, pp. 154, 367f. Tillich, rather interestingly, links this ethnic and nationalistic particularism to the claim that Judaism fails to relate itself fully and completely to the God of time and history. The particularistic ethnic element is seen as a residue of paganism. Cf. *Die Judenfrage* (Berlin: Deutsche Hochschule fuer Politik, 1953).

16. This view can be found e.g. in Karl Barth's writings. Cf. the exposition of his ideas, in F. W. Marquardt, *Die Entdeckung des Judentums fuer die christliche Theologie: Israel im Denken Karl Barths* (Munich: Kaiser, 1967), esp. pp. 59-68. In fairness to Barth, however, it should be added that he also held a more positive view of the people of the old covenant, cf. *Against the Stream* (London: SCM, 1954), pp. 197-201. Barth's view here is that the role assigned to the people of the old covenant is to witness to the state of salvation by possessing a presentiment of it already in this world. The Jew exists outside the world—he is a stranger to the world. In his electedness he reveals the truth and power of being rooted in no worldly security but only in the grace of God. And that precisely is the state of salvation—to exist outside the world and to say "no" to it. In this context, the role of Christianity seems to be the role of disseminating this truth and bringing it to the world at large. This view seems very similar to Rosenzweig's understanding of Judaism and to his notion of the "division of labor" between Judaism and Christianity in the economy of redemption.

17. *Israel en de kerk* (cf. note 12). Cf. also the statement by the Dutch

Reformed Church, of 1970: "Israel: People, Land and State," in Helga Croner, comp., *Stepping Stones to Further Jewish-Christain Relations,* See Unabridged Collection of Christain Documents (Stimulus Books: New York, 1977) pp. 91-107.

18. It seems that the repeated accusations in the Tanakh against the people for sins committed—accusations by the way which always mention the same transgressions and have every appearance of being set formulas—were provided by the biblical writers after the destruction of the temple, as justification and explanation for the catastrophe that befell Israel rather than as firsthand reports of the reality of Israel's behavior. Israel's record was probably by no means as bad as all that. Cf. Yehezekel Kaufmann, *op. cit.,* vol. III, chap. 15, where he makes a very strong case for this view.

19. For an excellent examination and refutation of the "substitution" formula, cf. John Oesterreicher, "Unter dem Bogen des Einen Bundes—Das Volk Gottes: seine Zweigestalt and Einheit," in Clemens Thoma, ed., *Judentum und Kirche: Volk Gottes* (Zurich: Benziger, 1974), pp. 27-69.

20. TB *Berakhot* 31a.

21. It must be admitted that Jeremiah 31:30-35 does not reflect this position. Jeremiah seems to hold there that man in his present constitution cannot fulfill the covenant, hence the need for a new heart. This outcry of Jeremiah does not reflect, however, the considered position of Judaism. It should be seen as reflection of the prophet's deep personal disappointment, bordering on desperation, at man's continued failure to fulfill the covenant. We have here an instance in which the basic trust and optimism of Judaism in man as he is at present, are lost.

22. Cf. e.g. TB *Menahoth* 38b; *Sukkah* 9a.

23. Indeed, the tendency of Christianity, when it does not set itself in contradistinction to the old covenant, is to relate in the main to Abraham rather than to Sinai. Thus, the discontinuous formulations relate mainly to the covenant of Sinai, i.e. the covenant of law, while the continuous formulations relate to Abraham, i.e. the covenant of promise. This is understandable because the covenant of promise formulates itself in the direct vertical relation, i.e. in the same context in which Christianity formulates its faith. It is further understandable because of the messianic claim, the claim of realized eschatology which Christianity makes. The new covenant because it claims to usher in a realized eschatology can relate itself very conveniently and logically to that which preceded it, i.e. the old convenant, when the latter is conceived as a covenant of promise. That could not very readily be done were the old covenant perceived as a covenant of law. The notion of promise lends itself, indeed invites, the claim of fulfillment. Yet most fundamentally it is understandable because in the covenant of promise and in that which Christianity introduces the respective roles assigned to God and man are the same, speaking formally rather than contextually. God is the main if not the sole actor while man is essentially the passive recipient and beneficiary. It is God who promises, it is God who saves—man must only trust and accept. This is in clear opposition to the covenant of law where the burden of action falls upon man—it is man who must carry out and fulfill the demands and stipulations.

24. Still, from the Jewish point of view there is an all-important difference because in this formulation the individualistic basis is not applied universally, i.e. the ethnic reality of Israel is not abrogated.

25. As such, it should be clear that we are referring, not to a hellenistically grounded Christianity but to that grounded in the Bible. For a more detailed attempt at differentiation between the two, cf. Manfred Vogel, "The Problem of Dialogue Between Judaism and Christianity."

26. This formulation reminds us very much of Franz Rosenzweig, except that it is here applied in reverse. For Rosenzweig, it is Judaism that is marking time while the work toward salvation is carried out by the world outside.

27. It becomes even more grievous if redemption may be an ideal never to be realized. In that case, the neglect of humanity would be not just provisional but permanent.

28. On the problem that the ethnic factor introduces into the process of conversion and the way in which Judaism handles it, cf. Manfred Vogel, "Some Reflections on the Question of Jewish Identity," in *Bijdragen*, January 1970, pp. 2-32.

29. The mere availability of the Thou-God here cannot determine whether man is to be viewed as an It-Thou or as pure Thou. However, the fact that the refraction of the direct vertical relation in the horizontal dimension is not explicitly included here suggests that man is viewed as a pure Thou. Thus, this formulation which purports merely to extend the old covenant to the world at large while retaining its content leads, in the last analysis, towards its coalescence with the formulation which changes the very content of the old covenant by envisioning redeemed man to be a pure Thou.

30. This formulation is very similar in its format to that proposed by Franz Rosenzweig. He, too, sees Judaism and Christianity as identical regarding the content of faith, the difference lying merely in the function they are assigned within the economy of redemption. Yet, there is a fundamental difference between Rosenzweig and the formulation presented here. It refers to the all-important question of what actually is the content of the covenant? According to Rosenzweig it corresponds to what we would view as the Christian perspective, i.e. the content of redemption being the ontological transformation of man to a pure Thou. Rosenzweig, in spite of his profundity and perceptive insight into Judaism, achieves the identity of the two covenants by reducing Judaism, so to speak, to Christianity.

31. The first alternative mode of the second formulation, by which Christianity is to bring only the Thou-God to the world, is subsumed in the first formulation whereby Christianity offers man an ontological transformation to a pure Thou.

II. WITNESS AND MISSION

4.

Witness and Mission in Judaism

Ben Zion Bokser

1. The Biblical Dimension of Witnessing

The concept of religious witness designates a responsibility invested in a religiously committed person to share his truth with people outside his faith community.

The Jewish tradition from its inception recognized the duty which devolves on the Jewish people to share the essence of their faith with the outside world. The Bible is the account of God's covenant with the people of Israel, but it presents its theme in a context which makes the covenant an incident in God's plan for world redemption. It begins with the creation of the world and the emergence of man on the world scene, and his history is presented as a series of strayings and stumblings which frustrate God's intention in having created man in His own image, and which frustrate man's growth toward the full potential of his humanity. God finally chooses Abraham as His emissary to call man to an awareness of his true destiny as child of God. Abraham and his children after him are graced with God's call, but it is not a private beneficence. It is a call to serve as a channel of world enlightenment. Thus does the verse describe it: "Be a blessing . . . and all the families of the earth shall be blessed through you" (Gn 12:2-3).

Obadya Sforno (1475-1550), one of the classic commentators on the Tanakh (Hebrew Scriptures), defines the call in these terms: Abraham was to be a blessing, "by acquiring knowledge and gaining perfection and teaching knowledge to the people."[1]

The call to Abraham which was repeated to his son Isaac and Isaac's son Jacob took the form of a covenant, which served as a foreshadowing of the covenant at Sinai, when the entire people of Israel pledged itself to God's service. The prelude to the Sinaitic revelation was Israel's pledged willingness to assume the covenantal obligations which Moses, speaking in God's name, summed up to them in these words:

> Now, therefore, if you will indeed heed My voice and keep My covenant, then will you be My own treasure from among all peoples, for all the earth is mine; and you shall be to Me a Kingdom of priests and a holy nation (Ex 19:6).

We quote Obadya Sforno again:

> You will be God's treasure if you serve as a kingdom of priests to enlighten and teach the entire human race to invoke God's name and serve Him with one accord as it is stated, "You shall be named priests by the Lord, men shall call you ministers of our God" (Is 61:6); and as it is also stated, "Out of Zion shall go forth the teaching and the word of the Lord from Jerusalem" (Is 2:3).[2]

It is in the writings of the prophets that this commitment is given explicit expression. The most celebrated of these is undoubtedly the vision in the second chapter of Isaiah:

> In the end of days, the mountain of the Lord's house will be established as the top of the mountains . . . and all the nations shall flow into it, and many peoples shall go and say, Come, let us go up to the mountain of the Lord, to the house of the God of Jacob, and He will teach us of His ways and we will walk in His paths. For out of Zion shall go forth the teaching and the word of the Lord from Jerusalem (2:2-3).

It is noteworthy that the Gaon of Vilna (1720-1792), in commenting on this verse in Isaiah, observed that the name for God, YHWH, used in the phrase, "the mountain of the Lord," is a universal term and it embraces in His concern, "all who inhabit the world."[3]

The second Isaiah lived after the destruction of the first temple in 586 BCE, at the hands of the Babylonians. His prophecies focused on the faith in the return of the Jewish people to their land and the rebuilding of the temple. But his vision of the restoration embraced all mankind in its beneficence. For he saw the Jewish people renewed in its vocation to serve as a source of illumination for the entire world.

In one passage the prophet put it thus:

> I the Lord have called you in righteousness ... and set you for a
> covenant of the people, for a light to the nations, to open the blind eyes,
> to bring out the prisoners from the dungeon and those that sit in
> darkness from the prison house (Is 42:6).

In another passage, Isaiah says:

> Listen, o islands, to me and hearken you peoples afar. The Lord called
> me from birth. . . .He said to me, "You are My servant, Israel, through
> whom I will be glorified". . . . And He said, "It is too light a thing for
> you to be My servant to raise up the tribes of Judah and to restore the
> offspring of Israel. I will also make you for a light to the nations, that
> My salvation may go forth to the end of the earth" (49:1.3.6).

The restored Temple which figures in Isaiah's vision of the future was
to be more than a Jewish sanctuary. Non-Jews, touched by the light of
God, will also be served by it. Here is how the prophet portrayed the
divine intention:

> I will bring them to My holy mountain, and will make them joyful in
> My house of prayer. Their burnt-offerings and their sacrifices shall be
> welcomed on My altar. For My house shall be called a house of prayer
> for all the peoples (56:7).

It was also Isaiah who expressed the duty of disseminating God's truth in
terms of witnessing, "You are My witnesses, says the Lord" (43:10).

The other prophets expressed essentially the same concept⁴, though
they often used varying idioms, reflecting the historical setting of their
own time. There is one prophetic book which is devoted entirely to this
theme of the need to serve the world beyond the confines of Israel's
fellowship. It is that of Jonah. A divine call pursues the prophet to go and
bring the people of the Assyrian city of Nineveh a message of penitence
lest they be destroyed for the evil of their ways. The prophet Jonah is
reluctant to go and seeks to evade the call pursuing him, but God prevails
and in the end Jonah goes, brings God's word to the people, and they
repent and are saved. Why did Jonah resist this call? Was it simply
another instance of the prophet's reluctance to undertake a burdensome
mission? Was it perhaps because the prophet did not initially feel the need
to concern himself with people not of his own faith? But the theme of the
book is clearly that God definitely is concerned and He expects those who

serve Him to share this concern. This book is read in the synagogue on the holiest day of the year, Yom Kippur, and it accents the larger vision as a basic commitment in Judaism.

The biblical vision of future world enlightenment and of the Jewish people's mediating role in bringing it about is stated in general terms. Does this mean that Judaism was expected to become the world religion, superseding other faiths? Was there another form of enlightenment that might be consistent with continued loyalty to other faiths?

The biblical authors did not engage in systematic expositions to define the precise dimensions of their ideas. But the answer to those questions emerges clearly in the pharisaic-rabbinic layer of Jewish tradition, where the implications of the concept of witnessing were examined in detail, and this became the formal position of Judaism on the subject.

The specific expression which is given in any religious tradition to the duty to witness will be conditioned by the conception which that tradition has of the particularities of its established system of rite and doctrine in other faiths. If it absolutizes its system and regards it as the only channel for winning acceptability to God, then witness will take the form of seeking to alienate a person from his own faith to make a formal convert of him. Conversion will then be the only efficacious way of bringing to him the indispensable treasure on which his salvation depends. Judaism in the rabbinic period did not regard its own system of rite and doctrine in such terms; it did not absolutize them and, therefore, did not seek to universalize them. The rabbis regarded them as channels for a transcendent light, as vessels containing a truth which is cultivated through them; but this truth, they held, has a life of its own capable of reaching and enriching other lives outside of its own system. Only truth which is abstracted from the forms through which it is expressed is universal and should be diffused by the act of witness: And this truth can enrich other lives regardless of any formal affiliation with a particular religious system.

There were channels for the basics of religion and morality even if one remained outside the Jewish faith. The rabbis believed that God revealed His will to prophets outside of Israel.[5] Some rabbis maintained that the basics of morality, the reprimanding role of conscience were present in man as part of his nature.[6] The universal substratum of faith as envisioned in Judaism consisted of the so-called seven Noachide laws. They constitute the substance of the revelation that came to Noah after the flood. These have been variously defined but generally they are said to include the demand to avoid idolatry, bloodshed, cruelty to animals and, on the positive side, the acknowledgement of a universal God and the pursuit of justice between man and man.[7] These were incumbent on all people, the specifics of the Jewish way of faith, with its rites, laws, customs, were held applicable only to members of the Jewish people.

2. The Rabbinic Dimension of Witnessing

Talmudic literature, which embodies the teachings of pharisaic-rabbinic tradition, reflects a profound awareness that the Jewish people were under a commitment to share the teachings of their faith with the peoples of the outside world. One of the most striking indications of this is the rabbinic reinterpretation of the career of the patriarch Abraham. He was envisioned as a missionary who engaged actively in disseminating his faith. Abraham's call is pictured as having been preceded by his deep frustration at seeing the world in its state of moral decadence. It seemed to him like a palace on fire, without anyone concerned to put it out. It was then that God summoned him to help put out the fire, to save His world. He was to serve as God's answer to the waywardness of man and commit his life, through teaching and example, to set mankind on the righteous course.[8]

The verse, "and Abraham took Sarah his wife . . . and all the persons they had acquired in Haran" (Gn 12:5) was taken as referring to the converts they had won for their faith. Abraham was said to have made converts among the men and Sarah among the women.[9] Abraham, we are told,

> extended hospitality to passersby, and after they ate and drank, he said to them, offer a prayer of praise. They asked him, what shall we say, and he told them: Praised be the God of the universe from whose bounty we have eaten.[10]

The rabbis suggested that the Torah was given while the Israelites sojourned in the desert of Sinai, a no-man's-land, to indicate that it was not meant to be the sole possession of the Jewish people but was to be offered to all who cared to live by it.[11] One rabbi stated that,

> every utterance from the Holy One, praised be He, (at Sinai) was divided into seventy languages.[12]

Another rabbinic source suggests that, "Moses expounded the Torah in seventy languages."[13] The term seventy languages is used in the Talmud to designate all the nations of the world. These pronouncements, therefore, mean that the Torah was seen as directed not only to Israel but to all mankind.

Judaism during the pharisaic-rabbinic period showed great concern to disseminate its teachings throughout the pagan world. It welcomed proselytes, and we have many expressions in talmudic texts showing solicitousness that proselytes be made to feel at home, that they be accorded a special love because of the depth of their commitment in having detached themselves from the roots of their ancestral faith, to come "under the wings of the shekinah."

The term *ger* which in biblical Hebrew meant a stranger was reinterpreted to mean proselyte and the thirty-six biblical repetitions to love a stranger were turned into a call to love a proselyte. A special prayer was added to the Jewish liturgy to invoke God's blessings on righteous proselytes, and converts from all strata of the Graeco-Roman world who joined the Jewish fold. Some proselytes after a time wavered in their new faith and reverted to their ancestral religion or joined other cults, especially after the Roman suppression of Judean freedom and the persecution of the Jewish religion. There were rabbis who expressed disillusionment with the efficacy of proselytism, but the general trend remained positive. Rabbi Elazar allowed himself to say that the dispersal of the Jews among the nations was providential since it brought them into greater contact with the non-Jewish world, enabling them to win proselytes for their faith.[14]

A candidate for conversion to Judaism was to be discouraged initially in order to test his sincerity. If he persisted he was to be taught the basics of the Jewish religion,

> the belief in the unity of God and the prohibition of idolatry, and some of the simpler and some of the graver commandments, the retribution for violating them and the reward for keeping them.[15]

The rite of initiation into Judaism consisted of circumcision in the case of males and, for males as well as females, immersion in a pool of water as symbol of purity and renewal. But while rabbinic Judaism was ready to embrace the sincere convert to its fold, it recognized a category of persons, Godfearers, who did not formally adopt Judaism but accepted its universal teachings about God and man, who acknowledged a supreme, universal God, and a sovereign moral order that derived from Him. These were summed up in the seven Noachide commandments referred to before.

We have a number of statements in classic rabbinic texts which extol the virtues and declare the sufficiency of the Godfearers who did not become full-fledged adherents of the Jewish faith. Perhaps the most striking is the following:

Rabbi Meir said, how do we know that if a gentile concerns himself with the Torah he is equal in status to a high priest? It is implied in the verse, "You shall therefore keep My statutes and My ordinances, which if a man do, he shall live by them" (Lev 18:5). It does not say, "which if a priest, a Levite or an Israelite do," but "if a man do," which shows that even a gentile who concerns himself with the Torah, he is equal in status to a high priest.[16]

Essentially the same statement appears in another context in the name of Rabbi Jeremia who cited additional proof texts for this position. After quoting the proof text given in Rabbi Meir's statement, he continues:

Similarly it is written, "This is the law of man, O Lord God" (2 Sam 7:19, a literal rendering of the Hebrew). It does not say, "the law of priests, levites and Israelites, but the law of man." Similarly it does not say, "Open the gates that priests, levites and Israelites may enter," but it says that "a righteous nation that keeps faith may enter" (Is 26:2). Similarly it does not say, "This is the gate of the Lord, priests, levites and Israelites shall enter it," but it says, "the righteous shall enter it" (Ps 118:20). Similarly it does not say, "Sing to the Lord, priests, levites and Israelites," but "Sing to the Lord O righteous" (Ps 33:1). Similarly it does not say, "Do good, O Lord, to priests, levites and Israelites," but "do good, O Lord, to the good" (Ps 125:4). Thus we infer that even a gentile, if he keeps the Torah, he is equal in status to a high priest.[17]

The boldest statement of this position appears in a comment on Psalm 132:9: "Let your priests be robed in righteousness." We are given a definition as to whom this verse applies:

This refers to the righteous among the nations who are priests of the Holy One, praised be He, in this world.[18]

Judaism during the Graeco-Roman period waged an active missionary campaign to win converts and Godfearers to its banner. In many cases, the missionaries were Jewish traveling merchants who propagated their beliefs among the people with whom they came in contact. We have the evidence of contemporary documents that these efforts were far-reaching. There is the well known testimony of the New Testament, accompanied by a gibe at the Pharisees:

Woe unto you, scribes and pharisees, hypocrites! For you compass sea and land to make one proselyte and when he is made, you make him two-fold more the child of hell than yourselves (Mt 23:15).

The Roman satirist Juvenal (60-140 CE), writing from another perspective, offers similar testimony. He alludes, moreover, to the process by which the Godfearer eventually became a full convert to Judaism or influenced his children to take this step. In one of his satires he mocks the Roman father who will not eat pork, who observes the Sabbath and worships only the heavenly God, but his son undergoes circumcision, despises the Roman laws and studies the Torah of the Jews.[19]

At times, the Jewish missionaries sought to discourage the would-be convert on the ground that the formal break with his ancestral faith was a needless severing of roots, of family ties. They pointed to the possibility of being loyal to the universal vision which is at the heart of Judaism within the structure and institutional framework of any other faith community.

Josephus reports such an incident involving King Izates of Audiabne. A Jewish merchant-missionary by the name of Ananias won him over to the Jewish faith, and the prince was ready and eager for a formal conversion. Ananias tried to dissuade him, telling him,

> that he might worship God without being circumcised, even though he did resolve to follow the Jewish law entirely; which worship of God was superior to circumcision.[20]

His mother Queen Helena, who herself had been an admirer of Judaism, also tried to dissuade him warning that,

> as he was a king, he would thereby bring himself into great odium among his subjects . . . that they would never bear to be ruled over by a Jew.[21]

Izates ignored the advice and became a full adherent of the Jewish faith.

But the turn to universalism in the Jewish conception of witness tended to blunt the potency of the Jewish missionary movement, especially after the emergence of Christianity. The latter inherited the concept of witness from its Jewish ancestry but turned it in a particularistic direction. Christianity proclaimed itself the sole path to salvation. An extremist ideology is always more potent in winning souls than one that recognizes the legitimacy of alternate paths to the desired goal. There were, of course, other factors which impeded the Jewish mission, e.g. the odium which fell on the Jews after the destruction of the Temple, and their ignominious defeat at the hands of the Romans. When Christianity became the official religion of the Roman empire, Jewish proselytism was declared a criminal offense against the state, and both the missionary as well as the proselyte were subjected to penalty, which in some cases was death. Yet, the universalistic terms in which Judaism defined its role of mission was also an inhibiting factor to the missionary effort. The realization that salvation may be attained without formal conversion necessarily robbed the drive for converts of at least some of its urgency.

3. The Post-Rabbinic Period

The concept of religious witness was further elaborated upon in the post-talmudic period. In a ninth-century midrash we have the statement that race, formal religious affiliation and social status play no part in qualifying a person for experiencing the "holy spirit." Only the quality of one's life is relevant:

> I call heaven and earth to witness that whether one be gentile or Jew, man or woman, male or female slave, in accordance with the merits of one's deeds does the Holy Spirit rest on him.[22]

Saadia ben Joseph Gaon (892-942) was even more explicit in interpreting this concept toward universalism. He denies categorically that God has favorites:

> All creatures are His creation and His handiwork and we may not say that He takes to Himself one to the exclusion of another, or to a greater degree than another. When biblical verses state that a particular people is His beloved, His possession, His portion and His inheritance, that "the portion of the Lord is His people, Jacob the portion of His inheritance" (Dt 32:9), this is only an expression of honor and respect, for we hold that the worth of every man and his inheritance is dear to Him. Moreover, in a figurative sense, the verses also make Him the portion of the pious. Thus it is stated: "The Lord is my portion, my share, my cup" (Ps 16:5). This, too, is an expression of distinction and exaltation. It is in the same way that He is called the God of the prophets, of those who believe in Him. Thus He is spoken of as the God of Abraham and the God of the Hebrews. He is the God of all, and these references are His way of showing honor and respect for the righteous.[23]

To the extent that a person rises in his spiritual development, he "possesses" God and is at the same time possessed by Him.

Maimonides (1135-1205) regarded the call to religious witness as a formal commandment which he derived from Leviticus 22:32, "and I shall be hallowed among the children of Israel":

The sense of this commandment is our obligation to disseminate our faith among all peoples.[24]

At the same time, Maimonides made it clear that people of other faiths need not necessarily enter the fold of Judaism to win acceptance before God. He formalized this into a doctrinal statement in his well-known letter to Rabbi Hisdai Halevi:

> As to your question concerning the other nations, you must realize that the Torah seeks the heart, and everything depends on the intentions of the heart. Therefore did the sages of truth, our masters, peace be upon them, declare that the pious (*hasidei,* but the text in Tosefta, San 13:4 has *zadikei,* the righteous) among the nations have a share in the world to come, if they have mastered what one can comprehend concerning the knowledge of the Creator, praised be He, and have refined their natures with sound principles of morals. There is no doubt about the matter, that whoever has perfected himself with good attributes of behavior and with sound principles of belief in the Creator, praised be He, is among those destined to have a share in the world to come.[25]

The Hasidic master Rabbi Nahman of Bratslav (1772-1810) called such a person a convert in essence, in contradistinction to a convert in fact. Here are his words:

> When we raise the conditions of our faith from its lowly state, converts come to us. . . . They either become converts in fact . . . or they only become converts in essence, and within their own faith as it is, they believe in the unity of God, the Creator, praised be He. This is prophesied in the verse (Mal 1,11), "From the rising of the sun to its going down shall My name be great among the nations, and in every place shall incense be offered to My name."[26]

4. A Contemporary View: The Thinking of Rav Kook

This concept received its fullest formulation in the thinking of Rabbi Abraham Isaac Kook (1865-1935), the late chief rabbi of Jewish Palestine prior to the birth of the state of Israel, one of the most sensitive religious spirits in modern Judaism. Rabbi Kook stressed often the classic doctrine that the Jewish people were the bearers of a heritage that proclaimed God's word with incomparable power, and that all mankind was meant to be nurtured by it. Yet, he took strong issue with those who disparaged other faiths. In all religions there are authentic elements, "a seeking after God and His ways in the world."[27] It is especially Jews, as the bearers of the universal vision, who should be the protagonists of this principle, but decadence obscured it for them:

> At a time such as this we must clarify the common elements of all religions, according to their degree of development, and not be intimidated by the customary disdain which lurks in the soul against everything alien.[28]

In Jewish tradition the feud between Judaism and Christianity, and Judaism and Islam, is sometimes projected back into the brotherly feuds between Jacob and Esau, and Isaac and Ishmael. Rabbi Kook seized on this projection and turned it into positive terms, the recognition of the essential brotherhood between the three faiths:

> The brotherly love between Esau and Jacob, between Isaac and Ishmael, will rise above the confusion fostered by the evil emanating from our creaturely character. It will rise above them and turn them to light and compassion without end.[29]

Rabbi Kook defined the essence of Judaism in terms of an existentialist philosophy which minimized dogmatic affirmations or ritual practices. For him, the essence of Judaism which flows from Jewish monotheism, is the passion to overcome the separatism which severs man from nature, from his fellow man, and from God. It is the passion to perfect the world through man's awareness of his links to all else in existence. It is the rejection of the alleged antagonism between the material and the spiritual. It is the rejection of nationalism as an ultimate center of moral values. It is the rejection of every parochialism which seeks to build man's spiritual home and his structure of values by taking to itself a fragment of life and ignoring the rest. "The Jewish outlook," he says, "is the vision of the holiness of all existence."[30]

Judaism has exerted an influence on the religious consciousness of the world but, for the most part this has been confined to the adoption of certain conceptual abstractions detached from the life context in which they appear in Judaism. These abstractions have been drawn into a religious system which centers its concern on a reverence for God as an exalted Being who exists in splendid transcendence from man's world, but which tends to separate religion from the ethical goals by which the world may be transformed toward righteousness. Judaism, on the other hand, centers its religious concern, not on the divine Being, but on divine ideals, on the goals which God has ever sought to realize in the world of His creation.

It is in the very concern to effectuate those goals in the context of a people struggling with the worldly problems of a nation functioning in history that the characteristic of Judaism is disclosed, and its cogency for a larger world service is indicated. At stake in the difference between the two approaches is,

> not the exalted metaphysical truth of the unity of God, but the divine aspect of the passion for equity and righteousness and the mighty aspiration to effectuate these divine ideals in all their strength.[31]

The crisis in Jewish peoplehood following centuries of exile and persecution and the resultant defensiveness which it fostered among Jews, has created a distortion in Judaism, and its authentic nature has been obscured, Rabbi Kook believed. His hope was that the return to Eretz Yisral and the Jewish renaissance to be engendered by it as a result of the Zionist endeavor would, in due time, also create a religious renewal enabling Judaism once more to be fully itself, and thus to assert a greater influence on world culture. The ultimate goal of the return to Zion is to enable the Jews once again,

> to bear the torch of holiness in all its purity before all the nations of the world. . . . It is to enable Judaism to bear witness to Torah in the world, both a political Torah which would foster peace and freedom . . . and a religious Torah enlightened by the knowledge of divine truth and the love of God's way in the life of the individual and society.[32]

Rabbi Kook did not proclaim that all religions are alike, but he held that they each had legitimacy, as the response of a particular people to the mysteries of God. In their value systems they may differ in the degree of universality attained, but each is to be seen as part of a larger whole. The interaction of religions will serve as a stimulus toward further growth, but none is to be supplanted. He states this bold position in clear terms:

> Conventional theology assumes that the different religions must necessarily oppose each other. . . . But on reaching full maturity the human spirit aspires to rise above every manner of conflict and opposition, and a person then recognizes all expressions of the spiritual life as an organic whole.[33]

Religions can serve one another as a stimulus, as a model to challenge and invite emulation. There are some elements in religion, too, which one faith may adopt from another. But in some fundamental respects every religion is integrally related to a people's historical experience, and a faith superimposed upon a people from without will, in a vital sense, remain alien to its life. Each religion is thus a permanent participant in the

> ensemble of faiths, and this domain also, where the feuds of the different faiths once raged will become filled with peace and light.[34]

The recognition that all religious traditions are channels through which the human spirit may grow in enlightenment is for Rabbi Kook the essence of the higher level of tolerance. As he put it:

> This concept of tolerance is aware that there is a spark of divine light in all things, that the inner spark of divine light shines in all the different religions, as so many different pedagogies for the culture of humanity, to improve its spiritual and material existence, its present and future, for the individual and society. But they exist on different levels. Just as there is only one force of germination, and it is manifest in the cedar of Lebanon as well as in the foliage on the wall, except that in the first instance it appears in a rich and beautiful form and in the second in a poor and limited form, so does the spark of divine light appear in the more advanced religions in a form that is rich and exalted, while in the less advanced religions in a form that is blurred, poor and lowly.... This type of tolerance is bound to spread so that the human spirit will be able to find the divine spark hidden in everything, and automatically discard every dross.... All the sparks will be joined into the mightiest torch, and all the nations will acquire "a pure language, to call in the name of the Lord" (Zeph 3, 9). "Take away the dross from the silver and there will emerge a refined vessel" (Prov 25, 4).[35]

5. Witness and Mission in Judaism and the Interreligious Dialogue

The concept of religious witness in Judaism is radically different from the same concept as it developed in Christianity. The primary goal of the latter is to win converts to faith in the messiahship of Jesus. This classic Christian position was reaffirmed by Vatican II in the following words:

> The missionary activity (of the Church) finds its reasons in the will of God, "who wishes all men to be saved and to come to the knowledge of the truth. For there is one God and one Mediator ... Christ Jesus who gave of himself as a ransom for all" (1 Tim 2:4f), "neither is there salvation in any other" (Acts 4:12). Therefore, all must be converted to Him as He is made known by the Church's preaching. All must be incorporated into Him by baptism, and into the Church which is His body.[36]

But be it noted that the Catholic Church has repeatedly condemned proselytism, the high pressure method of seeking to make converts to Christianity. Another document promulgated by the Second Vatican Council declares:

> In spreading religious faith ... everyone ought at all times to refrain from any manner of action which might seem to carry a kind of coercion or of a kind of persuasion that would be dishonorable or unworthy, especially when dealing with poor or uneducated people. Such a manner of action would have to be considered an abuse of one's own right and a violation of the right of others.[37]

The editor appends to this the following note:

> It is customary to distinguish between "Christian witness" and proselytism, and to condemn the latter. This distinction is made in the text here. Proselytism is a corruption of Christian witness by appealing to hidden forms of coercion or by a style of propaganda unworthy of the gospel. It is not the use but the abuse of religious freedom.[38]

The Vatican II position on the subject is made even more explicit in Tommaso Federici's study outline for the "Commission for Religious Relations with the Jews." The most emphatic statement on the subject is probably the following:

> The Church thus rejects in a clear way every form of proselytism. This means the exclusion of any sort of witness and preaching which in any way constitutes a physical, moral, psychological or cultural constraint on the Jews, both individuals and communities, such as might in any way destroy or even simply reduce their personal judgment, free will and full autonomy of decision. ... Also excluded is every sort of judgment expressive of discrimination, contempt or restriction against the Jewish people as such ... or against their faith, their worship, their general and in particular their religious culture, their past and present history, their existence and its meaning.[39]

The stress in the Jewish concept of religious witness is on the general illumination of people toward the recognition of the universal sovereignty of God and the primacy of the moral order. It does not call for the disappearance of diverse forms of religious expression but for the recognition that, transcending all these diversities, is the common reverence for a universal God in whom all life, including all manifestations of the religious disposition, can find its harmonious coexistence. The effort of any religion to supersede all others, with the claim that it alone offers the means of salvation, is from the perspective of Judaism a form of religious particularism due to be transcended as we grow toward true universality.

The Jewish conception of religious witness was invoked in modern times in the celebrated case involving Aimé Pallière, a French Catholic seminarian, who turned to Rabbi Elijah Benamozegh with the plea to convert him to Judaism. The Rabbi urged him to remain within the Church but to shed its particularism, such as belief in the divinity of Jesus, and to follow the seven Noachide laws as the principles of a universal faith open to all. Pallière's remarkable odyssey of faith is recounted in his *Unknown Sanctuary*. The formula by which he was taught to reconcile a formal allegiance to his native Catholicism with the universal vision of Judaism is well expressed in these words:

> The entire human race is thus united in a very real spiritual oneness even though there seem to be, because of the very nature of things, numerous and necessary differences. This does not deter the believer who lays claim to the prophetic tradition, from hastening, through his prayers, the coming of the day when God will be One and His name One.[40]

It signifies that the One God is really worshipped under many forms, in very different cults, but in the messianic era, the spiritual world will see unity of worship realized.

> Thus the believing Israelite attains through prophetism unto the loftiest divine Revelation in the past, and through Messianism, to the greatest religious hope in the future. His faith makes him a citizen of the world, and his hope of the Kingdom of God comforts him in the sorrows and shadows of the present, by making it possible for him to glimpse a complete manifestation of the eternal truth that is to come.[41]

There is a well-known adage in the Talmud, "adorn yourself, then adorn others."[42] The call to religious witness must be directed first to the Jewish people. Various levels of parochialism in Judaism have blunted the universal vision as it is conventionally understood. Centuries of persecution have made some Jews defensive, developing in them distrust, even hostility toward the non-Jewish world. Others have allowed the particular values of Judaism, its unique structure of rites and practices, to gain full domination at the expense of the universal vision, the spiritual and moral sensibilities immanent in it. As Rabbi Kook put it:

The love for people must be alive in heart and soul, a love for all people and for all nations, expressing itself in a desire for their spiritual and material advancement; hatred may direct itself only toward the evil and the filth in the world. One cannot reach the exalted position of being able to recite the verse from the morning prayer, "Praise the Lord, invoke His name, declare His works among the nations" (1 Chr 16:18), without experiencing the deep, inner love stirring one to a solicitousness for all nations, to improve their material state, to promote their happiness. This disposition qualifies the Jewish people to experience the spirit of the Messiah.[43]

The inner-directed application of the call to witness must have as its objective the strengthening of this disposition among Jews, that they may discover the full authenticity of their own faith.

The thrust of religious witness is to disseminate the recognition of the universality of God, yet this cannot be an isolated subject of belief dissociated from its conceptual and existential implications. In effect, this involves a whole philosophy of life and a way of life directed toward hallowing all existence. It takes an assiduous process of learning to achieve this and calls for continuous probing of one's self and the reality around him. The faithful witness of God's presence must therefore be a disciple simultaneously with being a master. Moses Cordovero (1522-1570) recognized this when he stated:

A person should face in two directions. Firstly, he must withdraw from worldly involvements to be with his Creator so as to increase his wisdom and to perfect it. Secondly, he is to teach other people of that wisdom which the Holy One, praised be He, bestowed on him. . . . He should be careful not to extend in excess of what the intellectual capacities of the recipient would allow, so that no damage might result. . . . Divine wisdom animates all beings with life, as it is written (Ecc 7:12): Wisdom gives life to all. Similarly he is to serve as a life-giving influence to the whole world, and enable all to possess life in this world and in the next.[44]

Divine enlightenment is also effected through people; in the mystery of divine creation, all persons are unique. We all see our world in a unique way and such perspectives are a means by which the many-sidedness of reality may gain greater clarification. Because men are unique, said Rabbi Judah Loew of Prague (1525-1609),

each one received a particular aspect of the truth in accordance with his mental perspective . . . and when these are gathered up, we have the truth in all its many-sidedness.[45]

One channel for enlightenment is the way of dialogue by the written and spoken word. A wise man is defined by the rabbis as one "who learns from all men."[46] The *Midrash Shmuel* comments on this statement:

> There is no limit to the divine service and to wisdom ... but who is wise? One who is always aware that he is lacking therein ... but one who thinks he has already attained it ... will not endeavor to gain more, thinking that he has already mastered it, and he will fall behind and not advance. . . . And how wonderful is the practice we find among the sages that they call the scholars *talmude hakhamin* (lit., disciples of the wise). . . . Whoever does not regard himself as a disciple is not wise.[47]

The call to dialogue as an important way to truth was sounded in bold terms by Rabbi Nahman of Bratslav:

> One must realize and believe that there is in every Jew some noble and very precious element lacking in his neighbor and he needs to be illuminated by him through this element. . . . Even when he meets a Jew of the lowest status he undoubtedly has something he can discuss with him and to receive from him or to enlighten him. Even when he meets a non-Jew he can receive from him.[48]

This theme is further amplified in another passage in which Rabbi Nahman sees the role of dialogue in more universal terms:

> In order to draw the whole world to His service, to serve Him in one accord, and that all discard their idols of silver and gold and direct their prayers to God, praised be He alone, this is effected in each generation to the extent that peace prevails in that generation. Through peace which prevails among people and they search and clarify the truth to one another, each person discards the falsehood of his silver idols and brings himself closer to the truth.[49]

It is to be noted, however, that one bears witness to one's faith not only in formal exercises of communication. When people live in an open society, the mere fact of one's being exerts an influence. The values embodied in one's life release vibrations that reach others and they respond subtly and sometimes even unconsciously, sometimes rejecting and sometimes adopting elements, as their inner sensibilities prompt them. Some people erect barriers around their lives to insulate themselves against influences from the outside. They doom themselves to stagnate in their own limitations. The life process itself, when it is experienced in free interaction between people, is the way to greater truth and a more dedicated service of God, including the fulfillment of the duty to bear witness to His truth, at whatever level of enlightenment one has experienced it.

Notes

1. Obadya Sforno, *Mikraot Gedolot* (Tel Aviv: Pardes, 1959), Commentary on Genesis, *ad locum.*
2. *Ibid.*, Commentary on Exodus, *ad locum.*
3. Elijah ben Solomon, Gaon of Vilna, *Mikraot Gedolot* (see no. 1), Commentary on Isaiah, *ad locum.*
4. Jer 1:9-10; 2:3; 3:17; Zech 8:2-23; Zeph 3:19.
5. TB *Baba Bathra* 15b.
6. *Genesis Rabbah* 1, 3; 33, 2.
7. TB *Sanhedrin* 56b.
8. *Genesis Rabbah* 39, 1.
9. *Ibid.*, 39, 14.
10. *Ibid.*, 54, 5.
11. *Mekilta* on Ex 19:2.
12. TB *Shabbath* 88b.
13. *Genesis Rabbah* 49, 2.
14. TB *Pesahim* 87b.
15. TB *Yebamoth* 47b.
16. TB *Baba Kamma* 38a.
17. *Sifra* on Lev 18:5.
18. *Yalkut Shimoni* (Jerusalem: Lewin-Epstein, 1951) on IS 26:4.
19. Juvenal, *Satires* 14, 96ff.
20. Flavius Josephus, *Antiquities* XX, 2.
21. *Ibid.*, XX, 4.
22. *Seder Eliahu Rabba*, M. Friedman, ed. (Jerusalem: Wahrmann, 1969), chap. 10.
23. Saadia ben Josef Gaon, *The Book of Beliefs and Opinions* (New Haven: Yale Univ. Press, 1948), p. 126. The book was originally written in Arabic. I followed the Hebrew translation of David Kapah.
24. Moses Maimonides, *Book of Precepts* (New Haven: Yale Univ. Press, 1961), 9th commandment.
25. *Igrot u Teshuvot Le-Rabenu Moshe ben Maimon Ha-Sefardi* (Warsaw: Teraklin, 1927), Letter 6, p. 16. But cf. *Mishne Torah, Hilkhot Melakhim* 8, 11 where Maimonides specifies that to be regarded among "the pious of the gentiles" one must believe, on the strength of biblical testimony, that the Noachide laws were divinely revealed. If he follows them on rational considerations alone he is to be regarded among "the sages of the gentiles." I follow the reading in the Yemenite manuscript, as cited in the edition of Mosad Harav Kook, Jerusalem 1962.

26. Nahman of Bratslav, *Likkutei Moharan* (Jerusalem: Yeshivat Bratslav, Bnei Brac, 1964) II:5:4.

27. *Abraham Isaac Kook* (The Lights of Penitence, The Moral Principles, Lights of Holiness, Essays, Letters, and Poems), Ben Zion Bokser, transl. (Paulist Press: New York, 1978), p. 12.

28. *Ibid.*

29. *Ibid.*, p. 339.

30. *Ibid.*, p. 26.

31. *Ibid.*, p. 27.

32. *Ibid.*, pp. 27f.

33. *Ibid.*, p. 28.

34. *Ibid.*, p. 29.

35. *Ibid.*, pp. 273ff.

36. "Decree on the Missionary Activity of the Church," in *The Documents of Vatican II*, Walter M. Abbott, ed. (New York: Guild Press, 1966) I:7.

37. "Declaration on Religious Freedom" in *The Documents of Vatican II*, pp. 682f.

38. *Ibid.*

39. Tommaso Federici, "Study Outline on the Mission and Witness of the Church," in *Face to Face*, an Interreligious Bulletin (New York: Anti-Defamation League of B'nai B'rith) Fall/Winter 1977, pp. 23-31; passage quoted is on p. 30. For additional documents by Catholic bishops' conferences in the United States and other countries, as well as position papers by the various Protestant churches, cf. *Stepping Stones to Further Jewish-Christian Relations: An unabridged collection of Christian Documents*, Helga Croner, comp. (New York/London: Stimulus Books, 1977).

40. Aimé Pallière, *Unknown Sanctuary*, Louise Waterman Wise, transl. (New York: Bloch Publ., 1928), pp. 237f.

41. *Ibid.*

42. TB *Sanhedrin* 18a.

43. *Abraham Isaac Kook* (see n. 27), p. 136.

44. Moses Cordovero, *Palm Tree of Deborah*, Louis Jacobs, transl. (London: Vallentine-Mitchell, 1960), chap. 3.

45. Judah Loew of Prague, *Beer Ha-Golah* (Pieterkov, 1910), p. 13.

46. *Avot* 4, 1.

47. *Midrash Shmuel, ad locum.*

48 Nahman of Bratslav, *Sipure Maasiot* (Brooklyn, N. Y., 1972), p. 181.

49. *Idem, Likkutei Moharan* I:27:1.

5.
Witnessing and Personal Religious Existence

Leon Stitskin

"Ye are my witnesses, saith the Lord, and my servant whom I have chosen; that ye may know and believe me and understand that I am He; before me no God was formed, neither shall any be after me" (Is 43:10).

1. Personal Witness to the Existence of the Divine

The intellectual mode of discourse articulated in the philosophy of Jewish personalism formulates propositions making claims about ultimate reality in personalistic terms. A basic assumption of personalism is that the most profound witness comes at the point of personalistic consciousness. Our humanity is a revelation of divinity, for at his highest state of authentication man is truly a mirror in which we can see reflected the image of God. The personalistic meaning of witness points primarily to the existential stance of each individual in his relationship with God. Even the collective witness of the people of Israel is grounded in the fulfillment of the covenantal challenge for self-authentication of individual members of the community.[1]

In this framework, the metaphysical is implicit in self-knowledge. The objective reference of thought is interpreted from the standpoint of the subject rather than the object. Rather than have a reflection of the object, it is the object who objectifies his thought. In self-knowledge and self-experience there is an identity of idea and object, a coalescence of self and experience.

While the logical positivists tell us that all ultimate questions are meaningless, and the scholastics claim that all ultimate questions are answered, we claim neither, except to state that the ultimate issue of transcendental awareness is at stake in our existence. The transcendental conceptual and moral nature of the human condition would fall into a contradiction with itself if there were no transcendent Being as the guarantor for the authentication of our cognitive identity and the fulfillment of our creative spirit, propelling us to transcend beyond ourselves and to participate in a genuine cognitive relationship. Indeed, the common refrain of Jewish philosophers, "know thyself and then you will know thy Creator," is the key to the generic and pervasive characteristic of reality.

Admittedly, the three traditional theistic arguments by classical and medieval philosophers have been largely refuted and fatally weakened by the criticism of Hume and Kant and some contemporary philosophers. The existence of God is consequently not determined by probing the nature of the world (cosmological),[2] the nature of the world's design (teleological),[3] or the nature of God (ontological),[4] but by the nature of man.

The existence of God is derived not from external accepted premises but from one's experiential reality and existential conditions. The pull is from within, existentially moving toward God rather than the push from without extending from God. We find the infinite not by looking away from the finite self but by looking more deeply into the finite self. To be human, in the personalistic sense, is to be potentially divine. Living is an experience which allows one a sense of unfoldment and fulfillment as one joins the inevitable evolutionary ascent toward a higher spiritual consciousness. The authentic self grasps its own life within a larger cosmic setting. It sees itself as part of a greater whole, as an existential demand of its finitude for the ultimate reality. Our built-in hierarchical quality to transcend beyond ourselves necessarily draws us to affirm the Ultimate Transcendent.

2. Valuational and Conceptual Response

Moreover, the built-in evolutionary thrust to transcend beyond ourselves necessarily draws us to make a two-fold response to God's challenge: a valuational and a conceptual. In the valuational, man responds by advancing from external compulsion to an inner-directed motivation and freedom. On the conceptual level, man responds by transcending from a state of potentiality to actuality culminating in a cognitive identification with the Divine Presence. As Maimonides (1135-1204) states, "the intellect which emanates from God unto us is the link that joins us to God."[5]

The dynamics for the double response to God's challenge is derived from the twofold meaning of reason: critical or discursive reason and personalized, actualized reason.

The Cartesian principle of *cogito ergo sum* reiterated the classical formulation that from self-knowledge we can proceed to a knowledge of God and the outside world. Inasmuch as self-certainty is predicated on self-awareness, reason becomes the basis for all knowledge. Religious truth does not simply find support in reason but is an outgrowth of it. Valid authority must itself be rational. But what kind of reason does the Cartesian principle imply? According to Descartes (1596-1650) it infers innate ideas put in our soul by God. Hence, Descartes attempted to probe God's existence by understanding the *idea* of God. We have an *idea* of God as infinite, omnipotent. But how can a finite being think of an infinite God, unless it is an innate idea? Kant refuted the argument by pointing to the inevitable contradiction we fall into when human reason goes beyond experience.

The Hebraic tradition, on the other hand, imputes two other qualities to reason which would tend to avoid Kant's refutation. First, discursive reason which attempts to establish God's existence by probing into the experience of the human condition to transcend beyond ourselves, in keeping with the personalist "not yet" ontology, necessarily affirms a Supreme Being. Second, actualized reason cognizes Supreme Thought when, by means of a conceptualization, ideas are not copies of phenomena but work together and become ultimate purposes, and thought takes on an objective content, a world of its own, resulting in an epistemological monism.

Scripture already refers to those two categories of reason. The psalmist speaks of *reishit hokhmah yirat Hashem*, "the first principle of reason is to use it as an instrument of reverence for God" (Ps 111:10). The Book of Proverbs, on the other hand, alludes to an ontological content of reason. *Reishit hokhmah keneih hokhmah*, "the first principle of reason is to acquire reason" (Prov 4:7). In the initial stage, critical reason employed as an instrument with which to probe man's essential nature draws man existentially to embrace the idea of God as the promise of our freedom. In the ultimate stage, reason as its own source of knowledge (hypostatized reason) necessarily validates the existence of God by cognitively identifying with Supreme Thought.

Manifestly, the content of faith in God is not drawn out of "feeling" or "the leap of faith" or reliance on "authority" but on the double implication of man's reason. Discursive reason, investigating man's transcendental quality is responsible for the existential approach, in its reliance on the incontrovertible assurance of transcending from an external to an inner-directed motivation. On the other hand, as an ontological content, reason affirms the Supreme Being by a cognitive kinship with the Divine Presence. Hence, the validation of God's existence is determined by a dialectic in the human condition requiring moral freedom and an independent inner-directed motivation in the valuational sphere and intellectual unification with the Supreme Being in the conceptual dimension. The existential approach requires critical reason for its validation, and the cognitive approach in the final stage is an outgrowth of "personalized," actualized reason. In the final dimension of conceptualization the dichotomy between subject and object, between separation and identification, is eliminated, and the dialectic common to all relationships is transcended in an epistemological monism.

3. The Nature of the Divine

Clearly, in the same manner as we determine God's existence we determine God's nature. The knowability and unknowability, the transcendentalism and immanence and attributes of God are some of the considerations involved in an investigation of God's nature. Since existence is drawn from the frame of reference of man's unique, irreplaceable selfhood, it follows that our relation to a divine presence grounded in man's double response requires a two-fold content—a valuational and conceptual, a knowable and unknowable, a *nigleh* (revealed) and a *nistar* (hidden).

From man's perspective, there are two aspects of viewing the Deity: God-in-Himself and God-in-Relation. In the first aspect, God-in-Himself as the transcendent, the *Ein Sof*, the Unknown, the absolute unity, the God-in-Essence beyond all categories of existence, man participates in the Divine Eternity. We experience God-in-Himself as the Pure Being, Being-Itself beyond the totality of beings, infinitely transcending finite beings in the immediate situation but providing, by virtue of His Essence, reinstatement with the Divine Presence in the ultimate situation, when transcending from a state of potentiality to actuality. On the other hand, in the God-in-Relation aspect, we experience God as the Creator, Being-in-Manifestation continuing His creative purpose for man's participation in the Supreme Value through *imitatio Dei*,[6] which cultivates in us a process of advancement toward an inner-directed motivation.

The double aspect of all beings to Being-Itself gives Being-Itself from our frame of reference a double characteristic. Pure Being is the unknowable devoid of any attributes. Creative Being denotes attributes derived from our finite experiences for man to imitate. Pure Being is Supreme Thought—the causal principle that is the source of theoretical knowledge. Creative Being is Supreme Value and Purpose as the paradigm of ethical action and as the goal of our consecrated experience.

According to Maimonides, knowledge of God's nature, as we experience it, is contained in the biblical dialogue between Moses and God. Moses makes two requests of God: "Show me thy ways" and "show me thy glory" (Ex 33:13.18). The first is a request for the knowledge of God-in-Relation by means of attributes, the second is for the knowledge of God-in-Himself, His Essence. In response to the latter, the response is that God is unknowable, "man cannot see me and live" (Ex 33:20). With regard to the first question, however, Moses received a positive reply, namely, "I will cause all my goodness to pass before thee" (Ex 33:19). This, in effect, infers that God can be known in His relation with man by His attributes, as the word "goodness" implies. This is borne out by the conclusion of the passage with the words, "and thou shalt see my back but my face (essence) shall not be seen" (Ex 33:23), and the proclamation of God's Thirteen Qualities (*middot*) in the remainder of the section.[7] Clearly, then, the Torah projects here the two-fold aspect of viewing the Divine. In-Himself, God is unknowable. To man on earth, in relation, God is manifest by His attributes, derived from our experiences.

To be sure, the attributes, according to Maimonides, are known to us only as the works or actions of God on the level of our experience. He writes:

> The words "all my goodness" imply that God promised to show him the whole creation, concerning which, it has been stated, "And God saw everything that He has made and behold, it was very good" (Gn 1:31).[8]

In other words, we can predicate of God certain actions, like Creation which was beneficial to mankind, although we cannot describe the disposition of the agent in producing the action or the manner of its production. The elements contained in God in order to produce the action of creation, such as mercy or graciousness are not known to us except the action or the effect as we read, "and thou shalt see my back . . ." In a previous chapter,[9] where he distinguishes between positive and negative attributes, Maimonides asserts that the content of the attributes by means of allusion come from the human side. They are predicated of God in a sense that is equivocal with its use in ordinary discourse. He writes:

You are, as it were, brought by the belief in the reality of the attributes to say that God is one subject of which several things are predicated.[10]

The inference is that the human condition necessarily evokes attributes in the Divine activity that constitute the regulative qualities for man to imitate. They surely do not tell us what God is within Himself but how He wills we should think of Him in order to guide our behavior. They are therefore moral, valuational attributes. When we attribute them to God we mean to affirm that they are of the same type as the actions of a person we would call moral.

By the same token, while on the level of philosophical analysis it is illogical and inconsistent to pray and speak to God in the certainty that He hears, it is plausible on the level of our moral needs for self-fulfillment and emotional quest for right choices and commitment to action. This constitutes our first response to God's challenge for self-authentication, impelling us to righteous conduct by a pull from within rather than a push from without.

Clearly though, our perception of God's attributes has no bearing at all on His Essence. In the ultimate situation God remains the Unknowable Infinity (the *Ein Sof*), and yet what we really strive for is to behold God's Essence. It is primarily toward this ultimate end that our transcendent condition of advancing beyond ourselves draws us. But this can be attained only by participation in the inevitable ascent toward a higher operational consciousness. Our innate drive, impelling us toward an appointed end of perfect correspondence to unchanging and permanent reality, cannot be made intelligible unless associated with the notion of an ever living God, who secures for man the possession of intellectual perfection and the participation of life eternal. The dynamic principle in this frame is not *imitatio Dei*, as in the first aspect, but theoretical knowledge of God who is beyond all categories of existence. As Maimonides states in the same context:

The words "that I may find grace in thy sight" imply that he who knows God finds grace in His eyes .... He who has no knowledge of God is the object of His wrath and displeasure .... The approach to Him and the withdrawal from Him are proportional to the amount of man's knowledge or ignorance concerning the Creator.[11]

This requires an ascending scale of the cognitive process of moving from perceptual to conceptual cognition, where we conceive universal laws rather than an image of an object governing existence, and moving on toward a philosophically abstracted Deity, the Divine Reality, the Ground of Life here and in the hereafter. While God-in-Relation reflects divine activity, God-in-Himself represents divine essence.

4. The Two Views of God Are Not Mutually Exclusive

Ostensibly some may argue that it is difficult to posit two seemingly opposite concepts of God—the Creator of whom we predicate attributes of a directly acting and communicative personality as depicted in Judah Halevi's *Kuzari* and the philosophically abstracted deity, the divine reality as the background of life here and in the hereafter.

In a personalistic framework no such dichotomy prevails. The two views are not mutually exclusive. From man's perspective two major patterns of the divine irrevocably emerge, the valuational and cognitive. Man, as a developmental, self-transcending being, requires a two-fold envisagement of the ultimate Being. When one looks at the facts of the world and tries to work back through them to a unified view of life, to a philosophical conceptual grasp of the world in the broadest sense, one must conclude that the basic issue is the frame of reference whence we take off to consider some basic philosophical propositions. Do we begin with external premises emanating from on high or do we commence on the level of human experience? Should not the underlying assumption for any meaningful search for the ultimate—like every other philosophical scheme of thought in our ideological construct, where propositions are significant when there is anything in human experience which is relevant to the formation of these propositions—begin with man's response to the encounter he experiences as a result of his "openness" and transcendental quality which is of a double nature? In the immediate situation, man responds to the challenge for self-authentication by striving for freedom of will and for an inner-directed motivation: in the ultimate situation, for the actualization of his potential.

It was indicated previously that when Moses inquired of the Divine "Show me thy ways," he was told "and thou shalt see my back, but my face shall not be seen." Implicit in this response was a two-fold existential experience, an operation and a cognitive relation. Propositions about God in the first type of experience are used to evoke conduct responses and stimulate emotional reactions. If one predicates of God, for example, the terms "wise" and "loving," one does not intend to assert a statement of fact, but the intention is to induce in oneself or others an attitude of "wisdom," of "loving-kindness." The logical status of such statements, as "God repented of having made man," is to produce in us the desired practical effect of being willing to confess to a mistake and to do something about it. In this context there is no reason for inquiring into the precise meaning of the words. All that is required is that the words be intelligible in terms of the experience of the listeners.

For this reason the attributes predicated of the divine were personalistic. They were meant to evoke proper conduct responses in the human personality. Since the mark of emphasis in Judaism was on the centrality of personality—personality being its own proof and the proof of its own right of existence—it was natural that in our valuational encounter with the absolute we should ascribe to Him the nature of a supreme personality. Consider the rabbinic interpretation of "This is my God and I shall glorify Him" as *ani vehu*, "I and He."[11a] The personalistic attributes predicated of the Divine were simply a fact of experience as each one of them were to every other. Only He was an overwhelming fact.

5. The Conceptual Dimension

But is the valuational quest the highest end of man in search of God? It is only a means to an end consisting in the perfection of man's specific form which is theoretical knowledge, cognizance of the true nature of things, when the empirical and transcendental self is realized in the unifying and self-identifying activity of consciousness. Knowledge on the level of consciousness, appropriated truth, securing for man the highest blessing of life eternal in the Divine Presence, can only be found in God as a Being-in-Himself, the Absolute Transcendent. The self is in knowledge a principle of unification, establishing a cognitive identification with God in the ultimate situation. In personalism it is through consideration of man's consciousness—the metaphysical reality is not a self-existent substance but a transcendent self that reveals itself in consciousness—that the idea of transcendent being tends to become the concrete idea of God rather than being reduced to a blank absolute, an impersonal abstraction. When man authenticates himself by reaching out beyond his present state he affirms God. There is a correlation between man's developmental endowments for intellectual actualization and the existence of the Supreme actualized Intellect. Aristotle states:

> Life belongs to God, for the actuality of thought is life; and God's actuality in virtue of itself is life most good and eternal.[12]

Accordingly, our apprehension of the knowability and unknowability or the transcendence and immanence of the Divine as well as His existence is determined by our investigation of the nature of man and his two-fold response to God's challenge for self-authentication.[13] In personalism the stress is on the kind of response evoked in man in terms of God-in-Relation and God-in-Essence. In-Relation the response is in *imitatio Dei*, designed to advance from an external to an inner-directed motivation, from a subject/object dichotomy to freedom of will. In this instance, then, God is viewed as Supreme Value and Purpose, the paradigm of ethical action and goal of consecrated deeds. In-Essence, the response is in the realization of the potential (the transcendence of the tension between conceptual possibility and perceptual limitation) and the advancement beyond ourselves in the unifying and self-identifying activity of consciousness, striving to be at one with ultimate Reality. Here we experience the Divine as Supreme Thought, the causal principle that is the source of theoretical knowledge.

Clearly, the promulgation of God's Unity in Judaism was not designed as a mere substitute for the multiple mythological gods whose arbitrary powers reduced the position of man to a puppet, a marionette dancing to the tunes of the gods. The concept of One God as the Uniqueness of God, initiated a new notion of man as the embodiment of a margin of sovereignty in the universe, and a new relation between God and man as challenge and response and not as cause and effect. In this frame of reference the focus of the challenge was on the authentication of the self evolving in knowledge as a principle of unification and the response of man, as indicated, was of a double nature.

6. Personal Religious Existence

Given this conception of God's existence and nature as grounded in man's valuational and conceptual dimensions, it follows that man alone is witness on earth to divine truth. Man alone can bring into being the kind of society which is worthy of being called the Kingdom of God on earth.

In his self-knowledge, man becomes aware of his possibilities and these, in turn, imply his responsibilities. As a divine potential, he cannot merely rest easy but he is driven to realize what is demanded of him first as an ethical personality, and secondly as a spiritual personality, and finally as a cognitive personality.

a. As an Ethical Personality

As an ethical personality, he must seek to unify his will with conviction as he advances from an external to an inner-directed motivation. Moral freedom is not a gift bestowed but an achievement earned. The tensions involved between heteronomous and autonomous sets of values are resolved in the personalistic focus on man's moral self-realization. As we ourselves discover the meaning of our existence and authentication, we evolve from "a push from without to a pull from within morality." In the immediate situation of man's developmental process, ethical guidelines externally imposed are required. In the ultimate situation, ethical judgments are the expressions of the rational character of moral cognition coinciding with the Divine Will.

b. As a Spiritual Personality

As a spiritual personality, the experience of the human personality to transcend beyond himself draws him existentially to embrace doctrinal beliefs and religious hypotheses and practices. The biblical notion of *zelem Elokim* (image of God), which constitutes a component *sui generis* of Judaism, embraces both properties of seeking the highest good in the path of self-authentication and believing that it is realizable. Otherwise the essential character of its nature would fall into a contradiction with itself.

It should be noted however that initially we are drawn by the evolutionary thrust of our existential condition into adopting an open-ended approach, an unconditional, intuitive compliance with the content of religious doctrine and practice for self-authentication. In the immediate situation one is required to venture the leap and stake one's whole existence of maximal practice, and it is only in the consummative stage when human reason actualized attests to the truth of doctrinal beliefs. Thus revelation for instance, accepted intuitively as a historical fact by the very nature of our human condition in the initial stages of self-development, constitutes a facet of the basic data necessary for the actualization of the faculty of reason. The revelatory material, which consists of firsthand expressions of religious apperceptions and fundamental facts of faith forms the experiential basis for the development of the dictates of reason. Just as our knowledge of the physical world is based upon our sense experience— since human thought, empiricism would argue, can only deal with material which has been given in experience—our religious knowledge, in the incipient state of our rational development, rests upon aspects of human experiences which are received by revelation. While in the early developmental process the validity of the revelatory act must remain an assumption in the subsequent involvement of one's inner world, the authentication of the canons of reason within us provides existential certainty for the historic act of revelation. Otherwise the human condition would fall into a contradiction with itself, as the logical order of the mind corresponds to the universal truths embodied in the revelatory act. At this stage the spiritual personality has blended into a single unity two fundamental issues of the philosophic enterprise, namely, what can I know and what can I believe?

7. The Mitzvah (Precept)

Consider further the nature of the *mitzvah* (precept) which in Judaism represents the unique mode of personal religious experience. Basically there are two overriding notions concerning the *mitzvah*. We can approach the significance of a precept from the perspective of either man or the deed itself. From the perspective of man, the *mitzvah* is merely a means to an end, serving the purpose of man's fulfillment. From the frame of the deed itself, the precept is an end in itself. According to Maimonides, this distinction hinges upon the general question whether the actions of God are the result of His wisdom or only of His will without being intended for any purpose whatever. Maimonides says:

> Some (theologians) hold that the commandments have no object at all and are only dictated by the will of God. Others are of the opinion that all commandments and prohibitions are dictated by His wisdom and serve a certain aim. Consequently there is a reason for each one of the precepts; they are enjoined because they are useful.[14]

Now if the emphasis is on the deed itself (apart from the mystical notion which invests the *mitzvah* with some magical power) some philosophers interpret the ritual act as a sanctum, a sacrament emobdying God's will. The law is divine when performed in a certain prescribed way designed to make the divine will and man's coincide. Thus we are reminded by Judah Halevi (1080-1142) that,

> man can only attain to divine order through Divine ordinance viz. through actions (*mitzvoth*) ordained by God.[15]

He is even more explicit in a later treatise of the *Kuzari* where he states that, "nearness to God can be achieved only through God's mitzvot."[16]

a. The Precept as a Means to an End

It would appear, however, that the more authentic attitude in the Hebraic tradition regards the *mitzvah* as a means to a higher end. The concern is with man's fulfillment and the ritual act is one of the spiritual instructional instruments toward that end. An affirmation of this thesis is the rabbinic statement:

It pleased the Holy One, blessed be He, to make Israel meritorious. Therefore He multiplied to them Torah and precept.[17]

Maimonides offers a classical philosophical example for the assumption of the ceremonial law as ministering to the perfection of man:

> For it has already been demonstrated that man has two perfections: a first perfection which is the perfection of the body; and an ultimate perfection, which is the perfection of the soul. . . . Once the first perfection has been achieved it is possible to achieve the ultimate, which is indubitably more noble and is the only cause of permanent preservation. . . . The true law then . . . has come to bring us both perfections. . . . The letter of the Torah . . . informs us that the end of this Law in its entirety is the achievement of these two perfections.[18]

The dynamics of the *mitzvah* in this context takes on a variety of forms. It may be psychological in that it aims to structure behavior, curb impulses, control compulsive drives. Or it may be of an ethical, intellectual nature striving for self-regeneration and self-authentication. In either case it sets up standards, relating each situation to some abstract rule or judgment.

In a more consequential manner, however, Jewish tradition regarded the *mitzvah* as a pedagogic vehicle to man's ethical uplift, spiritual purification, and self-redemption. We are told that,

> the mitzvot were conferred upon the children of Israel in order to refine human nature, as we read "all commandments of the Lord are for the purpose of purification."[19]

Under this conception, Jewish ritual is intended as a spiritualized device, each act is evocative of religious and ethical idealism. The key objective is the sanctification of life and the precept is the instrument designed to this end. Its effectiveness consists in employing the sound technique of action which is understood by all (the child and adult, the naive and the sophisticated) and it operates everywhere. It deals not in abstraction but in tangible expression.

b. Classical Jewish Philosophers and the Precepts

To Saadia ben Joseph Gaon (892-942), who distinguished between rational and conventional *mitzvoth*, the purpose generally is to affirm life. He states:

It is an act of Wisdom to prohibit murder in order to preserve the human species.[20]

He further writes:

> The ultimate aim of God's creation is the good of his creatures. Laws, ethical and ceremonial, are not an end in themselves but a means for the attainment of human happiness. The correct mode of life is that which leads to the satisfaction of man's needs and to the development of all his powers. . . . God has made man's happiness conditional upon the observance of His commandments, because man's pleasure, in the happiness granted to him, is increased by the recognition that he himself has earned it through his own deeds.[21]

Maimonides lists all *mitzvoth* under fourteen headings and distinguishes between observances relating to one's fellowman and to God. But, curiously, he defines the precepts governing man's relation to God (*bein adom l'makom*) in personalistic terms. He writes:

> The intention of those laws is to inculcate in man good qualities, sound thinking and perfected deeds that are designed to perfect man's personality and fulfill him—hence they are called laws relating between man and God.[22]

Positing the premise that all precepts, like all the actions of God, are the result of His wisdom, rather than His will, Maimonides maintains that the precept, "serves as a means to one of three ends: to impart some truth, to teach some morals or to remove injustice." He continues:

> There is no occasion to ask for the object of such commandments . . . as God is one; why we are forbidden to murder, steal and to take vengeance or to retaliate or why we are commanded to love one another. But there are precepts concerning which people are in doubt . . . believing they are mere commands and serve no purpose whatever . . . such as the prohibitions of wearing garments containing wool or linen; of sowing divers seeds or of boiling meat and milk together. . . . I am prepared to tell you my explanation of all these commandments, and to assign for them a true reason supported by proof, with the exception of some minor rules and of a few commandments. I will show that these and similar laws must have some bearing upon one of the following . . . things: the regulation of our opinions, or the improvement of our social relations which implies two things, viz. the removal of injustice and the teaching of good morals.[23]

With other cultic and ceremonial laws where such explanations were not applicable, Maimonides used the historical method exclusively to interpret them as defenses against pagan beliefs current in the biblical period. By way of the historical explanation, he attempted to discover the meaning of biblical commandments by comparing them with the cults recorded in Sabean (the biblical land of Sheba) literature.[24]

Strangely, to Maimonides who regarded the highest level of perfection the acquisition of cognitive thought, the law may be considered only a means to a means to an end. With the exception of some cases where,

> the law contains a truth which is itself the only object of the law as the truth of the Unity, Eternity and Incorporeality of God.[25]

all other laws serve as a means to an ethical component. And since the ethical is a means to theoretical, cognitive, contemplative knowledge, the *mitzvah* is only a means to a means to an end.

c. The Performance and the Internalization of the Precepts

This brings us to the personalistic approach which distinguishes between the performance of the precept (*peulat ha-mitzvah*), and the internalization and the personalization of the precept (*kiyyum ha-mitzvah*) investing it with man's own personality. In terms of the performance of the precept, it is purely a means to an end, an ethical end, in some instances, a conceptual end to authenticate the self. In terms of the internalization of the precept which involves a personal input into the *mitzvah* act by infusing it with *kavanah* (proper intention), *daat* (rational meaning), or any other appropriate subjective experiences, it becomes an end in itself, a sacrament serving, in addition to self-fulfillment, to validate empirically Sinaitic truths. This constitutes the authentic personalistic aspect of the *mitzvah*, which stresses the existential commitment and individual involvement man brings to all his actions. By virtue of man's contribution to the *mitzvah* action, the commandment assumes a higher dimension of value. Man's central position in the universe helps to invest the act with a sacrament—a unique content peculiar only to man's endowment of the divine image (*Zelem Elohim*).

Accordingly, it establishes a dialectic of authenticating the self and at the same time, by virtue of the self's contribution to the *mitzvah* act, the latter in a heightened dimension contributes to the verification of Sinaitic truths. Consecrated acts assume cosmic significance when man's response to them is an affirmation of his transcendental condition leading to self-authentication. The investment of one's own personality, subjective involvement, and creative spirit define the character of the activity. The internalization aspect of the personalistic perspective—stressing an additional level of existential certainty grounded in staking one's whole being, to penetrate one's life with purposeful ends, and setting forth the conditions for eventual self-authentication—endows the *mitzvah* with a transcendental content and an end in itself, thereby validating Sinaitic truths.

It is interesting to note that the nature of the observance of the Jewish New Year (*Rosh Hashanah*), with the exception of blowing the ram's horn (*Shofar*), is not mentioned in the Pentateuch but in the Book of Nehemiah, Chapter 8. On the first day of the seventh month (*Tishrei)*, we are told, the 43,000 exiles who returned to the Holy Land from Babylon in the year 538 BCE under the Cyrus proclamation, gathered before the water-gates and Ezra brought the *Sefer Torah,* the Scroll of the Law, and opened it before the eyes of all the people. He read therefrom and the people bowed their heads and prostrated themselves before the Lord with their faces to the ground.

Rosh Hashanah thus became the anniversary of the *Sefer Torah,* affirming the Sinaitic covenant. When on that holiday we offer the prayer to be inscribed in the Book of Life, we have reference to the commemoration of the anniversary of the Book of Law, we pray for renewed courage and wisdom to subscribe to the standards embodied in the *Sefer Torah.* When the book is lifted, "before the eyes of all the people" (Neh 8:5), we are enjoined to pass judgment on our actions in accordance with the standards set up in the Torah. This is then the *Yom ha-Zikaron*, the "day of remembering," the anniversary of the book, as it was observed at the time of Ezra.

It is also evident that there are two types of judges. One who hands down sentences, and another who holds up the Book of Law and asks the defendant to pass judgment on himself, by comparing his mode of behavior with the precepts embodied in the Book of Law. On our *Yom ha-Din,* the Day of Judgment, when we gather in our houses of worship to affirm our covenant with God's Law, we are exhorted to open the Torah before the eyes of all people so that we can properly look into it and compare our deeds with the exalted deeds set forth for us in the *Sefer* and then proceed to pass judgment on ourselves. This appears to be the meaning of the liturgical observation in the prayer *Unetane Tokef* of *Yom Kippur*: "Thou unfoldeth the Book of Remembrance and *it reads itself* (italics mine), for lo, the seal of every man's signature is contained therein."[26]

Clearly, the observance of the *Yamim Noraim,* the "Days of Awe," becomes compellingly meaningful when judged from the vantage point of personal involvement in its practice. It is lifted to a new dimension of sacredness by man's unique contribution to its fulfillment.

In addition, the categories which our rabbis have applied to the observance of the precept such as *hidur mitzvah,* "beautification of the commandment," *kavanah,*[27] "single-mindedness of fulfilling the precept," *zerizut,*[28] "eagerness to do the *mitzvah*," and *lishmah,*[29] "right intention," all indicate the distinct human contribution.

d. Some Derivative Philosophic Notions of the Mitzvah

The internalization aspect of the personalistic perspective, endowing the *mitzvah* with an end in itself by virtue of man's response to it as an affirmation of his self-transcendent condition, has given rise to several other philosophic notions that are crucial. In the first place, by adding the human ingredient, the real spirit of the Law is captured and man responds to the experiential scheme in the freedom and spontaneity of human conscience within the guidelines of the Torah.

Aware of the problem of relating the *mitzvah* to a philosophic framework, Saadia ben Joseph Gaon, in the Third Treatise of his book (cf. note 23), attempted to identify conventional *mitzvoth (mitzvoth shimeyot)* with the notion of reward as opposed to grace for the attainment of eternal bliss, and the rational commandments *(mitzvoth sikhliyot)* he related to the philosophic problem of freedom and determinism. He then proceeded to repeat his expositions on the *mitzvoth* in the Second Chapter, after he had thoroughly treated the subject in the first passage. Many scholars are baffled by the problem of repetition. Some even maintain that the two versions represent two lines of exposition. The first passage reflects the Motazelite (a contemporary philosophic school) influence and the second, Platonic and Aristotelian thought. An examination of the texts, however, suggests that the two passages represent both influences, and that both expositions are involved in the same perennial philosophic problem of freedom versus compulsion. While initially the corpus of the *mitzvah* denotes an external compulsion, when we examine the *mitzvah* under a two-fold aspect, Saadia argues, it is possible to ground its performance in man's free will. Accordingly, in the First Chapter he discusses the origin of the *mitzvoth sikhliyot* which he identifies with man's dictates of reason. The rational character of moral cognition thus assures man's freedom in performing the *mitzvah*. In the second exposition he is concerned with the result of the act, the end and purpose for which the *mitzvah* is performed. And when we are teleologically oriented and hold before us the end of the act, we do not feel compelled in its observance. For ends do not coerce. A teleologically-oriented act endows us with spontaneity and freedom even if at the time of its performance, according to prescribed guide-lines, it may appear temporarily compelled.

Thus, in the personalistic end which we ascribe to the *mitzvah*, apart from the concept of freedom, there are two other crucial notions which endow the *mitzvah* action with philosophical dimensions. First, the subjective internalization of the precept helps to sustain the experiences of Israel's historical collective encounter with the Divine at Sinai, or a personal, rare, intuitive apprehension of a Divine Presense in a moment of ecstatic rapture. The fleeting flash of a divine vision one may experience takes on enduring significance by means of the *mitzvah*. It helps to sustain the contemplation of the vision indefinitely and provides for continuous preservation of contact with the Creator. The moments of supreme meeting and relation are raised to constancy by means of the *mitzvah* action embodying every facet of life.[30]

Secondly, the *mitzvah* constitutes an empirical basis for the meaningfulness and verification of doctrinal concepts and historical allusions inherent in the *mitzvah* action. The truths of the theonomy were not pronouncements which took place once and for all in the past, and empirically validated by the collective body of Israel who stood at Sinai. They are gifts which are renewed whenever there is a human acceptance of them. The practice of the *mitzvah* represents such acceptance, inasmuch as the commandments contain the Sinaitic truths which in turn empirically validate them, just as the theonomy verified the eternal truths at Sinai. The God who commanded the precepts in the past is heard anew by the Jew at the very moment when he fulfills the *mitzvah*.

This is in keeping with the notion propounded by Franz Rosenzweig (1886-1929). He states that the content of the Law must be transformed into a personalized, inner power which will guide the individual to fulfillment of *mitzvoth*. What is "inner power"? It solves the problem of a subjective experiential aspect of observance vs. objective, conceptual formulation—personal direct experience—by stressing that "inner power" reflects not one's will but ability, religious ability to experience this Law as God's commandment to him.[31]

Rosenzweig makes a distinction between law which denotes a body of precepts and regulations with which to organize a life under God, and a commandment which signifies the experience of an immediate presence of God commanding him as at Sinai to obey it. He writes:

> No matter how well the written word may fit in with our own thoughts,
> it cannot give us the faith that creation is completed to the degree that

we experience this by keeping the Sabbath and inaugurating it with, "And the heaven and the earth were completed." Not that doing necessarily results in hearing and understanding. But one hears differently when one hears in the doing.[32]

Thus the *mitzvoth* which were revealed to us are themselves vehicles of further Revelation. The Revelation is latently hidden within the commandment. In the performance of the command by the Jew, the Revelation is actualized and completed. As an empirical experience it helps in a sense to validate the Sinaitic truths.

In sum, personalism maintains that the *mitzvah* in terms of the performance of the precept is a means to an ethical, and in some cases also conceptual end. In terms of the internalization of the precept the creative, personalized activity and subjective investment in the *mitzvah* is crucial. It serves to establish a dialectic whereby the specific quality of the human spirit transforms the act into a sanctum and in turn the act helps to full the self (*shleimut ha-anashi*) in an indentification of the cognitive process and the *mitzvah*, and sustains a dialogical relation with the Divine. As an end in itself, the *mitzvah* further serves to empirically verify the eternal verities of Torah for the individual, as the revelatory process served empirically at Sinai for the collective body of Israel.

e. Personal Religious Existence as a Cognitive Personality

As a cognitive personality, in the conceptual sphere, personalism by positing a teleological idealism as the ultimate metaphysical generic characteristic of reality, actualized reason by means of conceptualization, ideas work together and thought takes on an objective content, a world of its own, transforming ideas from being mere copies of phenomena to becoming ultimate purposes. As such they structure an internalized ideal order, relating the reality of its universal, unified concepts to the cosmic ideal order, and in the ultimate situation to a cognitive identification with Ultimate Reality, the Divine Presence and Supreme Thought. Here again we come to grips with a fundamental principle of the philosophic pursuit, namely, how to reorganize our thoughts as being part of and at the same time apart from all-encompassing nature and external experiences.

If the ultimate aim of man, according to Maimonides, is *yediat Hashem*, "knowledge of God," this can be attained by a process of self-authentication which leads to a knowledge of God. Martin Buber likewise asserted that, "God does not which to be defined, discussed or defended by us but simply to be realized by us."[33] For the ultimate issues of life, the existent individual's affirmed thought is decisive in establishing the best critera for the truth of the objective content. Truth is not merely a statement of fact. The individual's actualized thought modes are truth. The growth process, the dynamic realizable scheme in which man is existentially involved creates its own verifiability. Instead of believing that certain facts are the case, it is primarily the realizability of certain conditions of self-authentication that brings about its own fulfillment. The realizable is the verifiable.

9. The Historical Level

Lastly, on the historical level, the plain sense of the prophet's words, "Ye are my witnesses, said the Lord, and my servant whom I have chosen" (Is 43:10) tends to relate the meaning of witness also to the people of Israel. As a covenantal people, the Jews bear witness to God by their common descent grounded in a determination to obey the commandments of God and by a common faith based on the fulfillment of the laws of God. This biblical covenant was never renounced. While the price of keeping the Covenant is suffering, in the Judaic biblical perspective—in contrast to Christian theology—its content is not suffering but joyful obedience to God's command and compliance with God's laws by individual Jews.

The source of this covenant is two-fold: Abrahamism which is recorded in the biblical episode of the binding of Isaac (*Akedat Yitzchak*), and the Sinaitic covenant or Mosaism, as Samuel David Luzzatto (1800-1865), characterizes the dual aspect of Jewish religion,[34] which is marked by the giving of the Law.

With Isaac's binding, the history of Israel as the witness of faith really begins. In the terrifying hour of the "binding," Abraham was put to his most critical test of obedience to God's command. If he submits and obeys God's command Isaac, who was his only legitimate heir, may not remain alive and there would be no Israel. On the other hand, if he refuses to obey, Isaac and Israel may possibly live but certainly not as God's witnesses and God's people. This was the choice put before Abraham. He made his decision to sacrifice his son in his determination to obey God's command although with Isaac's death the whole people of Israel would perish and with them the possibility of bearing witness to God.

The gruesome hour had passed. Abraham's hand was stayed. Isaac remained alive and with him the people of Israel were destined to live as God's witnesses. From this very moment on they were to testify for Him through their very being.

Manifestly, the covenant of Abraham was one of common origin. This motif is dramatized by a midrashic comment on the verse, "and the angel of the Lord called unto him out of heaven and said, 'Abraham, Abraham, lay not thy hand upon the lad' " (Gen 22:11f):

> Rabbi Aha said, Abraham wondered: surely Thou too indulgest in prevarication. Yesterday thou saidest, "For in Isaac shall seed be called to thee" (Gen 21:12); Thou didst then retract and say "take now thy son" (*ibid.* 22:2); while now Thou biddest me "lay not thy hand upon the lad."[35]

One may wonder why Abraham did not raise this perfectly legitimate query in the beginning when he was to offer his son as a sacrifice. Surely, it would have been more appropriate to put this question to God before the retraction. But here again the rabbis give us a penetrating insight into the true meaning of the covenant. The fact that Abraham was puzzled by the retraction of the command to sacrifice Isaac as by the original command was an indication that the covenant was to be based on bearing witness not by a common heritage but by our very existential stance. Our mission to testify to God's glory rests on our common descent from Abraham.

Subsequently, the Sinaitic covenant which was made with the whole people of Israel was grounded in a commmon heritage. By virtue of the fulfillment of that heritage by every individual Jew, Israel as a people lives as God's witness. In order to stand the test as the bearer of God's witness, the Jewish heritage enjoins on its followers a discipline that is all-embracing. Every aspect of life from early childhood is moulded according to the prescribed pattern of the Law. But the Law does not possess any supreme authoritarian body which imposes religious duties on its adherents from without. Jewish Law is intellectually grounded requiring acquisition of knowledge to find a rational basis for each law. The validation of each law is derived by means of free discussion which tries to arrive at a consensus of interpreting the *Halakha*, The Written and Oral Tradition. Everyone who has acquired the necessary knowledge is obligated to participate in these discussions, including the most humble member of the community.

Accordingly, the meaning of our testimony is reflected in our commitment to our heritage as servants of God and an exemplary nation. While the people of Israel as a whole can never abandon the covenant, it devolves upon each individual member of the community to fulfill the Law and do God's will anew in each generation. The dual aspect of our covenant of Abrahamism and Mosaism has fashioned us as a community of common descent and common heritage which was always open to sincere proselytes. Depending upon the fulfillment of each individual's potential, the Jewish community never stressed its so-called race purity.

Moreover, the substance of our witness for God is not in suffering but in joyful commitment to the Lord's covenant. To be sure, the Fathers of the Church, beginning with St. Augustine,[36] interpreted the Prophet's words to mean that Israel's suffering testifies to the truth of God and that true witness implies suffering, but Judaism projected its content as obedience to God born of our common descent and common heritage.

In sum, on a valuational level we bear witness to God when we respond to His challenge for self-authentication. On the conceptual level our testimony to God's presence is reflected in the establishment of a cognitive affinity with the Divine. On the historical level, our witness is grounded in the covenantal community shaped by devotion to God's law and obedience to His will, by each member of the community.

Notes

1. Significantly our sages, in the only two references in the Talmud to the verse in Isaiah, "Ye are my witnesses saith the Lord," implied that it points to the relationship of the individual Jew to his God. They observe, "You yourself, the limbs of your body or the soul of your being are my witness before Me, the Lord" (TB *Taanit* 11a; *Hagigah* 16a).

2. One of the oldest attempts to demonstrate the reality of God was the cosmological proof from the nature of the world which originated with Aristotle's doctrine of the four kinds of causes. We find that everything that happens around us comes into being as the result of the activity of other things. These activities, in turn, are themselves the result of other causes and so on, in a causal series which must be either infinite or have a first cause which is not itself caused by any preceding activity or member. But since we must exclude the possibility of an infinite regress of causes—such a causal series cannot "go back to infinity" and remain eternally inconclusive, inasmuch as to trace back the causal sequence endlessly, there would be no beginning to the series; and if there were no beginning there could be no succession, since each cause must follow after its predecessor— we must conclude that there is a first of uncaused cause responsible for the initiation of the series of events which we call God. (Aristotle's proof from the fact of motion inferring a first mover is basically similar.)

The weakness of the cosmological argument lies in the difficulty of accepting an assumption of the impossibility of an infinite regress of events requiring no beginning. Indeed, David Hume (1711-1776) thought that proofs from the nature of the world are *a priori*, implying that their conclusions—that the world could not bring itself into existence and that there is a source of existence outside the universe always in existence itself—are assumed in the very statement of the argument. Beyond this, Hume's general critique of causality (that every event must have a cause) rejected the fundamental premise of the cosmological proof. From his analysis there is no reason to conclude that the sequence of constantly conjoined events must have a cause to account for the effect. We can only determine what events occur in regular sequences with other events in our experience. By why must we conclude that the succession of these events has had a beginning?

3. The teleological argument purports to establish God's existence from the character of the natural world. The argument occurs in philosophical treatises from Plato's *Timaeus*, to Saadia's *Emunot v'Deot*, Aquinas' *Summa Theologica*,

Hume's *Dialogues on Natural Religion*, and W. Paley's famous exposition in his *Natural Theology*.

The argument which causes us to regard the universe as a great machine gained momentum as an outgrowth of the modern scientific mechanistic accounts of physical phenomena, as for example Newton's account of planetary motion. Nature, it is asserted, is not a mere jumble of accidents, a mere chance collection of parts but machinelike, all the parts fit together in one vast machine. Everything in this gigantic order of nature conforms to pattern and is governed by law, just as the formation and assembling of many parts in a functioning machine necessitate the presence of a structure and pattern.

Paley's (1743-1805) analogy of the watch conveys the essence of the argument. Suppose that while walking in the desert we see a rock on the road. We can readily attribute its presence to chance, to such natural forces as wind, rain, heat, and volcanic action. But suppose we see a watch on the ground consisting of a complex structure of wheels, cogs, axles, springs, and balances, all operating to provide a regular measure of the lapse of time. Surely we cannot attribute this orderly operation to the chance action of wind or rain. We are obliged to postulate an intelligent mind which is responsible for the phenomenon.

Now if the natural world is a complex mechanism, an interesting analogy follows. It must have been made. Just as a watch implies the existence of a watchmaker, the existence of a universe-machine, which reveals an orderliness in the physical, chemical, and biological aspects of the world whose complex structures function together in a coordinated system, implies the existence of a universe-machinemaker, a designer or architect whose purpose it was to create this machine.

Hume's criticism of the argument from design is first levelled against the central claim and its fundamental contention that since there is a resemblance between effects of human planning and natural effects, the same applies to the cause of human artifacts and the universal causal agency. Thus if we assume that like effects prove like causes and that the more similar the effects the more similar are the causes, then we would have no ground to accept the traditional religious conclusions about the nature of God, such as infinity, absolute perfection or the moral attributes of the designer of nature.

Another difficulty lies in the very analogy between the universe and a machine. One could equally liken it to an animal or to a vegetable. But in this case the design argument fails. For like the animal or vegetable world, the entire natural world may possess some built-in factors for growth, as one finds in carrot seed, that orders the direction of its development. "The world," Hume says, "plainly resembles more an animal or vegetable than it does a watch or a knitting-loom." Its cause, therefore, may be some innate principle of development and order rather than an intelligent and conscious architect of nature.

Finally, Hume suggests that the Epicurean hypothesis that projects a universe consisting of a finite number of particles in random motion which in due course, after going through every possible combination, arrives at an orderly cosmos, may have the same appearance of being designed as the traditional postulate of a deliberate, conscious designer. The same applies to other naturalistic explanations of the world.

4. The ontological argument which constitutes a proof from the nature or the idea of God was first developed by Anselm of Canterbury (1033-1109) in his *Proslogion* and later used by Descartes and even by a naturalist like Spinoza.

The argument begins by defining God in the way we talk about Him as an all-perfect Being containing all conceivable perfections, including the property of existence. The idea of absolute perfection being non-existent is self-contradictory for not to exist is not to be an absolutely perfect being. It is an imperfection not to exist. The very definition of God as "that Being than which none greater can be conceived" guarantees His existence just as the definition or essence of a triangle necessarily implies three sides. Moreover, by the very definition of God as the Supreme Being, God must exist in reality, independently of my ideas, or else something greater than God can be conceived, since it is greater to exist both as an idea and a real thing than merely to exist as an idea.

The ontological argument considered as a purely *a priori* demonstration was rejected by several philosophers. Gaunilon, a contemporary of Anselm in the Middle Ages, pointed out that if this sort of reasoning, i.e., to establish God's existence from one's definition of God, were legitimate, one could also demonstrate that all kinds of imaginary or unreal objects such as a perfect island somewhere beyond man's reach must exist since existence necessarily follows the concept of perfection. St. Thomas Aquinas levelled his criticism against the assumption that we can know the nature of God, that He is a perfect Being, before knowing whether He existed. Actually the opposite is true. We must first establish His existence by other means and then proceed to define His properties. The most telling criticism of the ontological argument was advanced by Immanuel Kant (1724-1804) who rejected the basic assumption that existence, like triangularity, is a predicate which something can have or lack, and which may be analytically connected with a subject. Does the idea of existence enlarge or add anything to the concept of a particular thing as a predicate or property like blue or square adds to the idea we have of anything? If we conceive of something and then conceive of it as existing, is our idea of the thing at all different? An imaginary one hundred dollars, for example, consists of the same number of dollars as a real one hundred dollars. Its monetary value that can be broken down into one hundred one-dollar bills or equivalent coins is the same as a concept in my mind or as money in my pocket. The concept is the same whether one merely thinks of it or thinks of it as existing. Hence, the property of existence cannot be part of the concept of the all-perfect Being any more than the existence of the one hundred dollars can be derived from one's concept of a hundred dollars. Existence is not a predicate or quality that enlarges a concept and cannot be part of any concept.

5. Moses Maimonides, *The Guide of the Perplexed*, Shlomo Pines, transl. and annot. (Chicago: University of Chicago Press, 1962), CXI, 51. Henceforth cited as *Guide*.

6. This is reminiscent of Plato's ideal archetype in which phenomenal objects participate and imitate. By the same token, Aristotle and R. Joseph bar Hiya speak of two forms, a relative form for every object—that of realizing the form, proper to its species—and an ultimate, pure form—that of realizing a state of complete rest from which it will be impossible to change. An object by becoming pure form completely devoid of matter can arrive at this final state where there is no change, alteration or divisibility.

7. Maimonides, *Guide*, I, 54.

8. *Ibid.*

9. *Ibid.*, I, 50.

10. *Ibid.*, I, 52.

11. *Ibid.*

11a. *Mekilta* II, 25.

12. Aristotle, *Metaphysics*, XII, 7. Curiously, the sages interpret the very construction of the Tabernacle as evidence of the desire of the Unknowable God to limit His Infinity within the confines of the Holy Temple in order to manifest His divine purpose for man.

"When Moses heard the command, 'And they shall make me a sanctuary and I shall dwell in the midst of them' (Ex 25:8), he was startled and said, 'Behold the heavens and the heavens of heavens cannot contain thee; how much less then this house that I have built' (1 Kgs 8:27). How then can you instruct me now to construct a holy temple for you to dwell in? And the Lord replied, I do not have in mind your concept of me as the Infinite Being, but when you will proceed to construct the tabernacle consisting of ten cubits the length of the board in the south, twenty in the north and eight in the western side, I shall confine my infinite essense as I descend and you will view me in the aspect of God-in-Relation, as we read 'And I will meet with thee there' " (Ex 25:22); *Yalkut Shimone* (Jerusalem: Lewin-Epstein, 1951), on Ex 25, chap. 365.

13. Cf. Joseph Ibn Zaddik (d. 1149), *Sefer ha-Olam ha-Katan* (Book of the Microcosm), S. Horowitz, ed. (Breslau: 1903), Introd.: "Do not imagine, however, that the Almighty is either near or removed, attached or aloof from any object to change, perception, relation or any of the other accidents. . . . The notion of God's abandonment of aloofness is found only in the hearts of fools and in slumbering, indolent minds, intoxicated with lust which is worse than being inebriated from wine. This is what the philosophers refer to when they speak of hearts of men in pursuit of lust who are far removed from the Creator."

14. Maimonides, *Guide*, III, 26.

15. Judah Halevi, *Book of Kuzari*, Hartwig Hirschfeld, transl. and annot. (London: M. L. Cailingold, 1931; republished New York: Pardes, 1946), I, 98. Henceforth cited as *Kuzari*.

16. Halevi, *Kuzari* III, 23. The *mitzvah* act, according to Halevi, is the sole instrument in man's ultimate purpose of establishing a relationship with the divine. Philosophers agree, including Halevi, that such a relationship depends upon man's preparation to receive the divine influence. The initiative, in a philosophic frame, lies with the recipient rather than with the dispenser. But, while other philosophers

maintain that man's intellect is the basis for a cognitive identity with the divine, Halevi projects the *mitzvah* as the ground for such a relationship.

The *mitzvah*, as an agent leading to a kinship with God, however, presents two problems. First, unlike the intellect which can cognitively identify with an incorporeal spiritual divine being upon the actualization of its faculty, the *mitzvah*, as a tangible, practical act can hardly be said to become one with such a divine spirit. To this Halevi responds that, inasmuch as the *mitzvah* is equated with Torah, and since the Torah is divinely inspired as is evidenced by the empirical proofs grounded in the historical episodes of Scriptures, the *mitzvah* act, like the Torah, is sanctum. It is an end in itself by virtue of possessing traces of the divine influence. As such, the commanded divine act helps to spiritualize man so that, as Halevi says, "the human soul becomes divine, being detached from material senses, joining the highest world, and enjoying the vision of the divine light, and hearing the divine speech. Such a soul is safe from death, even after its physical organs have perished. If thou, then, findest a religion and knowledge and practice of which assists in the attainment of this degree, at the place pointed out and with the conditions laid down by it, this is beyond doubt the religion which insures the immortality of the soul after the demise of the body" (I, 103). This aspect of the *mitzvah* Halevi discusses in the first treatise of *Kuzari*, Chapters 98-104.

The second aspect of the *mitzvah*, which he describes in the second treatise, Chapters 46-49, involves the distinction between rational and conventional laws. He argues that the conventional law—*torah ha-Elohit*—which constitutes the unique posssssion of Israel and is, consequently, an end in itself, is more likely to bring man nearer to God and lead him to ultimate kinship with the divine in the hereafter. The rational law—*ha-bukim ha sikhliyot*—is merely, "the preamble of the divine law preceding it in character and time" *(Kuzari,* II, 48). See also *Kuzari* I, 79, 98-104; II, 46ff; III 23-32, 50.

17. *Mishnah Makkoth*, 3, 16.

18. Maimonides, *Guide*, XXVII, 3.

19. *Genesis Rabbah*, 44, 1.

20. Saadia ben Joseph Gaon, *Emunot v'Deot* (The Book of Beliefs and Opinions), Samuel Rosenblatt, transl. (New Haven: Yale University Press, 1948), III. It should be noted that Saadia's distinction between *mitzvoth sikhliyot* (rational laws) and *mitzvoth shimeyot* (revelational laws), is drawn from the Talmudic statement in TB *Yoma* 67b.

21. Saadia, *op.cit.*, Introduction. The revelational precepts, although they are not grounded in the dictates of human reason, may nevertheless be linked, according, to Saadia, to the philosophical notion of *olam habah*, eternal bliss of the soul. Refuting the Christian doctrine of grace, Saadia posits reward for the performance of *mitzvot* as the gateway to immortality. The conventional commandments, Saadia argues, may serve as a means to an ultimate end, "on account of the service thereby rendered." If immortal life depends on reward and not on grace, then all *mitzvot*, even those devoid of conceptualization, may legitimately be included in a philosophic exposition.

22. Maimonides, *Guide*, III, 35.

23. *Ibid.*, 26.28.

24. *Ibid.*, 29ff.

25. *Ibid.*, 28.

26. *High Holiday Prayer Book*, Philip Birnbaum, transl. (New York: Hebrew Publ. Co., 1951).

27. TB *Berakhot* 5b; 13a; 31a; *Erubin* 95b; *Megillah* 20a; *Pesahim* 114b.

28. TB *Pesahim* 98b; *Yoma* 84b; *Menahoth* 43b.

29. TB *Menahoth* 38b; 50b; *Sukkah* 9a; *Gittin* 20a; *Abodah Zarah* 28a.

30. Cf. Martin Buber's notion of "moment God," in *I and Thou*, Ronald G. Smith, transl. (New York: Scribner, 1958), pp. 109f. The succession of such meetings in the I-Thou relationship eventually determines for us "the Lord of the Voice." Each new encounter of the Thou renews the past experiences of Thou, so that the moments of the past and the moment of the present become simultaneously present and joined in living unity.

31. Franz Rosenzweig, *On Jewish Learning*, Nahum N. Glatzer, ed. (New York: Schocken, 1955).

32. *Ibid.*, p. 122.

33. Martin Buber, *On Judaism*, Eva Jospe, transl. (New York: Schocken, 1967) pp. 93f.

34. Samuel D. Luzzatto, "Yesode ha-Torah" (The Foundations of the Torah), transl. in, Noah H. Rosenbloom, *Luzzatto's Ethico-Psychological Interpretation of Judaism* (New York: Yeshiva Univ., 1965).

35. *Genesis Rabbah* 56, 12.

36. Augustinus, *De civitate Dei* IV, 34; XVII, 7.

6.
Witnessing God after Auschwitz

Daniel Polish

Witness, as a theological term, has no cachet in the religious language of the Jews. Its appearance in our conversation is an importation from neighboring territory. In its most elemental sense, redolent, as it is in English, with overtones of legal process, it is, of course, familiar. The Hebrew equivalent of "witness" *ed*, carries a network of associations in its wake. Isaiah 43:10—" 'you are my witnesses' says the Lord," sounds a central chord of the Jewish experience. To decipher it, to break that chord down to its component notes, is to penetrate the heart of the questions posed in these pages.

The witness, in the strictest sense of the term is not simply one who speaks for another. Rather he is one who takes formal oath and gives testimony to some fact concerning the other. Such oath in biblical theology is serious business indeed, with immediate implications for the witness and consequences for future generations. Biblical oaths have a physical component: the witness places his hand under the thigh of the one to whom he is swearing. This is what Eliezer does to Abraham in Genesis 24 as he is about to embark on the mission that will assure his master of the descendants whom he had been promised. This graphic act has its counterpart in the Roman practice that provided the etymological root of the English word testify: the witness takes the preliminary oath with his hands clutching his own testes. The implication of these acts underscores the dreadful seriousness of witnessing. To witness is to declare that upon which one

134

would stake, not his good name alone, but something far more serious—the existence of his progeny and their descendants.

Perhaps the real question posed by the *shoah*[1] is not what we can witness to, but the starker one, can we—or dare we—make witness at all? If the Jews of today do not consciously base their answer to this question on the Nuremburg laws[2], their collective unconscious knows only too well the hideous implications of Jewish affirmation. Jews of even the most marginal identification died in the *shoah* because of a grandparent's faithfulness to the inherited witness. Every decision to circumcise a son, every act of bringing a daughter into the line of Sarah, is made despite the consequences that can flow from it, and as a repudiation, both joyous and terrified, of that evil decree.

Witness itself has been rendered problematical, no less so the contents of our witness. Perhaps Jewish understanding of the world and its Maker have been altered by the experiences of this generation. Perhaps faith after Auschwitz will differ from that of our ancestors. Can we speak about the religious understanding of those events? It has been stated that it is blasphemy for us to speak about the effects of the *shoah* on Jewish faith. And, though it appears paradoxical for one writing about witness after the *shoah*, I agree with this.

I do not imply that we should not speak of the *shoah*, that we should brush it aside as an unpleasant memory, or as an aberration in Jewish history and human behavior. To be silent is a sin, doing violence to the Jewish imperative to remembrance, and making possible the *shoah's* re-enactment. No, we must speak of the *shoah*. Indeed, as with the events of the exodus, "to dwell on it at length is accounted praiseworthy."[3] So it is not silence that I counsel.

And yet, even as we talk, some critical portion of our minds should be skeptical about the contents of our words. I cannot believe that already, barely three decades after the events, we can presume to understand what they mean. One sits with a friend who has lived through trauma, and hears the friend out. Victims' words do not always attest to reality, most likely not even to reality as it will come to be understood with distance from the traumatic events. The words are cathartic, spoken to help ease the pain. Their truth is tentative: they represent an effort to grasp onto shards of shattered reality. They are products of the work, quickly begun, to grope towards what will later be an understanding of the trauma.

Had the generation of the Exodus been allowed the final say in understanding their experience, we would have found no redemption in it. Instead, the heritage left us by the liberated slaves would have been one of humiliation, despair and terror. They knew only the anguish (and the fantasized glory) of their degradation, and the hardship of their desert trek. A *haggadah* of their composition would be only the fearsome rehearsal of their own pain, tragedy, and suffering and the obduracy of a silent God. Even their sons and daughters, had they been empowered to speak the last word, would have left us a legacy far different from the one we inherited. Though those children of slaves did enter the land of promise, they saw little of the promise's fulfillment. They had to live through the terrible battles of conquest and the hardships of reclaiming the soil. Whatever glimmer of reward they experienced could not but have been colored by bitterness on behalf of their parents. How they must have railed at a God who tantalized them with the promise of the milk and honey of their ancestral land without allowing them to taste it.

These generations lived through the experience of that central event, but they could not have seen its full reality. That had to wait. So, too, with our words about the *shoah*. We speak because we must speak. But we cannot speak about what these events will come to mean to Jewish faith. God knows—and keeps as a secret—how the *shoah* will be understood generations hence. Our words can only reflect the groping for truth that engages us now. Our insights remain merely timely. They are situation reports about our current state of mind. Whatever rays of timelessness shine from their darkness will be perceived only later. And so we blaspheme; not in speaking the words, but in believing them to possess ultimate reality.

As a result of the *shoah*, some ideas of recent generations have been repudiated altogether. Jewish thought since the emancipation reflected the optimism of the general intellectual climate. A mood prevailed which affirmed human nobility. Reason was celebrated, and with it a sense that human moderation and understanding would carry the day for the cause of virtue. Mankind, it was felt, had virtually approached the limits of its perfectability. Pockets of corruption may have persisted, it was believed, but they would be quickly overcome by the forces of right. Humanity shines less radiant now than to those teachers of hope, many of whom, themselves, perished in the cataclysm. Our eyes have been seared by the flames of hell. Whether they see more clearly for that, or suffer a painful stigmatism, we cannot say. But to us, humanity appears less noble and less the proper object of veneration. We see the human spirit as capable of base depravity as of elevation. We see human actions as readily responsive to the impulse for evil as to the good.

Our predecessors might have echoed Shakespeare's tone of veneration:

> What a piece of work is a man!
> how noble in reason!
> how infinite in faculty!
> . . . in action how like an angel!
> in apprehension how like a god![4]

We are likely to find our text in the Talmud's account of a debate between the schools of Hillel and Shammai:

> For two and a half years, the school of Shammai and the school of Hillel debated a major point. The school of Hillel maintained that it would have been better if man had never been created; while the school of Shammai maintained that it was better that he had been created. The count was taken and the majority decided it would have been better if he had not been created. But since he has been created, let him examine his actions.[5]

Human power and its capacity for evil, alike, are evoked in Wiesel's account of mankind's taking the place of God, and the fearsome implications of that reversal of roles:

> Legend tells us that one day man spoke to God in this wise:
> "Let us change about. You be man, and I will be God. For only one second." God smiled gently and asked him, "Aren't you afraid?"
> "No. And you?"
> "Yes, I am," God said.
> Nevertheless he granted man's desire. He became a man, and the man took his place and immediately availed himself of his omnipotence: he refused to revert to his previous state. So neither God nor man was ever again what he seemed to be.
> Years passed, centuries, perhaps eternities. And suddenly the drama quickened. The past for one, and the present for the other, were too heavy to be borne.
> As the liberation of the one was bound to the liberation of the other, they renewed the ancient dialogue whose echoes come to us in the night, charged with hatred, with remorse, and most of all, with infinite yearning.[6]

To the more hopeful spirits of those earlier times it must have appeared that we were standing at the very gates of the Messianic Kingdom. A general air of expectancy prevailed for that long-awaited day. In the city of Augsburg, in the year 1871 a rabbinic synod asserted:

> A new, highly important turning point in history is now at hand. The spirit of true knowledge of God and pure ethics fills more and more the consciousness of humanity in government, art and science. Judaism cheerfully recognizes in this the approach of its ideas which have illuminated its historical march.[7]

How premature was the rapturous optimism, and how different the nature of the world waiting to be born. The outlines of that world were anticipated in the vision of Kafka's *Trial*, dismissed initially as distorted, but in time revealed to be tragically lucid. There the world is far from redeemed. In place of the perfected reign his co-religionists were announcing, Kafka saw a world of disorder and wanton cruelty; or, from a different vantage, a world of perfectly ordered process, finely tuned to the achievement of its true goal. Kafka prophesied the kingdom of night in which his community, including his own family, would perish: an array of irrational and implacable accusers, overseeing a machinery which only seemed unresponsive but was intended all along to lead inexorably to the destruction of one who at the last instant would recognize himself to be deemed a "dog"—a less than human intrusion into human society.

This darker vision of human nature, of our world, and perhaps of the Jew's place in it, is part of the legacy we inherit from the *shoah*. It is part of the witness that the Jew makes today, witness to a world still unredeemed, a world removed even further from redemption by its ignorance of—or refusal to acknowledge—how remote it is from perfection.

There is in this message something of precedent and paradox. Over the centuries, as Judaism and Christianity encountered one another on various levels, one element of contention has been the Jewish insistence that the messiah had not come. Perhaps an aspect of the Christian response to Jewish faith has been a resentment of the denial of this important tenet of Christian doctrine. Now, the Jewish message is once again of the world's unredeemedness. And because of the experience it has visited upon the Jews, the world may be prepared to hear that message more clearly. For Christians this calls for more serious attention to the implications of the events that can occur in a *parousia* delayed.

As a part of the ideogram in which he enunciates Israel's role as witness, Isaiah 43:10 identifies Israel as "my servant whom I have chosen." Integral to any authentic understanding of Jewish witness must be the fact of Israel's role as witness itself. The concept, for all its familiarity, constitutes a "scandal" for Jewish thought. Part of the Jewish religious inheritance to be sure, part of the Jewish understanding of God—God as capable of choice, able to choose a people, perceived as having chosen us— the idea is, none the less, profoundly disconcerting. Reacting against the idea of special election, many modern Jewish thinkers before the *shoah* virtually jetisoned the idea. Mordecai Kaplan had the courage to do explicitly what many of his confreres had done implicitly: he excised any reference whatever to chosenness from the liturgies of his Reconstructionist movement. Others, while avoiding such a thoroughgoing revision of classical texts, elected to remove it from their universe of discourse.

Reform Judaism effected its change by transvaluating the idea of election to that of the "Mission of Israel." Purged of anything that might be interpreted as chauvinistic or self-serving, mission was represented as bespeaking Israel's role as light to the nations, or conscience of humanity. Israel's place was understood in terms of service to others. Whatever might imply validity in its existence for its own sake was dismissed or derided. Even before the *shoah*, Achad Ha'am took vigorous issue with this "invention":

> the Jews as a people have always interpreted their mission simply as the fulfillment of their own duties, and from the earliest times to the present day they have regarded their election as an end to which everything else was subordinate, not as a means to the happiness of the rest of humanity. While it is true that the Prophets expressed the hope that Judaism would have a good influence on the morality of the gentile world, their idea was that this result would follow automatically from the existence of a superior type of morality among the Jews, not that the Jews existed solely for the purpose of exerting themselves to bring this result about.[8]

Achad Ha'am, though hardly from a theistic stance, enunciates the belief that the Jewish people has a right to survival for its own sake.

The *locus classicus* for understanding the condition of the Jewish people in our day is Ezekiel 37:1-14. We have seen the piles of bones of those who will not rise in this world. And we have seen, too, the survivors of the camps of death reduced virtually to skeletons, summoned to new life. The world has stood on that crest above the valley as the sundered bones of the people reassembled themselves into a re-animated body. The question the world is asked is: "Have these bones a right to live?"

Since the *shoah* the Jewish people has fixed its eye upon its own enfeebled hand grasping at the tenuous piton of survival. At times this has led the Jewish community to castigate itself for reducing its horizons to "mere survivalism," or left it open to the accusation that it has removed itself from the affairs of the world for the sake of "turning inward." However depicted, the fact is that the *shoah* has re-awakened a sense that there is value in the survival of the Jewish people for its own sake. As we articulate the elements of Jewish faith after Auschwitz, this compelling commitment cannot be ignored.

We are all familiar with the fact that many have interpreted this renewed concern with the life of the Jewish people in strictly secular or nationalistic terms. Of more immediate concern to our discussion of witness are the voices which, echoing the formulations of earlier times, have articulated the commitment to Jewish survival as an article of faith, inextricably interwoven with our understanding of God and God's will. This is the issue Emil Fackenheim raises with such telling clarity as he finds his tracks circling back repeatedly to the question of the religious imperative for Jewish survival, not despite, but in the face of Auschwitz:

> Once there was a sharp, perhaps ultimate dichotomy between "religious" and "secular" Jews. It exists no longer. After Auschwitz the religious Jew still witnesses God in history, albeit in ways which may be revolutionary and the "secular" Jew has become a witness as well. . . .
> His mere commitment to Jewish survival without further grounds is a testimony; indeed, Jewish survival after Auschwitz is neither "mere" nor without grounds.
> Jews throughout the world—rich and poor, learned and ignorant, believer and unbeliever—were . . . responding to Auschwitz. . . . Faced with the radical threat of extinction, they were stubbornly defying it, committing themselves and their children as Jews. . . . Why is there this response when there might have been, and by all logic should have been, total disarray? I believe that whereas no redeeming voice is heard at Auschwitz, a commanding voice is heard, and that it is being heard with increasing clarity. *Jews are not permitted to hand Hitler posthumous victories.* Jews are commanded to survive as Jews, lest their people perish. . . . They are forbidden to despair of God, lest Judaism perish. . . .
> Jewish survival, were it even for no more than survival's sake, is a holy duty. . . . [9]

Fackenheim is sensitive to the limits of what might decently be spoken without breaching the boundary of blasphemy. Yet, there is implication, in his asserting a command to live, of a divine warrant for Jewish life—with its attendant sense of a bond between God and the people which persists even after the *shoah*.

This commitment to the life of the Jewish people has expressed itself most tangibly in terms of support for the State of Israel. In pre-Hitler Europe and America there existed principled dissent from the idea of a Jewish State. The question was an emotional, and a divisive one. After the *shoah* that debate stopped. The labels non-Zionist and anti-Zionist became irrelevant, as virtually all Jews bent their efforts, almost reflexively, to the creation of a homeland for the remnants of European Jewry, and to the legal establishment of a Jewish State. The ensuing decades have not diminished the commitment or the efforts of Jews throughout the world to sustain and defend that State. Nor have they eroded the centrality Israel has assumed in Jewish thought and emotion in so brief a time.

It is hard to speak distinctly of God's role in creating the State of Israel in the aftermath of the *shoah* without falling into blasphemy. One runs the risk of depicting God, as some have done, as an ethical "monster" or of doing affront to the sacred memory of those who perished in the *shoah's* demonic devices. We stand too close to the events to address them dispassionately. We cannot speak of our own dead, or of the wounds of those close to us, in clinical terms; nor of their fate as part of some larger process. It is scarce comfort to mourners of one who perished in a plane crash to have explained the mechanical forces, physical laws, and biological processes that eventuated in their loss. Such discourse would require us to sever ourselves from our own humanity, and such a price is beyond reason.

At most, we can acknowledge dim resonances of a classical archetype for formulating Jewish history: *meginut l'shevach*—from degradation to exaltation. No recounting of the Exodus can be complete without first dwelling on the horror of the slavery that preceded it, called it forth, and was, in its own way, necessary to the greatest glory of Jewish experience— the covenant at Sinai. Already, in our day, the cataclysm of the *shoah* is bound inseparably to the epiphany of the re-establishment of a Jewish State. These two events of such immeasurable magnitude for the life of the people within a single generation are increasingly spoken of *b'dibur echad*—"in the same breath." The creation, and unique role, of *Yad Vashem*—the holocaust memorial—in the capital of the third Jewish commonwealth, and the establishment of a day of remembrance for the victims of the *shoah* immediately prior to the observance of *Yom Ha'atzmaut*—Israel Independence Day—bespeak the awareness, on all levels of Jewish life, of the organic relationship of these two events: the death and resurrection of the Jewish people.

To move closer to blasphemy, we cannot help but see the birth of the State of Israel as causally linked to what preceded it. We are told by some students of political history that the State could not have been reborn except as the world's atonement for the destruction it inflicted, and allowed to be inflicted, upon the children of the European exile. We know that without the recreation of the Jewish State, the shattered body of the Jewish people would not have had the will to climb out of the pit. We fear any threat to the welfare of the State as portent of a second *shoah*, one that the people could not survive. A theology of these historical events will emerge among Jews who believe in the God of history. But it cannot be written by us who have lived through the history.

We have, thus far, isolated two strands of Jewish witness after the *shoah*: a recognition of the darker side of the world and human nature; and a commmitment to the life of the Jewish people. The interweaving of these two strands yields a peculiar thread that runs through the psyche of the Jewish community and of individual Jews in our day. This is the frame of mind which is specially attuned to threat to Jewish life, a mind-set often derided as "Jewish paranoia." The latter phrase seems to demean the emotion it purports to describe and evokes Saul Bellow's response, "even paranoiacs have enemies," or simply the epigram, "paranoia is only heightened awareness." Jews continue to have a sense that whatever the evil was which erupted in the *shoah*, a remnant of it—like a remnant of us—is left in the world, lurking in wait. This sense of brooding menace is evoked in Amos Oz's description of another, far-removed, scene:

> A few times it happened that darkness fell while they were still in the depths of the forest. Then they would light a great fire in the middle and surround the camp with a close circle of small bonfires for fear of vampires, wolves, and demons.
> If one looked upward one could see how the light of the fire was broken by the thick ceiling of leaves. Round about, wolves howled, foxes' eyes glinted, an evil bird screeched and shrieked. Or was it the wind? Or sinister imitations of the sound of fox, bird, and wind? Even the rustling of fallen leaves hinted perpetually at the certainty of another, a hostile camp whispering round about us and hedging us in.[10]

Jews still seared by the experience of this generation are painfully vigilant to the possibility that the sentiment "the Jews are our misfortune," and the actions that flow from it, are liable to surface wherever the social order is strained.

The sense of the imperative to Jewish survival, and of the threat to it, express themselves in the exclamation in America of "never again" and in the activities, of whatever ilk, associated with it. In Israel the resolve was expressed when archaeologists unearthed the last Jewish outpost to perish in the Roman destruction of the second commonwealth: "Masada shall not fall again."

"My servant whom I have chosen" (Is 43:10) is understood after the *shoah* with a renewed sense that there is something divinely special about the Jewish people and something singular—even hellishly so—about Jewish history. Something beyond discourse was visited on our people in our time; an evil of unequaled magnitude. And something remarkable happened to our people that has happened to no other people, even as it has happened to this people before in the span of time since it entered history at the dawn of human recollection—it died and lived again. The events of our lifetime call us to affirm anew the special role of the Jewish people in God's design.

The reappropriation of this classical formulation is not an act of simple nostalgia, nor, dare it be, even worse, the expression of some atavistic impulse to tribal pride, group chauvinism, or, in the term bandied about too loosely in this time, racism. The singularity of Jewish peoplehood makes sense only in the context of divine imperative. It can be understood only in the light of the promises made to Abraham for his descendants, and of the covenant which God cut with that first Jew, which was re-enacted by every generation of his heirs and attested at Sinai, and which is sealed by the blood of all the martyrs who perished rather than forsake it.

The theological core of Jewish peoplehood—as well as our capacity to lose sight of it—is reflected in the consistency with which we understand and express the major events of Jewish experience in biblical idiom. Scriptural citations, if in "apocopated" form, remain a primary vehicle of self-interpretation even in our own age. At the end of the last century the First Aliyah—the first great wave of emigration—to Palestine from eastern Europe called itself BILU. This name, the rallying cry of that great movement, was derived as an acronym of the first letters of the words of Isaiah 2:5: *Bet Ya'acov l'chu v'nelcha . . .*—"O house of Jacob let us walk . . ." [i.e. "let us be on our way"]. Throughout the Jewish communities of the free world today, the watch word of the heroic efforts to liberate the Jews of the Soviet Union is taken from Exodus 7:16, "let My people go. . . ." By the same token, the remnant community which escaped destruction in the *shoah* finds expression for the celebration of its own survival in the words of Psalm 118:17, "I shall not die, but live. . . ."

The phrases are audacious, and even in their abbreviated form, stirring enough. Yet the emotional response they arouse can finally be explained not in their rhetorical force, but their evocation of a fuller meaning to which they are allusion. These more complete meanings persist in the folk-memory—and constitute the final rationale of Jewish people-hood. The true nature of Jewish life can be found in reading the full citation. Thus we read the constitution of Jewish life in the Isaiah verse: "O house of Jacob, come let us walk in the light of the Lord." We hear the supreme summons to Jewish freedom in Exodus: "let My people go that they may serve Me." And we confront the challenge of Jewish life after the *shoah* in Psalm 118: "I shall not die, but live, and declare the works of the Lord." The life of the Jewish people, undiminished, indeed made more urgent, by the *shoah*, is bound up with its role as chosen witness.

The renewed affirmation of the legitimacy of Jewish survival should not blind us to the very darkest implications of the *shoah*. One pattern of Jewish history reveals that what first befalls the Jew, soon enough becomes the lot of other parts of humanity. Assyrian barbarity, Roman cruelty, medieval superstition, inquisitorial repression, the wanton destruction of rapacious mobs, were not the exclusive experience of Jewish communities. These forces of darkness, having been initiated and perfected with their application to Jews, soon enough found wider arenas of expression. The horror of this age teaches not simply that the world can be inhospitable to Jews, but that it can be hell for all people. That too must be part of Jewish witness in our day.

In asserting this wider sense of the *shoah's* message I do not wish to participate in the disturbing tendency to erode the particularity of that event by reducing it to another tragic instance of "man's inhumanity to man." No, it was a specific expression of animus against the Jew. Nor would I want to be understood as engaging in that semantic devaluation of the coin of the *shoah* which renders every human indignity a holocaust, and every social evil a genocide. These terms deserve the dignity of their specificity. To trivialize them abets in obscuring the full monstrosity of what they convey. But there is cause to understand the holocaust as a paradigm of what humanity can do to the dispossessed of our age. Here Jewish experience of our day, as in earlier times, itself becomes witness.

Jews have exhibited the paradoxical quality of treating the events of their collective life in terms we would least expect. Thus the experience of Egyptian servitude. It would not be unnatural for a people to attempt to obscure its humble origins, or invent a noble pedigree for itself. The Jews chose to hold onto the memory of their degradation and define themselves in reference to it: "a wandering Aramean was my father, and he went down into Egypt and sojourned there . . . and the Egyptians dealt ill with us, and afflicted us, and laid upon us hard bondage. . . " (Dt 26:5-6). The reiteration of those events became an integral part of Jewish life. By the same token, we might expect that the transcendence from such a lot, and the attainment of a higher status, would make a people self-righteous, and proportionately unconcerned with the plight of others who were not able, as readily, to extricate themselves from diminished circumstances. Yet rather than making Jews insensitive to the hardship of others, the memory of their own enslavement became the cornerstone for a system of ethical responsibility:

> For I am the Lord that brought you out of the land of Egypt, to be your God: You shall therefore be holy as I your God am holy. (Lev 11:45)
> The stranger that sojourns with you shall be to you as one of your own, and you shall love him as yourself for you were strangers in the land of Egypt, I am the Lord. (Lev 19:33-34)
> A stranger you shall not oppress for you know the heart of the stranger seeing that you were strangers in the land of Egypt. (Ex 23:9)
> If your brother should become poor and be without means, then you shall uphold him and enable him to live beside you. . . . I am the Lord your God who brought you forth out of the land of Egypt, to give you the land of Canaan, and to be your God. (Lev 25:35-38)

By the same token, the experience of the Babylonian exile produced quite the opposite effect we might have predicted. According to most historical reconstructions, Jewish religion prior to that first exile consisted of the same essential patterns as neighboring faiths: belief in a deity who was associated with a particular geographic territory; who was related exclusively to a single nation, or people; and whose fate was determined, or reflected, by the fate of that people in its military and political engagements. When the Jewish nation was defeated in battle and led captive from its homeland, we might have expected it to respond as its neighbors did under similar circumstances: recognize that its deity had been defeated; seek cultural identification with the newly dominant society; and the protection of the "conquering" deity through the adoption of his cult.

What the Jews did seems to have been without precedent, and to have resulted in the survival of the Jewish people. Rather than interpret its changed political circumstances in the light of the prevailing theological constructs, it evolved a radically new way of understanding the role of the God it worshipped. Thus the great "prophetic" transvaluation of Jewish thought. The God of Israel, rather than being confined to the borders of Israel's land, is more clearly perceived as the creator of the entire world, who stretches His hand over all lands and nations. Rather than relating to the people of Israel alone, the God of Israel came to be understood as the Father of all humanity, the controller of the destiny of all peoples.

The radical junctures of Jewish life precipitated the articulation of new and pregnant modes of thought. Significantly, the two instances with which we have dealt betray the same pattern of response. Each could have yielded a narrowing of the horizon of Jewish concern, an introversion in response to threat. Instead both resulted in the dialectical movement of holding onto the particularity of the experience itself, while universalizing its implications.

Thus the *shoah*. Without relinquishing an iota of the particularity of the evil visited on the Jews, we must proclaim its portent for all humanity. If in the face of the *shoah* we did not learn the lesson of Jewish survival we have learned nothing. If we learned only the lesson of Jewish survival we have not learned enough. The *shoah* bespeaks the horrors that are possible when humanity's technological progress outstrips the development of its moral understanding. It testifies to the fact that even in a "civilized" age, ancient and uncivilized animosities persist and to the consequences that flow inevitably from such hatred between groups of people. It cries to heaven about the de-sanctification of human life and the fate that befalls the children of men when life itself loses its ascription of supreme worth. It damns human indifference in the face of manifest evil, the impassiveness with which people knew and understood about monstrosities unfolding, and kept silent. "Never again" cannot just mean never again for the Jews, but never again for any of God's children. This, too, is the witness of the *shoah*.

"That ye may know and believe Me, and understand . . ." is the final facet of the ideogram of Isaiah 43:10. How indeed are we to know and understand God, let alone have faith in the aftermath of the *shoah*? This is perhaps the hardest question confronting the religious person today. In its starkest form, the problem has been posed: "How can we pray to the God of the gas chambers?" For many, the answer is that we cannot. The traditional notions of an omnipotent God, "mighty to save", seem incompatible with the monstrous evil that befell the people of Him who is called "the guardian . . . who neither slumbers nor sleeps (Ps 121:4)." To some thinkers the *shoah* bespeaks the "silence" of God, or His "eclipse."[11] A deity who could let such horrors occur and not stop them can, to many, be seen only as a "monster," or a null idea, bereft of reality.

The absence of God in the *shoah* demands the attention of religious thinkers, even as it eludes the conventional categories of thought. Richard Rubenstein identifies the *shoah* as the background against which to understand the idea of "the death of God." While Rubenstein does not use the phrase in a literal sense, he does posit that the *shoah* and the age which followed it are a time in which the God of traditional belief is without relevance. The notion is put more graphically in another narrative by Eli Wiesel:

One day when we came back from work, we saw three gallows rearing up in the assembly place, three black crows. Roll Call. SS all around us, machine guns trained: the traditional ceremony. Three victims in chains—and one of them, the little servant, the sad-eyed angel.

The SS seemed more preoccupied, more disturbed than usual. To hang a young boy in front of thousands of spectators was no light matter. The head of the camp read the verdict. All eyes were on the child. He was lividly pale, almost calm, biting his lips. The gallows threw its shadow over him.

This time the Lagerkapo refused to act as executioner. Three SS replaced him.

The three victims mounted together onto the chairs.

The three necks were placed at the same moment within the nooses.

"Long live liberty!" cried the two adults.

But the child was silent.

"Where is God? Where is He?" someone behind me asked.

At a sign from the head of the camp, the three chairs tipped over.

Total silence throughout the camp. On the horizon, the sun was setting.

"Bare your heads!" yelled the head of the camp. His voice was raucous. We were weeping.

"Cover your heads!"

Then the march past began. The two adults were no longer alive. Their tongues hung swollen, blue-tinged. But the third rope was still moving; being so light, the child was still alive. . . .

For more than half an hour he stayed there, struggling between life and death, dying in slow agony under our eyes. And we had to look him full in the face. He was still alive when I passed in front of him. His tongue was still red, his eyes were not yet glazed.

Behind me, I heard the same man asking:

"Where is God now?"

And I heard a voice within me answer him:

"Where is He? Here He is—He is hanging here on this gallows. . . ."[12]

Put most nakedly, one stance of modern man is that the idea of God is untenable in the face of such monstrous evil: God cannot be affirmed, cannot be said to exist. God is as irrelevant in human concerns as he was in the salvation of the victims of the *shoah*.

Such a stance, if it is not merely a variant expression of the general atheist position which has wide currency in the modern age, rests on a specific perception of the *shoah*. To substantiate the position that the evil of the *shoah* is cause for a radical revaluation of Jewish faith, or for a principled abandonment of faith, one must assert that it was an event *sui generis*, without precedent or parallel. The *shoah's* utter novelty, in this view, warrants the articulation of a wholly new theological vision. This, indeed, is what many theologians have done. It may also be the implicit view of many Jews whose theology is written on their hearts rather than being articulated propositionally. The singularity of the *shoah*, I sense, is an idea of wide, if not always stated, constituency.

I disagree with this position. That disagreement needs qualification, which, while it might appear to the casual reader to be a quibble, is of fundamental importance to my understanding of God in the face of the *shoah*. It is clear by now that I do not dismiss the *shoah* as an event of profound significance in our lifetime, or, for that matter, in the history of the Jewish people as it will henceforth be written in that people's chronicles. Nor do I underestimate the meaning of the scope and intent of the *shoah's* perpetrators. I recognize, and am overwhelmed by, the enormity of the evil—there are times when it grips me unexpectedly in my waking moments, or invades my sleep, shocking me into unwelcome consciousness. It is painful for me to take issue with the conventional wisdom.

I do not belittle the reality or the implications of the *shoah*. But I cannot view it as an event of singularity in the sweep of Jewish experience. To my eyes, the *shoah* was unique in its extent, not in its intent. I cannot fathom the numbers of dead—six million eludes my comprehension. Yet I know that in the annals of Jewish life, millions have perished because they were Jews. It has been estimated that in the rebellion against Rome, and its aftershock, two million of the people died. How many millions more perished in the endless night of medieval Europe or the pogroms of more recent eastern Europe? The destruction was greater in number, but not in kind. I am staggered by the geographical scope of the *shoah*, and its completeness. But I know too well, also, of the destructions of whole communities before it, or the utter extirpation of entire Jewish populations. We speak of the fiendishness of the technology employed in the *shoah*. Still, to depict it as singular does injustice to the ingenuity of

Israel's persecutors in the past. Pharaoh's chariots, the battering rams of the Roman legions, the devices of the Spanish Inquisition, all in their own times represented the furthest reach of human inventiveness. The *shoah's* instruments of death were fashioned with greater absolute skill, but not relative—to the societies that created them. The cold-hearted evil of the agents of the *shoah* exceeds our comprehension. Yet even it finds precedents in Jewish accounts from the earliest times. God help us, but Hannah and her sons and the martyrs of *Eleh Ezkara* do not sound out of place beside narratives from the *shoah*.[13] It seems the same spirit expressed itself in our day as in the lives of even our distant ancestors.

Some have suggested that the *shoah* stands alone in Jewish history as the only attempt to completely destroy the entire Jewish people. Sadly, I demur. I believe what, for all its foolishness, the Megillah of Esther communicates to us with great force. That force, I feel, comes from the fact that we, the readers, comprehend what is not said in the text itself. We know, even if we are not told, that we are to understand Haman's goal as precisely the annihilation of all Jews. In this regard, it is instructive that Jews in the death camps had to create copies of Esther from memory and smuggle them about because they were specifically prohibited from reading that work. It is said that Hitler boasted, "I am the second Haman; if we lose they will celebrate another Purim."[14] It may be that the account is apocryphal, but if it is, its author correctly saw into the heart of the Megillah. There is, of course, an earlier, absolutely explicit, account of a genocidal plan. The intent of the Pharaoh in Exodus 1:15-22 is clearly the destruction of the whole people. The chilling evil, as well as the efficiency of his plan cannot be lost upon anyone who hears the story with ears unjaded by familiarity. There is precedent in the people's self-understanding, even for the demonic intent of the *shoah*.

The *shoah* exceeded everything that came before it in the actual magnitude of its enactment. It reached new limits in the real devastation it succeeded in inflicting. But it is, tragically, but a piece of Jewish history in being a life-threatening trauma to the body of the Jewish people, and in having as its goal, Israel's destruction.

The perception of the *shoah* as within, rather than removed from, the flow of Jewish history is reflected poignantly in a *responsum*—an answer to a specific *halakhic* question—from within the nightmare kingdom:

> Rabbi Ephraim Oshry was asked whether a Jew condemned to forced labor could honestly recite the daily benediction, "Blessed art Thou, who has not made me a slave."
> The rabbi replied:

Heaven forfend that they should abolish the saying of this benediction, which was instituted by the great sages of old. On the contrary, especially at this time is the obligation upon us to cite this benediction; in order that our enemies and oppressors recognize that, in spite of the fact that we are in their power to do with as their evil desires dictate, we still see ourselves not as slaves, but as free men, temporarily in captivity, whose salvation will speedily come and whose redemption will soon be revealed.[15]

The prescription, in this opinion, is against adopting behavior which would treat that strand of circumstance, insane as it was, as different in kind from the whole fabric of Jewish experience.

As we reflect on how to understand God after the *shoah*, then, I reject the proposition that we treat it as being of a different order of reality from anything that preceded it, thus needing theological responses of a wholly new order. I regard it as being different in magnitude but not in kind, from cataclysms that the people had known before in its history. Thus, in framing an answer to our question, it is instructive to review the theological responses of the people to those earlier events.

Psalm 137 bespeaks the disorientation of the generation of the destruction of the first Temple. We err in not appreciating sufficiently the enormity of the event and the profound sense of dislocation it must have inflicted upon those who lived through it. They had been of the belief that their God would protect them from all misfortune, avert any disaster. They had believed that their God was to be found only in a chosen land, in a particular city, and within one specially sanctified building. Now devastation had befallen them, and that building was razed, the city devastated, and they themselves led away from the land. If a god ever was thought to have died, or become irrelevant for a people, certainly these people had reason to imagine so; and indeed they did question. We have already alluded to the answers germinated in Babylonia, the nature of the question itself is fascinating. As recounted in verse 8 of this Psalm, the concern was not "how can we sing a song of the Lord after what has befallen us," but, "how can we sing of the Lord here?" The locus, rather than the possibility, of prayer was the concern of those survivors of a cataclysm, the accessibility, not the existence, of God.

More remarkable still, are the accounts in the chronicles of medieval Jewish communities, places like Mainz or Worms, where in the same year—1096— 1,100 Jews were killed by a mob in the one city in a single day, and 800 in two days in the other. In the face of such enormous devastation, we might expect questioning of religious principles, even rejection, at the very least indifference about the God who did not save. Instead, we find expressions of a very different kind:

> . . . they made their way to the gate to battle against the vagabonds and the towns people. . . . But oh, because of our sins the enemy prevailed and captured the gateway. . . . Their voice rang out because all hearts were at one: 'Hear O Israel, the Lord . . . is One.' Ours not to question the ways of the Holy One, blessed be He and blessed be His name. . . . Oh, our good fortune if we do His will! Oh, the good fortune of everyone slain and butchered and killed for the Unification of His Name. . . .[16]

Incredibly, that devastated generation viewed its tragic history within the structure of its inherited theology, not as cause to abandon it.

Can we make such affirmation? Most of us do not. If it is not meet to respond to the *shoah* by denying God, it is not possible to so acclaim Him. It is appropriate that Isaiah 43:10 employs the categories of belief and understanding. In the wake of the *shoah* it is not necessary, nor, I feel, proper to abandon belief in God. But understanding is different from belief; and in the wake of the *shoah*, understanding is difficult. We cannot, as some prophetic voices suggest, accept the "because of our sins" formulation of the biblical and medieval periods and its attendant interpretation of events as theological explanation of the *shoah*. Nor have we the confidence to assert with Joseph, "you meant it for evil against me, but God meant it for good . . ." (Gen 50:20). We read Leo Baeck's Kol Nidre prayer of 1935, with its echoes of Psalm 121, "He that keeps Israel neither slumbers nor sleeps," and can only gasp in amazement.[17] The words are, assuredly, heroic; but they seem, like the words of the Mainz Chronicle, to come from a world wholly different than our own. We cannot utter them without reservation.

The *shoah* leaves us theologically tainted. Even in our most fervent moments we cannot be wholehearted. Like the shadow of a cloud, on a spring day, the memory of the *shoah* darkens our every thought of God, raising an awful "yes, but . . ." in the back of our minds even in the midst of our most devout affirmation. Words of praise or theological confirmation come out of our mouths with less ease than we would wish. Burrs of recollection cause them to stick in our throat, taking more effort and intention to move them along than we imagine would be necessary for the truly pious. We resist the idea of full obedience or self-abnegation on His behalf. We reserve the right to examine the "divine decree" before accepting it for ourselves. We feel entitled to resist "His will" from being done. We have, in short, for worse or for better, lost the ability to speak smoothly the language of the faithful. But we persist in speaking it, if with difficulty.

The state of Jewish belief, or rather Jewish understanding, after the *shoah* seems characterized by the way we hear Maimonides' credo, *Ani Ma'amin*—I believe. First, we recite it not for ourselves, but for the victims of the *shoah*. That is, we sing it, not because we feel it to be an eloquent expression of our own affirmations, but because they sang it on their way to the camps of death. Secondly, the emphasis of our age seems not to be on the opening words "I believe with perfect faith. . .," but in those that come later, *ve'af al pi*—"even though. . . ." That is the way even the most devout of us believe today, *af al pi*—even though . . ., nevertheless . . ., despite. . . .

Isaiah 43:10 demands of us not only to believe in and understand God, but to know God as well. We might assume that the terms understand and know are redundant, both implying some kind of a cognitive comprehension, if we were not already sensitive to the fact that in the biblical idiom know implies not intellectual perception, but relationship. So we are commanded to engage God and be engaged by Him. What is the climate of that engagement in the days of the aftermath of Auschwitz? If acclaim of God is hard for us in this time, so is love. This is not to imply that the relationship is cool or indifferent; far from it. On the contrary, it can be characterized by a peculiar intensity, the intensity not of rapture, nor of hatred, but of anguished questioning, even recrimination: a lover's quarrel, if you will, but of a most violent sort.

The stance of engaging God in confrontation is, of course, no novelty. It is the stance of Abraham in Genesis 18, as it is of Job—not in the sense of the erroneous cliché "patient"—but as he is depicted in the Bible, adamant in his insistence of innocence, heatedly demanding an explanation from God. This role of adversary to God, though hardly articulated, can, nonetheless be sensed. Like a raging underground river churning beneath the earth's shell, it pulses just below the surface of Jewish thought. That is the spirit which is reflected in our appropriating to ourselves the figure of Levi Yitzchak of Berdichev, a Hasidic rabbi of the eighteenth century. It is related that on one Yom Kippur, Levi Yitzchak halted the service just prior to the *Kaddish* and refused to continue. Instead he mounted his pulpit and offered up direct challenges to God:

> Good morning to You, Lord of the world!
> I, Levi Isaac, son of Sarah of Berdichev, am coming to You in a legal
> matter concerning Your people, Israel.

What do You want of Israel?
   It is always: "Speak unto the children of Israel!"
   It is always: "Command the children of Israel!"
   Merciful Father! How many people are there in the world?
   Persians, Babylonians, Edomites!
   The Russians—what do they say?
     Our Emperor is the Emperor!
   The Germans—what do they say?
     Our Kingdom is the Kingdom!
   The English—what do they say?
     Our Empire is the Empire!
   But I, Levi Isaac, son of Sarah of Berdichev, say:
     Yisgadal ve'yiskadash shmei rabbah—
     Glorified and sanctified be His great name!
   And I, Levi Isaac, son of Sarah of Berdichev, say:
   I shall not go hence, nor budge from my place until there be a
   finish
   Until there be an end to the suffering of Thy people, Israel.
   Glorified and sanctified be His great name![18]

We find ourselves in Levi Yitzchak. He does not deny God, neither does he ignore Him. He understands himself to be living in relationship to God, and feels entitled to exercise the rights that accrue to him because of that relationship. He believes in God, but is perplexed by Him. He praises God—for the *Kaddish* is pre-eminently an expression of praise, as well, appropriately enough, as a memorial to the dead—and demands an explanation for the unspeakable evils that have befallen his community.

There is, in the end, a paradoxical quality in our role as divine adversary. For it may be that our stiff-necked refusal to abandon faith in God, our insistence on clinging to belief *af al pi*, is perceived by us as being some ultimate act of disobedience, a defiance of some incomprehensible plan of His. Again, we invoke terminology from Maimonides' formula—Whatever God has done to us, for whatever reason, *im kol zeh ani ma'amin*—"in spite of it all, I believe." This, and other elements of our generation's profoundly complex relationship with God which we have noted, is given voice in one of the most moving theological reflections on the *shoah*, a literary creation put into the mouth of one of the last survivors of the Warsaw Ghetto—"Yossel Rackover's Appeal to God":

I am proud that I am a Jew not in spite of the world's treatment of us, but precisely because of this treatment. I should be ashamed to belong to the people who spawned and raised the criminals who are responsible for the deeds that have been perpetrated against us . . . .

I believe in You, God of Israel, even though You have done everything to stop me from believing in You. I bow my head before Your greatness, but will not kiss the lash with which You strike me.

You say, perhaps, that we have sinned, O Lord! And therefore we are punished? But I should like You to tell me—Is there any sin in the world deserving of such punishment as the punishment we have received?

You assert that You will yet repay our enemies? I should like You to tell me, however—Is there any punishment in the world capable of compensating for the crimes that have been committed against us?

I die peacefully, but not complacently; persecuted, but not enslaved; embittered, but not cynical; a believer, but not a supplicant; a lover of God, but no blind amensayer of His.

I have followed Him even when He repulsed me. I have followed His commandments even when He castigated me for it; I have loved Him and I love Him even when He has hurled me to the earth, tortured me to death, made me an object of shame and ridicule.

And these are my last words to You, my wrathful God: Nothing will avail You in the least. You have done everything to make me lose my faith in You, but I shall die exactly as I have lived, crying:

"Hear, O Israel, the Lord our God, the Lord is One."

"Into Your hands, O Lord, I consign my soul."[19]

We are, this generation after the *shoah*, in all that befalls us, not singular. Even in our adversary stance to God we cannot claim peculiarity, but find paradigms in our history. We have, perhaps without consciousness of it, appropriated the role invoked upon our Father Jacob when, after his night of violent encounter with a "man"—or was it God—he assumed the name Yisroel. We have become what we were then called to be— wrestlers with the divine, just as we have been wrestlers with man. Even as our lot must confront the conscience of humanity, so does our very faith confront God Himself. Would that we prevail.

What then of God in Jewish witness after the *shoah*? Our belief is not without adulteration: it is never free of the possibility of unbelief, and not fully beyond the desire not to believe. The incompleteness of our understanding torments us. The contradictions of our experience mock our efforts at affirmation. But despite it all we find ourselves to be locked in embrace with God, inescapably bound up with Him for eternity. For we recognize, no less than our ancestors, even in the face of what has befallen us or whatever may yet befall us:

I am He
Before Me there was no God formed
Neither shall any be after Me
I, even I, am the Lord . . .
Therefore ye are My witnesses
Saith the Lord
and I am God (Is 43:10-12).

Notes

1. The word *shoah* expresses the sense of devastation and ruin like that brought on by a fire storm such as evoked in Isaiah 10:3. It is a destruction of this magnitude which was visited upon the Jews of Europe in our days.

2. On November 14, 1935 the first ordinance of the Reich Citizenship Law was enacted, which established the method of determining who was to be considered a Jew. Under the terms of these "Nuremberg Laws" one was regarded as Jewish if they were descended from a Jewish grandparent—if even one of their grandparents had made the decision to remain within the Jewish community.

3. The phrase echoes the words of the Passover Haggadah which assert that to dwell at length on the events of the Exodus from Egypt is deemed praiseworthy.

4. Shapespeare, *Hamlet*, II, 2.

5. TB *Erubin* 13b.

6. Elie Wiesel, *Town Beyond the Wall* (New York: Avon Books, 1964).

7. CCAR Yearbook, vol. I, 1890, pp. 115/116.

8. Cited in *Contemporary Jewish Thought*, Simon Noveck, ed. (Washington: B'nai B'rith Dept. of Adult Jewish Education, 1963). p. 18.

9. "The people of Israel Lives," in *Christian Century,* (May 6, 1970), p. 567. Emil Fackenheim, *Quest for Past and Future* (Bloomington: Indiana University Press, 1968), pp. 19f; *idem, God's Presence in History* (New York: New York University Press, 1970), p. 86.

10. Amos Oz, "Crusade," in *Unto Death,* Nicholas de Lange transl. (London: Chatto & Windus, 1976), p. 26.

11. The question, "how can we pray . . ." was posed by Martin Buber who titled his book about the dilemma of the modern person of faith, *The Eclipse of God* (New York: Harper Torchbooks, 1957).

12. Elie Wiesel, *Night* (New York: Hill & Wang, 1960), p. 71.

13. 2 Maccabees, chapter 7 tells of the martyrdom of seven brothers who were executed by Antiochus Epiphanes in a cruel manner for refusing to compromise their devotion to the One God. The medieval composition *Eleh Ezkara,* recited as part of the Yom Kippur liturgy, recounts the torture and deaths of ten great sages whom the Romans killed for their fidelity to the teaching of Torah. Cf. *High Holiday Prayer Book,* Philip Birnbaum, transl. (New York: Hebrew Publ. Co., 1951), pp. 841f.

14. *Interpreter's Bible* (New York: Abingdon Press, 1954), Introduction to Book of Esther.

15. Irving J. Rosenbaum, *The Holocaust and Halakha* (New York: Ktav, 1976), p. 65.

16. "Mainz Chronicle," cited in Shalom Spiegel, *The Last Trial*, Judah Goldin, transl. (New York: Pantheon Books, 1967).

17. The great scholar, Leo Baeck, composed a special prayer to be read just before the recitation of the *Kol Nidre*. It was pronounced in all the synagogues of Germany on the Eve of Yom Kippur, 1935.

18. The great Hasidic Rebbe (d. 1809) is renowned for the challenges he hurled at heaven about the straits of God's covenanted people.

19. This appeal, a fictionalized testament of one of the last survivors of the Warsaw Ghetto, appears in Zvi Kolitz, *The Tiger Beneath the Skin* (New York: Creative Age Press, 1947).

7.
The Mission of
Israel after Auschwitz

Martin A. Cohen

Dedicated to those members of my family
Who disappeared from the face of the earth
When the Nazis stormed into Riga, Latvia,
And of whom a single piece of correspondence,
Now in my possession, remains the sole memorial.

1. Post-Auschwitz Theology and the Mission

Although three and a half decades have passed since the Holocaust, it is perhaps still too soon for Jews to plumb its meaning with academic distance. The events are still too close, the memories too searing, the billowing emotions of repugnance, revulsion, abhorrence and revenge too refractory to look at that tiny lustrum *sub specie aeternitatis*.

Yet until we do we stand removed from the theological tradition of our faith, which speaks unequivocally of an omnipotent, omniscient and omnipresent God who cares for His creatures and dispenses justice in an ordered universe. Until we do we may in our fathomless pain and anger rebelliously proclaim both the annulment of this millennial affirmation and the inauguration of a qualitatively new era in the Jew's address to God. Jews who have taken this course are spread across an entire spectrum of belief and disbelief, ranging from a categorical rejection of faith to a variety of alternative propositions which reveal the burdensome influence of recent non-Jewish thinking and a cavalier dismissal of the powerful challenge of our traditional modes of thought.

Among the most noteworthy of our new theologies, those of Richard Rubenstein, Emil Fackenheim and Irving Greenberg have rightfully and representatively commanded the greatest notice. All presuppose the fragility of traditional belief in the face of the Holocaust. Rubenstein goes so far as to state that, "a void stands where once we experienced God's presence." He characterizes God as the

> Holy Nothingness . . . out of which we have come and to which we shall ultimately return,

and emphasizes the need for,

> Torah, tradition, and the religious community far more than in a world where God's presence was meaningfully experienced.[1]

Emil Fackenheim, though sharply critical of Rubenstein, similarly stresses the importance of the survival of the Jew, and articulates it in his now famous "614th commandment":

> The authentic Jew of today is forbidden to hand Hitler yet another, posthumous victory.[2]

For his part, Greenberg posits a dialectical or "moment faith," in which an awareness of God fades in and out of the clouds of human experience. Greenberg raises the role of the individual's faith-response to at least parity with that of divine demonstration. He sees a new human-divine relationship whose practical consequence will be "the reaffirmation of meaningfulness, worth and life—through acts of love and life-giving."[3]

It is noteworthy that the majority of Jewish thinkers, though stunned by the enormity of the Holocaust, have not been moved to radical theologizing. This is apparent in the creative theologies of Arthur J. Lelyveld, Eliezer Berkovits and Elliot Dorff. Lelyveld rejects special providence, emphasizes life's inherent contingency and rededicates himself through the covenant "to battle evil and perfect the world."[4] Berkovits retains faith in God's goodness even if during the Holocaust God, so to speak, were "silent" and "hid His face," and insists that indeed "there is a judgment and there is a judge in world history."[5]

Dorff reaffirms the traditional Jewish antinomy of a just God responsible for evil and concentrates on, the classical Jewish commitment to constructive work in this world, through both the ritual and moral *mitzvot*, ... on the faith that our action can make a difference.[6]

An abiding faith is evident as well in the more conventional analyses of the divine role by an entire panoply of thinkers, liberal and orthodox.

Thus, Ignatz Maybaum, emphasizing the role of the Jews as the Suffering Servant, views the Holocaust as a divine visitation to bring an end to a decaying era and to usher in a new, utopian world.[7] Menahem Emanuel Hartom explains the Holocaust as punishment for Jewish assimilation and sees the state of Israel as its intended outcome, although the Jewish people, "was not worthy of it by its conduct."[8] Bemoaning the tendencies to irreligiosity in Israel's secular nationalism, Harton warns against another retributive visitation.

Joel Teitelbaum, leader of the anti-Israel Satmar Hasidim, goes so far as to blame secularist Zionism for the divine visitation of the Holocaust.[9] David Chomsky shares Hartom's faith, but rejects his fear of the assimilative trends in Israel. On the contrary, he sees the possibility of the Jews in secular Israel becoming "a kingdom of priests and a holy people."[10] Issachar Jacobson hears in the Holocaust a call for Jews to renounce all attempts at rational explanations of its events and to reaffirm their Jewish belief,

to remain people of faith, fearing God and always doing good, for in these ways alone can we grasp something of God's wisdom.[11]

Similarly, Jacob Rothschild calls on the Jew to rise above the naturally human desire for explanation of daily events to a strong and unquestioning faith in human history under the guidance of God.[12]

If contradictory in their causality, these positions all fully sustain the traditional conceptions of God's nature and involvement in the universe. By implication, they all furthermore challenge the oft-enunciated principle of the Holocaust's utter incomparability.

It would be otiose to deny a uniqueness to the Holocaust in the range and degree of its destructiveness. But this distinction is one of magnitude and not essence. To equate the Holocaust's excess in the formalization of evil with a qualitative change in the nature of evil itself is a tragic mistake. It betrays an insensitivity to the fundamental fact that since the days of Job, and beyond to the archetypes of the human species, insofar as can be fathomed, the pernicious substance of evil has remained essentially the same and has regularly expressed itself as demoniacally as possible within the material limitations of every given age. In this sense, every great catastrophe of the Jewish past is substantively akin to the Holocaust, as is the wanton destruction of any individual Jew because of his or her Jewishness.

It is no coincidence that the radical Jewish responses to the Holocaust either deny the concept of the mission of Israel or relegate it to the periphery of our theological concern. The mission of Israel is a concept which makes sense only in connection with traditional Jewish theological categories. It presumes a just and caring God, possessor of a progressively unfolding universal plan which is at least in part actualized by the faith-community of Jews.

Except in reductionist minds this is not a naive concept, oblivious to the actualized or potential evil of the human psyche. While it entertains, "visions girt with beauty and with wonder lit," to borrow the words of Louis Untermeyer's *Prayer*, it never dismisses, "the dirt, and all that spawn and die in it."[13] Anything but doctrinaire, the concept represents a commitment to the highest possibilities of human nature after a comprehension of its complex dialectic of evil and good.

2. The Centrality of the Mission in Jewish Theology

In the tradition of Judaism, the word "Israel" bears three simultaneous meanings. It denotes the individual Jew (who in our sacred writings is designated not a *Yehudi* but a *Yisrael*), our faith-community and our Holy Land. The individual Jew is the terrestrial source of our faith, the people its corporate embodiment, and the land its millennial nourishment and hope. The subject of the mission of Israel is the faith-community, or, as it is usually called, the Jewish people. Israel the people possesses a distinctive characteristic and bears a special obligation. The characteristic is called the election of Israel; more popularly it is referred to as Israel's chosenness or its status as the Chosen People. The obligation is its mission. Election and mission constitute the inseparable obverse and reverse of the same theological coin.

According to Jewish tradition, Israel's mission is pragmatic and verifiable. Its content is ethical, its orientation societal, its teleology universal. The classical expression of this mission still remains the opening words of the forty-second chapter of the Book of Isaiah:

> Behold, my servant, whom I uphold;
> Mine elect, in whom my soul delighteth;
> I have put my spirit upon him,

He shall make the right to go forth to the nations. . . .
I the Lord have called thee in righteousness,
And have taken hold of thy hand,
And kept thee, and set thee for a covenant of the people,
For a light unto the nations,
To open the blind eyes,
To bring out the prisoners from the dungeon,
And them that sit in darkness out of the prison house.

Through the ages the concepts of Israel's chosenness and mission have remained central in its theology. Without both, the distinctive dimensions of other theological affirmations in Judaism, including revelation, the covenant, the messianic age and even God, are immeasurably compromised. Until our own times these concepts have occupied a central place in the various orders of Jewish prayer. In recent decades Reconstructionist Jews have drastically altered their total theology of Judaism by abandoning these concepts. But Reform, Conservative and Orthodox orders of prayer still voice the age-old conviction that God has chosen us, sanctified us and delighted in us.

Yet, of all Jewish theological concepts, this pair stirs the greatest discomfort. Not uncommonly Jews who repeat them mechanically in prayer reject them as foundations of their personal belief. At the same time, increasing numbers of Jews, recognizing their centrality, are prepared to accept them provided that they are couched in rational explanations congenial to modern thinking.

3. The Reality of the Mission Past and Present

Elsewhere[14] I have presented such an explanation utilizing the disciplines of contemporary social science and seeking conformity with the four conditions implicit in any effort at contemporary explanation. These are, first, that the explanation must conform entirely to the traditional explanations in the mainstream of Judaism; second, that in accordance with the tradition, Jews be shown to be the subjects of an election beyond their initiative and control. Chosenness entails reception and not donation. The conceit that Jews are a chosen people because they chose God runs counter to the tradition. Third, that the concept of chosenness embrace all Jews, for tradition exempts none from chosenness. Finally, that a justification for the choice be given. Only two such justifications constitute serious possibilities: either the Jews had merit or they were chosen by grace.

These conditions can all be satisfactorily met by recourse to the experience of the Jewish people. Like that of every other group, the history of the Jews is fully explicable by contemporary social scientific norms, and

like that of every other, its total configuration is distinctive, resulting from
the interplay of the particulars of environmental determinism and human
volition. The distinctiveness of Jewish experience lends itself remarkably to
an understanding of the concepts of chosenness and mission.

The Jewish experience is divisible into two phases: the formative,
when the Hebrews became conscious of their mission and articulated its
implications, and the experiential, when the Jews found themselves driven
to its fulfillment.

As certified by our religious tradition, Jewish history begins with the
Exodus and the Wilderness, where the egalitarian-utopian slave ethic of
the refugees became the ideological foundation of their society and the
content of their covenant with their God. If other groups begun with
similar ideals have seen them dissipate as they became stable polities,
Israel's chronic instability, preconditioned by the strategic geography of
the Holy Land, kept the Wilderness Ethic in the forefront of Hebrew
consciousness and enshrined it in the Bible as the basic ethos of the
Hebrew tradition.

The importance and instability of the Holy Land led to the conquest
of its northern Hebrew kingdom of Israel by the Assyrians in 722/721
BCE and to the subsequent buffeting of the kingdom of Judah from one
great power to another. In this process Jews gained not only the latest
knowledge and techniques from the advanced, conquering nations, but the
realization that only through service could they continue miraculously to
survive.

Their miraculous survival despite the disappearance of larger polities
around them led Jews to the conviction that their God was the most
powerful of the deities in the region and even God universal. If so, their
covenant with the universal Deity implied the Deity's choice of them from
among all the peoples of the earth. The idea of chosenness was given
classical articulation by the prophets, who emphasized that the choice was
by grace and not by merit, that it implied duty rather than privilege, and
that this duty was nothing short of showing the Wilderness Ethic in every
corner of the world.

Attempts by Jews to fulfill this task by active proselytization failed as
the Roman empire declined and Christianity spread. Jews were soon to
learn that their mission was to be accomplished compulsorily in a strikingly unusual way.

After Rome's destruction of the Jewish State and Temple in the year
70 CE, the center of Jewish life, definable as the place of greatest Jewish
population, wealth and creativity, began to move—to Babylonia, Africa,

western, central and eastern Europe, and ultimately to the United States of America, a route roughly paralleling that of western civilization. Simultaneously, the Jews became a wandering people. Although not all Jews actually wandered, and some families remained rooted in the same land for centuries, no sensitive Jew (and indeed no sensitive former Jew or non-Jewish descendant of Jews) could fail to realize that potentially he or she was a wanderer too.

Jews could wander only to those places that were prepared to accept them. Invariably this acceptance came from polities that were new or in the process of renewal and therefore in dire need of the accumulated knowledge and skills of this people, who furthermore, because of the paucity of their numbers admitted, could never constitute a political threat. At all times, the host polities of the Jews determined the range of their occupational activity and the social and political roles they were to play.

Though always a small minority, our roles and our achievements have held us prominently before the public eye and therefore facilely targeted for the frustration, envy and hatred of all the disadvantaged and oppressed. Understandably, therefore, wherever we have gone, our corporate well-being has always been directly proportional to the implementation of the Wilderness Ethic by society as a whole. The greater the practice of justice, brotherhood and general human concern, the happier the lot of the Jew; the more pronounced the frustration and disorientation of the people, the greater the likelihood for the projection of hostility onto the Jew.

Antisemitism can be understood as a societal disease deriving from an environmental insufficiency of the Wilderness Ethic. Every human being deprived of the fruits of the Wilderness Ethic becomes a potential antisemite. Accordingly, Jews cannot rest secure until their mission of the universal implantation of the Wilderness Ethic has been fully accomplished.

It is no coincidence that Jews have traditionally and perennially, wherever possible, been in the forefront of movements designed to further the ideals of the Wilderness Ethic. Many have even been deluded into following movements that have made no more than rhetorical use of these ideals. The Jewish role in these areas has not always been calculated; it is primarily the result of a conditioning now deeply imbedded in the subconscious of the Jew.

As a people, we Jews have not always wanted this role. We have not sought to be different, much less heroic. Wherever we have wandered, we have tried to be like everyone else and to live unobtrusively in tranquility and peace. But, as sensitive Jews have come to learn, our ultimate salvation as a people is bound up not with escape into the ease of rootedness, but with our restless struggle to universalize the Wilderness ideal.

Such is our chosenness. It is the kind of chosenness which, if we Jews had had the choice, we might possibly never have chosen. Yet this chosenness has not been without its rewards. It has experientially given us a universal outlook on life and a respect for the equivalence and dignity of all humanity. It has also compulsorily made of us a learned, creative and sensitive people, who keep ever before us the concept of the world perfected by the Wilderness Ethic and the desire to bring that world a bit closer each day.

The renowned sixteenth century Italian rabbi, Raphael ben Gabriel Norzi, aptly summed up the mission of Israel when he said that,

the purpose of serving God is to promote the perfection of humanity.[15]

The mission of Israel is unequivocally a worldly mission, *l'taken olam b'malkhut Shaddai*, "to perfect the world under the kingdom of the Almighty,"[16] and to do so not through the uniformity of reiterated creed but through the unity of realized human aspirations. This is the goal of the traditional Jewish High Holyday prayer, *U'vekhen Ten Pahdekha*, which petitions God to animate all His creatures with awe and reverence, "that all may form a single band to do Your will wholeheartedly."

Never before in our millennial history have we Jews faced the opportunity and obligation to implement our mission that we possess today. Until modern times it was impossible for us to advance our mission beyond the confines of Jewish society: We lived in the main in autonomous communities with little power to influence the world outside. When we became citizens of modern states, where we enjoyed at least a theoretical equality with everyone else, our power of influence increased and our advocacy of the Wilderness Ethic spread. But the articulation of our mission in the two centuries that elapsed from the first dawn of our so-called emancipation from the old way of life until the black midnight of Auschwitz was decidedly limited. Countless Jews tenaciously held to the belief that modern science and reason were irreversibly propelling the Wilderness Ethic toward its proximate fulfillment in a utopian society. At the same time the eagerness of these Jews for the realization of what they believed to be the strong possibility of full acceptance by non-Jews inhibited them from dwelling on those aspects of our mission which might offend non-Jews by their implicit criticism of their contemporary society.

Auschwitz has shattered these doctrinaire illusions. It has brought painfully home to all humanity the realization of the moral primitiveness of human civilization and the miraculous unassimilability of the Jew. It has left little doubt that the Jew's best option is to reconcile himself with his mission, and to proclaim openly, as the prophet Jonah was constrained to do, "I am a Hebrew and I serve the Lord" (Jon 1:9).

4. The Moral Crisis of the Post-Holocaust World

By synecdoche Auschwitz has come to represent the Holocaust as a whole. But because the Holocaust has generally been regarded by the world as a parochially Jewish phenomenon, the range of its synecdochic significance has been overlooked. No serious study of the events, of which the Holocaust was the sad culmination, can overlook the fact that it concentrically marks the destruction not only of one third of the world's Jewish population and of the centrality of European Jewry, but also the end of the hegemony of Europe and of western civilization. It therefore complementarily signals the inauguration of a new epoch in human history.

Although we are still living amidst the debris of the world the Holocaust symbolically ended, the contours of the new era are slowly but unmistakably appearing in a delicate interplay of international politics, social change and individual reorientation. The chief catalyst in this process is the miracle of communications, which has already shrunk our planet to a maximum distance of well under twenty-four hours and has put the sounds of its remotest corners well within our reach.

Geopolitically, the new world, according to some of today's most penetrating thinkers, is characterized by a movement toward global unification.[17] This movement is led by the great powers, under the apparent leadership of the United States of America. The process is necessarily plodding, since it involves a complexity of polities, vested interests and group sensibilities. It entails the abolition of colonialism and the creation of a post-nationalist world of nation-states increasingly dependent upon one another and hierarchized in regional alignments susceptible of global integration. All of this, say such thinkers, is to be accomplished with the maximal containment of armed conflict and the eventual sublimation of group hostilities into ventures of group cooperation.[18]

Public information, stressing only the immediate and surface events, appears to belie such movement. The media have a tendency to present national and international events as fortuitous and their creators as impulsive decisors. Behind these showcase presentations can be discerned a deeper reality, where diplomacy is a science and vital information is incubated until innocuous. The dichotomy between the surface and the depth of political events is certainly nothing new. It is not tantamount, as some ingenuous generalizers would have it, to a conspiracy theory of history, though conspiracies may also reveal this divergency. It is rather an aspect of normal corporate practice common since the beginning of time; only today it is more sophisticated and writ universal.

Societally, a transformation is taking place in harmony with the geopolitical revolution. Traditional loyalties are fading: nationalism is losing to regionalism and ethnicism, and established religions are ceding to new emotional commitments. Churches headquartered in Europe are having a difficult time untying themselves from that continent's connection with exploitative colonialism. In addition, greater mobility, a by-product of industrialization, has weakened ties to community and family and is one of the root causes of nuclear family fission.

Obviously corollary to all of this is the increasingly intensive disorientation of the individual occurring at different velocities around the world, but fastest in the most advanced nations. In their ever more difficult and even hostile transitional environments, individuals bereft of the support of traditional structures, institutions and ideologies are seeking to construct new personal worlds of material well-being and emotional balance. This goal is universally replacing the quiescent hope nurtured by many religions of extra-worldly compensation for terrestrial disadvantage. In this quest for a new and better life there is an increasing sensitivity to the global interdependence of all people and therefore to global problems which must cooperatively be resolved in order for individual goals to be attained.

It is to the ethical and moral challenges of this post-Auschwitz world that Israel must direct its mission. Though the culmination of an historical era, Auschwitz, it must be emphasized, hardly marks the termination of the forces of darkness that consume the marrow of human life. These organisms continue to flourish, some in their conventional forms, others in new and fearsome strains, increasingly resistant to our ethical antibodies and noxious to the spirit of human dignity. In the light of tensions generated by the dual process of societal unification and individual reorientation, a universal Armageddon looms between the values of the Wilderness and the mechanisms of human oppression.

Of these organisms, the first and most fundamental constellation, sparing no one, are those involved in the destruction of the earth's ecosystem, plunging it precipitately and irresponsibly toward what Ron

Linton so aptly calls "terracide,"[19] through atmospheric and sub-surface pollution. Characteristic is the survey at the beginning of this decade which revealed that air pollution alone damaged up to fifty per cent of the basic crops on the eastern shore of the United States, more than fifty per cent on the western shore, and some eighty per cent of the acreage in the San Bernardino National Forest. Ward and Dubois estimate that the health problems related to pollution in the United States alone cost some six billion dollars a year.[20]

This reality renders even more ominous the depletion of terrestrial resources through the unchecked proliferation of the human species. It is no coincidence that Malthusian pessimism, thwarted by two centuries of unprecedented technological achievement in food production, has revived in the face of the incapability of the earth's resources, however stretched, to maintain pace with its exponentially expanding population. That the urgency of the problem has not escaped responsible political leadership is evident from the warning of United States Senator Gaylord Nelson read into the Congressional Record in 1970 to the effect that,

> unless something is done about the population explosion, we will be faced with an unprecedented catastrophe of overcrowding, famines, pestilence and war.[21]

Next are the manifold frustrations of the six basic human needs for physical survival—food, raiment, shelter, medicine, education and employment. The still sufficiently abundant stocks of all these resources are in the most inhumane fashion inequitably distributed. Four hundred and sixty million people on this earth are malnourished, and at least that number are deprived of their other basic rights. Millions live unnecessarily in population densities that breed physical and emotional disorders, not the least of which are frustration, hatred and the urge to destroy. This situation of "blocked opportunity" is endemic to all societies, even the most advanced. Particularly distressing in some of the more fortunately provisioned countries of the post-Auschwitz world are the powerful efforts to market health-care as a luxury rather than distribute it as an inherent right and the ugly maneuvers which have eviscerated their once effective systems of public education, the only gateway to the healthy combination of productive employment and democratic living. Equally applicable to all these areas is the conclusion by Harry Walters in his discussion of world food problems that,

> lasting solutions require changes in social and economic imbalances and in political decisions.[22]

Next are the seemingly ineradicable plagues of discrimination against people who belong to disadvantaged races, nationalities, faiths or castes. We Jews continue to be the paradigm for such discrimination in each of these categories. Even in advanced countries like the United States, we continue to suffer insidiously interposed disabilities in business, the professions and leisure activities. We even find ourselves in the forefront of those affected by reverse discrimination. In addition we often find ourselves in the condition of a caste, not entirely dissimilar to the Eta of Japan or the untouchables of India. We can therefore readily feel the plight not only of the traditionally designated out-groups in various places around the world, but of innumerable others almost ubiquitously and perennially disadvantaged, such as the physically handicapped, the aged and women.

The extent of the blight of discrimination in our time is seen in the proliferation of movements for political and cultural self-determination by minority groups all over the world, perhaps the most universally known in our times being the struggles of African blacks in areas still dominated by European whites. The human resources lost in the morally indefensible repression of the countless millions thus affected stagger the imagination.

Next are the manifold new organisms that bring about the dehumanization of individuals, now being added to the perennial forms of dehumanization by self-abuse through a variety of dissipations and abuse of kith and kin through various displacements of hostility. The new forms have found a multiplicity of carriers. They include practitioners in various fields and public agencies of social service that digitize, computerize, and depersonalize their clientele, arrogantly refusing them the respect and self-worth that every human being deserves. Even more tragic, they include as well the institutions of national states that intimidate, incarcerate, muzzle, torture and destroy those regarded as politically threatening or otherwise undesirable, by means that are best and most comprehensively depicted in Aleksandr Solzhenitsyn's *Gulag Archipelago*,[23] but which, it must be emphasized, are by no means limited to totalitarian lands. Far more frightening and ultimately even more dehumanizing than this modern pursuit of heresy is the increasing imposition of scenario wars on unsuspecting and idealistic individuals by international consortia for recondite political ends.

Finally, there is the degradation of the human personality through the moral corruption of societal institutions whose examples are decisive for individual behavior. The failure of institutions of business, labor, the professions, education and government to curb the natural tendencies toward corruptibility that afflict all human structures has posed history's greatest challenge to the Wilderness Ethic and projected the specter of humanity's retrogressive descent into primal barbarity. Strikingly painful in this regard are the shortcomings of religious institutions, dramatized by their silence in the face of the Holocaust and ever since by their general myopia toward the moral and ethical aberrations within their own ranks and in the world around them. The preference of numerous religious bodies to avoid full and dedicated involvement in the field of social ethics and morality and to focus their attention instead on the harmless disquisitions of esoteric theology constitutes one of the most tragic and cynicism-breeding realities of our time.

5. The Demands of the Mission Today

To struggle for the eradication of these manifold deterrents to the full humanization of our species is the sacred task of the post-Auschwitz Jew. To proclaim to the world, courteously, calmly, but courageously and cogently our commitment to the Wilderness Ethic is an indispensable prerequisite for the survival of the values of western religion which are constructed on its base. It is no less necessary for the reestablishment of the general credibility of religion in a world where through the default of its institutions and the power of its threatened opponents such credibility totters near its historic nadir.

This, of course, is a task of overwhelming arduousness. It involves taking a stand on every conceivable public issue, from the right of all humanity to peace to that of the living to die and the not yet born to live. It entails a commitment to a constant search for new structures and institutions of community, national and international life to provide substance, security and fulfillment for every segment of humanity. It demands a responsible but dauntless critique of the shortcomings of contemporary institutions and a willingness to name names and specify situations. Above all, it calls for a girding for battle with the real adversary, in the form of a variety of political, social, economic and even religious institutions. Driven by selfishness, greed and misanthropy, these vested interests, like their counterparts in every past, are prepared to sow discontent, hostility, oppression, and, in every sense of the word, an irreligiosity which contradicts the basal ethical and moral principles of the Jewish and Christian faiths.

To engage in this task is to accept in its broadest sense for our day what Judaism calls the *ol malkhut Shamayim*, the yoke of the kingdom of Heaven. To flee its imperious demands or to compromise its directives so that it has no effect but to leave the world unchanged is to descend into the deepest troughs of hypocrisy.

The possibility of the eventual fulfillment of the task is no longer a rootless dream, nor is it one in which we Jews with our miniscule numbers need see ourselves struggling alone. Countless people adversely affected by the organisms of oppression in every area of the earth are striving, much more often than not peacefully and prayerfully, for the recognition of their humanity. They are also drawing closer to the realization of all humanity's common ethical concerns.

The outspoken religiosity of the Jew carrying the banner of the Wilderness Ethic can serve as an invaluable catalyst in this process. It can encourage humanity's truly religious struggle for the recognition of its inalienable dignity and for the creation of what Abraham J. Maslow calls a "good society," by which he means, speaking not politically but ethically, "ultimately one species, one world."[24]

6. The Internal Mission

Laborious as this post-Auschwitz mission intrinsically appears, the greatest obstacle to its fulfillment lies not in the impediments placed by others, but in the psyche of us Jews ourselves. It is axiomatic that the mission of Israel can be achieved only by a people strong enough for the task. Yet the sad fact of Jewish existence in the post-Auschwitz world is that we are far from strong enough numerically, psychologically and religiously for the effective pursuit of our sacred obligation. To reach an effective level of serviceability to humanity we Jews must first therefore strengthen ourselves. The mission of Israel to the body of the world must therefore necessarily be preceded by the mission of Israel to the heart of the peoples, as the great Iberian philosopher and poet Judah Halevi, recognizing the nature of the mission, called the people of Israel itself.

Numerically, the Jewish people has always been miniscule. This makes the effect of the Holocaust, which consumed more than thirty-seven percent of the sixteen and a half million Jews in the world all the more difficult to bear. In the three and a half decades that have elapsed since the Holocaust, we have been unable to recoup our losses. Besides, the infinitesimal percentage of the world population that we constitute is becoming progressively smaller. The 14,200,000 Jews scattered across the globe now constitute only four-tenths of one percent of the rapidly expanding world population.

Of greater concern than our faith-community's modest numbers is the persistent danger of their further reduction. In open, democratic societies the Jewish population is eroding through defection, chiefly by way of intermarriage and a declining birthrate characteristic of the middle class. Suggestions that Jews in these countries increase their birthrate have not unexpectedly fallen on deaf ears because, like other middle class people, Jews reduce family size in order to assure a reasonably good life for their offspring. Many Jews, however, are beginning to realize that the time has come to stop being squeamish about tapping the one reservoir which alone can provide the certainty of continuity. That is the reservoir of prospective proselytes, whose entrance into the Jewish fold, in accordance with traditional Jewish experience, can serve to fortify the people Israel for its mission.

A certain number of proselytes, perhaps in excess of three thousand, enter Judaism each year. We Jews do not solicit conversions and look with abhorrence at all efforts to dissuade people from retaining their commitments to another faith. All our proselytes come on their own initiative, and most because conversion has been raised as a condition of their desired marriage to a Jew. According to traditional Jewish law, conversion for the sake of marriage does not constitute a sufficient reason for acceptance into the fold; but most Jewish leaders today, rather than seek a legal subterfuge, recognize the reality and accept those who have gone through the requisite studies and rites. Increasingly, however, responsible leaders in the community have come to realize that besides these self-motivated candidates, there are hundreds of thousands of spiritually sensitive people without religious denominational roots or affiliation in the various free countries of the world, and that these people might be interested in joining the fellowship of Israel if information about it were disseminated to them. Such leaders not incorrectly point out that in the long course of our history, Israel has frequently been enriched by the incorporation of considerable numbers of converts.

An even more urgent aspect of our mission is the protection of the various Jewish communities in danger of spiritual or physical extinction. The prime example of the first category is the Jewish community of the Soviet Union, the second largest in the world, with 2,680,000 souls. Almost to the last person this community would welcome a lifting of a ban on their unfettered religious expression and a significant percentage would take advantage of an open door to emigration.

In addition, thousands of Jews are in danger of persecution in various parts of Latin America. This is also the case in the Moslem countries of Africa and Asia, where the remnant of Jews who have remained have for the most part been reduced to pariahs and find themselves in constant danger of arrest, persecution and death.

The task of saving these Jews and securing for them the ideals of the Wilderness Ethic must occupy the attention of Jews in happier circumstances and all the allies whom they can muster for this humanitarian cause.

The natural refuge for these beleaguered children of Israel is the State of Israel. Theologically, the State of Israel may be described as the miraculous haven created by God for the remnant of the Holocaust, "a firebrand plucked out of the burning" (Am 4:11). Although the origins of the modern State of Israel lend themselves readily to naturalistic explanations, their sum is not the less miraculous. Were it not for the State of Israel, the survivors of Nazi barbarity would for the most part have had no place to go, for even the most democratic and freedom-loving of nations, though proud of their philanthropy, hardened their hearts at the plight of the European Jews during the Holocaust and icily turned their backs to their survivors' desperate pleas for massive admission to their shores.

The importance of the State of Israel for the internal mission of the Jews cannot be overemphasized. For the disillusioned Jews of the post-Holocaust world Israel represents the last hope of rootedness for their people. It does so not merely because it was and remains the only land on earth open freely to every Jew, but because from the very beginnings of the Jewish tradition the Holy Land formed the territorial component of the covenant between the people Israel and God. The transcendent significance of the land Israel is indelibly stamped upon the psyche of all self-respecting Jews, even those who claim to be irreligious. To be sure, the State of Israel is not the ideal messianic state promised in Scripture and Tradition. In some ways we would have to admit that it may as yet be far from that ideal. Yet who will deny that it is the closest that we have come to the messianic state for at least the past nineteen hundred years? And who knows but that it is the messianic state in time that will yet develop into the messianic state of eternity?

Today the State of Israel serves as a major source of identity and pride, a fountain of Jewish culture and potentially a well of universal spiritual refreshment.

The spiritual reawakening that Israel potentially offers suggests the next priority of the Jewish mission after Auschwitz. Naturally consequent upon the physical security of Israel the land and Israel the people is the spiritual continuity of Israel as a faith-community. Without the tradition and faith which have informed the people Israel through four millennia any talk about Jewish survival is a blatant contradiction in terms. The loss of spiritual identity among the Jews of free societies poses a danger to Jewish continuity no less ominous than the Damoclean sword of persecution and oppression in societies that are closed.

The spiritual drain of the Jewish community is a direct consequence of what has come to be known as the Jewish Emancipation. The phenomenon of Jewish "emancipation" belongs to the eighteenth and early nineteenth centuries. When, in the process of their emancipation, Jews acceded to the dissolution of their organic communities, they left the tender shoots of piety and faith exposed to the outside world. The great peril of this world lay not in its secularity but in its philosophies and theologies, religious as well as secular, which began to exercise the natural pressure that any majority imposes upon a minority culture. Even the emancipated Jew who continued to cling to the traditional Jewish notions of God, the soul, immortality, revelation and other cardinal ideas of the faith of Israel found it difficult to resist the philosophical categories and theological presuppositions of the non-Jewish world around him. Often these ideas were absorbed subconsciously by a natural process of mental osmosis.

An even more potent influence than alien concepts on the faith of the Jew is the general lack of piety and spirituality pervading today's open societies. In the case of the Jews the problem is complicated by the tendencies toward centrifugality inherent in all minority groups and by the continuing pressures of anti-Semitism and the social and occupational barriers that even the freest of societies continue to put into the path of the Jew.

Many Jewish intellectuals have fled Judaism for a variety of psychological reasons, but their rationalized complaint that it is ideologically bland and unsatisfying should not be cavalierly and depreciatingly dismissed. The fact is that Jewish theology is weak and outdated in many of its formulations.

For those left in the synagogue, the religious focus of Judaism has concentrated on ritual and fellowship. To complicate matters, religious institutions have gradually yielded their traditional position of centrality in Jewish life to a panoply of secular organizations, local and international, which make the most important decisions and usually offer the most cogent programming in Jewish life.

Much remains to be done to restore a healthy spiritual life to the average Jew. The synagogue must be restored to institutional primacy in Jewish life, the theology of our tradition must be couched in contemporarily relevant frames of thought, and the religiously faint-hearted must be brought back to our religious preserve through education, service and concern.

These tasks are not limited to the Jewish community of the United States of America. They belong as well to the Jewish communities of all other open societies, and especially that of Israel. There Jewish spirituality remains underdeveloped as many Israelis eschew a committed contact with their religious heritage because of a political situation which permits the dogged retention of power over religion by one segment of the religious community. Only when the leadership of this segment is prepared to yield some of its power for the sake of the broadest religious expression of Judaism can the deep hunger for faith present in Israel be relieved.

7. The Mission To Seek Answers

Not only the theology of mission, but all theological statements, however transformed, reflect a societal reality. The comprehension of any theology is therefore inconceivable without a clear perception of the society of its birth and the successor societies of its survival. Indispensable for this perception are the formal disciplines by which society is measured. These include history, sociology, social psychology, economics, politics (especially, today, the dimension of geopolitics) and the intersecting realms of philosophy. These disciplines are in many ways more complex than the natural sciences, and perhaps primarily for this reason, less precise. But their increasing sophistication facilitates an understanding of the nature of society and suggests sound and realistic parameters for the implementation of Jewish theological ideals. Much theologizing today about the world of individual and institutional interaction is regarded as fey and ungrounded precisely because it is innocent of the knowledge these disciplines can provide.

For the religiously committed Jew, the *hohmat ha-adam*, or human science, and the *hohmat elohut*, or divine science, are not mutually exclusive alternatives moving with hostile parallelism into an obscure infinity. They are rather complementary and interpenetrating perspectives on life. The mainstream of the Jewish tradition has seen little confrontation and no antithesis between the sacred and the secular disciplines into which human knowledge is so often arbitrarily compartmentalized. It views the result of every worthy quest for knowledge as a discovery in God's domain, as Torah in the broadest connotation of the word.

This fact bears emphasis today, because a number of Jewish theologians have explicitly or implicitly condemned the societal disciplines. Some, in flagrant disregard of the mainstream of Judaism's millennial tradition, have gone so far as to compromise the use of reason in the discernment of God's will.

It is this tendency which portrays the Holocaust as utterly beyond the canons of objective analysis. This is what is meant when theologians label the Holocaust as incomprehensible or absurd. Emil Fackenheim even goes so far as to state that it is immoral to search for meaning in the Holocaust.[25] Such pessimistic thinking is a derivative of the broader concept of the absurdity of the human condition so prevalent today and perhaps nowhere better expounded than in Albert Camus' *The Myth of Sisyphus.* This is, however, not the direction of the mainstream of the Jewish tradition.

Nowhere is the need for the theology of mission to combat such despair better seen than in the case of the Holocaust. The eminent Jewish historian Ellis Rivkin, in his challenging work, *The Shaping of Jewish History,* justifiably takes sharp issue with the fatalistic implications of the concept of the Absurd related to the Holocaust and insists not only on the possibility, but on the necessity of explanation in a traditional Jewish sense:

> If there is no answer [to the Holocaust], then there is no hope; for if there is no discernible cause, there can be no way of offsetting the effect. But if the Holocaust can be explained, if this evil, like other evils can be accounted for, then there may indeed be hope.[26]

To find the explanation of the Holocaust, to reexamine the society that spawned it, to reconstruct the motivations of its generators and agents, constitutes a quintessential element of Israel's post-Auschwitz mission. For if such probings have any merit, they will forewarn even when they cannot forearm against any tendencies that may lead, heaven forbid, to a Holocaust of the future. No less important, they will give us a deeper insight into the raw stuff of human nature and therefore a more realistic understanding of ways to coax it, in ethical terms at least, toward the *malkhut Shamayim,* the yoke of the kingdom of Heaven.

To attain such understanding, however tentative and provisionary, entails the ability to communicate it to others. As fundamental as any other aspect of the mission after Auschwitz is the obligation of the Jew to dwell in Auschwitz, to reflect on Auschwitz and to transmit the lesson of Auschwitz to Jew and non-Jew alike. Not for naught does Israel's Holocaust memorial in Jerusalem, the Yad Vashem, bear the motto "Remember." To forget Auschwitz is to forget the diabolical power of evil and to neglect the questioning of its role in the divine scheme of life. To dwell on Auschwitz is to remember that the ominous threat of genocide of minority groups branded as the enemy has not been removed from the world, that the oppression of such groups, be they the Gypsies and Poles slaughtered by the Nazis, the Nisei interned by the Americans, or the Blacks, so frightfully disadvantaged in various parts of the world, has become ubiquitous and perennial. To dwell on Auschwitz is also to remind us Jews of our inevitable vulnerability and indispensable centrality in the struggle for the

Wilderness Ethic, which alone can bring the ultimate manumission and vindication not only of the oppressed but of humanity as a whole.

In this light, it is difficult to understand how any contemporary theologies, particularly those of the western European tradition, can neglect the example of the Holocaust in their discussions of the various theological coordinates which seek to describe the meaning of contemporary life. No less regrettable is the minimization or omission of Auschwitz in textbooks of European and general world history of the twentieth century.

8. The Mission and Christian Ideals

There is yet another dimension of the mission of post-Auschwitz Israel and this, perhaps, is the most sensitive dimension of all. It involved an address to the value system of the Christian faith and to their theological spokespeople. From an ethical point of view, we could hardly deny a dichotomy between the lofty values of the Christian tradition, exemplified resplendently during the Holocaust by the actions of ecclesiastical and lay individuals and groups, and the silence if not hostility of the majority of Christian institutions and the people who pledged allegiance to them. We may perhaps correctly explain the dichotomy as a rejection of Christianity by the people involved, possibly decided upon for the practical purpose of personal or institutional security. But the fact remains that for this majority the lofty ideals of Christianity were overpowered in the incandescent heat of challenge.

Having suffered from this breakdown of values, we Jews have an understandable interest in the strengthening of the practical potency of Christian ideals. In this sense Christian thought ceases to be merely a Christian matter as far as Jews are concerned and becomes a Jewish problem as well.

It requires little delving into Christian theology to recognize that three of its basic formulations have for centuries served to depreciate, ostracize and condemn the Jew. These are the ideas of a Christian covenant superseding the older covenant of the Jews; of a messiah already come, rejection of whom carries the stigma of purblindness, and a salvation (as the various developing groups of Christianity interpreted this word) restricted to the professors of the Church.

Some Christian thinkers, among them notables like Johannes Aagard, Jean Daniélou and Kurt Hruby, continue to nurture the belief in the fulfillment of the Hebrew covenant in a Christian successor, and other related ideas which in the sphere of practical life can only promote depreciation, conversionism and persecution, regardless of any disclaimers to the contrary. The emergence in Christian theology of new directions with evident anti-Jewish thrusts, like the Latin-American Catholic theology of liberation, reveals new settings for the old patronization of the Jewish faith and the Jewish people. The implications of the concept of liberation in the Latin American theology are incidentally chasms apart from the concept as present in the tradition of Judaism.

Other contemporary Christian theologians, sensitized by the enormity of Auschwitz, have sought to reunderstand the relationship of Christian revelation to the religious position of other groups, of whom the most conspicuous as well as closely related are, of course, the Jews. As a result, they have moved toward a recognition of the continuing validity of the Jewish covenant and therefore the Jewish faith. This, in turn, has impelled them to wrestle with other cardinal elements of Christian theology. The resulting insights into Christianity by theologians like Peter Chirico, Eva Fleischner, J. Coert Rylaarsdam, Gregory Baum, Rosemary Radford Ruether and John T. Pawlikowski, for all the differences in their respective approaches, are united in envisioning the continuity of the Hebrew covenant, either as part of a single covenant embracing Judaism and Christianity, or with its Christian counterpart, as one of two parallel covenants, which together and, one may add, only together, reflect God's continuing concern on earth.[27]

Simultaneously with these new considerations, many such thinkers have extended a friendly hand to their Jewish counterparts to discuss in an atmosphere of appreciation for our respective traditions what they correctly and clearly perceive as our mutual problems of theological concern.

Jewish theologians would do well to accept such fraternal overtures with alacrity. The position of some Jewish thinkers that no benefit can be derived from a Jewish-Christian theological dialogue reveals a short-sightedness if not a fear of the fragility of their own theological superstructures.

9. Caveats on the Dialogue

Only in two circumstances could such dialogue prove ineffective. The first is if the intent of the Christian interlocuters is conversionist. The Jewish side will hardly be. Nothwithstanding previous remarks on conversion which apply to religiously non-committed persons Judaism's goals are neither exclusivist nor imperialistic. The aim of its mission is to effect a united humanity under God and not the synagogue. With its primary emphasis on deed rather than creed, Judaism evinces an inherent regard for the earned worth of individuals regardless of their religious denomination and expresses this regard theologically by its assurance of "the world to come" to "righteous of all nations." Ironically, some Christian circles have frequently misrepresented the election and mission as exemplifying a religious exclusivism and imperialism which in reality was a mere projection of their understanding of the Christian faith. To this day some Christian theologians, including a number who are sincerely sympathetic to Jews, believe with George A. F. Knight that,

> there is one thing, and only one thing, that we must communicate to Jews, as to all men, and that is Christ. To refrain from doing so . . . is a form of religious anti-Semitism which is as basically evil as the philosophy of the Nazis.[28]

Such a position makes dialogue useless.

Second, the dialogue would prove ineffective if either Christians or Jews fail to respect the differences in the theological contexts of their respective faiths. Basic to any meaningful Christian-Jewish dialogue must be a recognition that Christianity and Judaism order their theological concepts in different configurations and with different priorities; that terms identical to the two groups often possess divergent connotations; that their respective theologies transcend the elements they hold in common; that it is thus impossible to discuss Jewish theology in any rounded way without a consideration of concepts like *halakhah, mitzvah* and Zion; that similarly, concepts like covenant, messiah and salvation, for all their importance to Judaism, lack there the central position they hold in the Christian faith. The variety of theological approaches within both Judaism and Christianity does not essentially alter this fundamental fact.

The *Zohar*'s comment that God's spirit alights only on people who have made an effort to receive it[29] may well point to the intended meaning of the enigmatic talmudic story of the four second century sages, Ben Azzai, Ben Zoma, Elisha ben Abuya and the incomparable Rabbi Akiba, who entered the "Garden." The Talmud reports that on beholding the Garden's glistening stones of pure marble, Ben Azzai died, Ben Zoma became mad and Elisha ben Abuya lost his faith. Akiba alone left the Garden unscathed.[30]

No one knows for sure to what the Garden, or as it is termed in Hebrew the *Pardes*, alludes. Suggestions that it refers to paradise or to the garden of esoteric philosophy do not readily commend themselves to acceptance. Surely no less plausible is the possibility of the Garden as a parable of life's maturity entered by youth's innocent doctrinaires. On seeing the glistening stones of life's bared realities, some are destroyed, others maddened, still others perverted. Only the small percentage of Akibas retain their idealism and proceed constructively to an address to the world.

In the face of Auschwitz, it is the mature mission of Israel to address the Garden of Life as did Akiba, to retain idealism, reject despair, and serve as a light and inspiration. In this way, above all, the people of Israel can witness that God lives, and that where God lives, hope resides.

Notes

1. Richard L. Rubenstein, *After Auschwitz*, (Indianapolis: Bobbs-Merrill, 1966), p. 154, also pp. 227ff.

2. Emil Fackenheim, "Jewish Values in the Post-Holocaust Future," in *Judaism* 16 (1967) p. 272. Cf. also *idem, God's Presence in History* (New York: New York Univ. Press, 1970), pp. 84ff.

3. Irving Greenberg, "Cloud of Smoke, Pillar of Fire: Judaism, Christianity, and Modernity after the Holocaust," in *Auschwitz: Beginning of a New Era?*, Eva Fleischner, ed. (New York: KTAV, The Cathedral of St. John the Divine, Anti-Defamation League of B'nai B'rith, 1977), pp. 7-55, esp. pp. 26ff.

4. Arthur J. Lelyveld, *Atheism is Dead* (Cleveland & New York: World Publ., 1968), esp. pp. 175ff.

5. Eliezer Berkovits, *Faith After the Holocaust* (New York: KTAV, 1973), pp. 50ff., 94ff., 120.

6. Elliot N. Dorff, "God and the Holocaust," in *Judaism* 26 (1977) pp. 27-34.

7. Ignatz Maybaum, *The Face of God after Auschwitz* (Amsterdam: Polak & Van Gennep, 1965) esp. pp. 81-84.

8. Menahem E. Hartom, "Hirhurim al ha-Shoah" in *Deot* 18 (1961) pp. 28-31.

9. Joel Teitelbaum, *Al ha-Geulah ve-al ha-Temurah* (Brooklyn, N. Y.: Jerusalem Publ., 1967) e.g. pp. 10f, 18, 29, 58.

10. David Chomsky, "Hirhurim al ha-Shoah u-Tekumat Yisrael," in *Deot 19, (1962) pp. 28f.*

11. Issachar Jacobson, "Ha-hashivah ha-Mikrait ve-ha-Shoah," in *Deot* 19 (1962) pp. 26ff.

12. Jacob Rothschild, "Od le-Inyan ha-Erkatah ha-Datit shel ha-Shoah," in *Deot* 20 (1962) pp. 39f.

13. Louis Untermeyer, "Prayer," in James Dalton Morrison, ed., *Masterpieces of Religious Verse* (New York: Harper, 1948) p. 369.

14. Martin A. Cohen, "Are the Jews the Chosen People?" in *Dimensions* (Spring 1968) pp. 1-5.

15. Raphael ben Gabriel Norzi, *Orah Hayyim* (Venice: G. di Gara, 1579), p. 2b.

16. The phrase, found in many places in the literature, is recited daily in the Aleynu prayer; cf. Solomon Schechter, *Some Aspects of Rabbinic Theology* (New York: MacMillan, 1909), pp. 89ff.

17. For examples, cf. Ellis Rivkin, *The Shaping of Jewish History* (New York: Scribner, 1971), esp. Chapters 9 and 10; also Victor C. Ferkiss, *Technological Man* (New York: New American Library, 1969), pp. 205ff.

18. In addition to the works mentioned in note 17, cf. Leonard C. Lewin, *Report from Iron Mountain on the Possibility and Desirability of Peace* (New York: Dial Press, 1967), esp. pp. 57ff. If fictional this report is nonetheless significantly reflective of contemporary geopolitical reality.

19. Ron M. Linton, *Terracide: America's Destruction of Her Living Environment* (Boston: Little, Brown, 1970).

20. Barbara Ward and René Dubois, *Only One Earth* (New York: Norton, 1972), p. 57.

21. *Congressional Record*, February 27, 1970, pp. S2611f.

22. Harry Walters, "Difficult Issues Underlying Food Problems," in *Science* 188 (1975) pp. 524-530.

23. Cf. e.g., Aleksandr Solzhenitsyn, *The Gulag Archipelago* (New York: Harper & Row, 1973), pp. 103-117.

24. Abraham J. Maslow, *The Farther Reaches of Human Nature*, quoted in Gerald and Patricia Mische, *Toward A Human World Order* (New York: Paulist Press, 1977) p. 19.

25. Emil Fackenheim, "The People Israel Lives," in *Christian Century* 87 (1970), pp. 563-568.

26. Ellis Rivkin, *op. cit.*, p. 216.

27. For an excellent survey of these dimensions of Christian thought, cf. Michael B. McGarry, *Christology After Auschwitz* (New York: Paulist Press, 1977), pp. 56-107. On the concept of liberation in Jewish theology, cf. Levi A. Olan, "A Theology of Jewish Liberation," in *Judaism* 27 (1978) pp. 25-32.

28. George A. F. Knight, "Beyond Dialogue," in *Jews and Christians: Preparation for Dialogue*, (Philadelphia: Westminster Press, 1965), pp. 174f.

29. *The Zohar*, Harry Sperling and Maurice Simon, transl. (London: Soncino Press, 1934).

30. TB *Hagigah* 14b.

Rabbinic Literature quoted in this Volume

Avot, The Ethics of the Fathers, Melvin J. Glatt, ed. (New York: Burning Bush Press, 1971)

Mekilta de Rabbi Ishmael, Jacob Z. Lauterbach, transl. and annot., (Philadelphia: Jewish Publ. Co., 1949)

Midrash on Psalms, W. G. Braude, transl. and ed. (New Haven: Yale Univ. Press, 1959)

Midrash Rabbah, H. Freedman and Maurice Simon, transl. and ed. (London: Soncino Press, 1939)

Midrash Shmuel (Crakow, 1893; photo-reprint: Jerusalem, 1964/65).

Mishnah, H. Danby, transl. and annot. (Oxford: Oxford Univ. Press, 1933)

Sifra on Leviticus, S. Koleditzky, ed. (Jerusalem: Hatchiya Press, 1960)

Sifre Deuteronomy, L. Finkelstein and H. S. Horovitz, eds. (New York: Jewish Theological Seminary of America, 1969, reprint)

Talmud Bavli, The Babylonian Talmud, I. Epstein, ed. (London: Soncino Press, 1935/48)

Talmud de Jérusalem, M. Schwab, transl. (Paris: Maisonneuve, 1932, reprint)

Yalkut Shimoni (New York: Horeb, 1925; reprint: Jerusalem: Lewin-Epstein, 1951)

Notes on the Contributors

BEN ZION BOKSER is rabbi of Forest Hills Jewish Center and Adjunct Professor at Queens College, New York. He is editor of the Eternal Light radio program and has published many books, incl. *The Wisdom of the Talmud, Judaism and the Christian Predicament,* and *Jews, Judaism and the State of Israel.* His latest book, a translation of the major writings of *Abraham Isaac Kook,* with a biographical introduction and commentary on his religious philosophy, was published by Paulist Press in 1978.

RABBI MARTIN A. COHEN is Professor of Jewish History at Hebrew Union College-Jewish Institute of Religion, New York. He has written extensively on biblical, rabbinic and early modern history. Dr. Cohen serves as chairman of the national committee on Jewish-Catholic relations of the Anti-Defamation League of B'nai B'rith.

ELLIOT N. DORFF is Associate Professor of Philosophy and Dean of Graduate Studies at the University of Judaism, Los Angeles. He was ordained at Jewish Theological Seminary of America in 1970. His publications include *Jewish Law and Modern Ideology; Conservative Judaism: Our Ancestors to Our Descendants;* and a number of articles on topics in Jewish philosophy and Jewish law, in *Judaism, Conservative Judaism,* and *Hastings Law Journal.*

RABBI LEON KLENICKI is Director of the Department of Jewish-Catholic Relations, Anti-Defamation League of B'nai B'rith. He is Associate Editor of *Face to Face: An Interreligious Bulletin* and teaches at Immaculate Conception Seminary, New Jersey, on "Rabbinic Judaism and Early Christianity" and "Jewish Understanding of Christianity, from Rabbinic Times to the 20th Cent."

LEONARD KRAVITZ is Professor of Midrash and Homiletics at Hebrew Union College-Jewish Institute of Religion, New York. He has published articles in the *Journal of the Central Conference of American Rabbis, Hebrew Union College Annual,* and others. He was ordained by Hebrew Union College-Jewish Institute of Religion in 1954.

DANIEL POLISH is Associate Executive Vice President of the Synagogue Council of America and Director of its Washington office. He serves as rabbi of Temple Beth Ami in Potomac, Md. Dr. Polish was ordained at Hebrew Union College—Jewish Institute of Religion, Cincinnati in 1967. He has taught at Harvard and Tufts Universities and lectured at Boston University and Brandeis College. He has published articles in the *Journal of the Central Conference of American Rabbis, Christianity and Crisis, Reform Judaism,* and *Face to Face.*

The late LEON D. STITSKIN was Professor of Jewish Philosophy at Yeshiva University's Bernard Revel Graduate School, New York, and Dean of West Coast Teachers College, a Los Angeles affiliate. His last book, which was greatly acclaimed, was *Jewish Philosophy, A Study in Personalism* (1978). He wrote a number of other books and articles and was associate editor of *Tradition.* Dr. Stitiskin was ordained at Rabbi Isaac Elchanan Theological Seminary, New York, and served as rabbi in various cities, from 1934–1953.

MANFRED H. VOGEL is Professor of Modern Jewish Thought in the Department of History and Literature of Religions at Northwestern University. He has contributed articles in Jewish philosophy and theology to various learned journals, such as the *Harvard Theological Review, Journal of Religion, Concilium, Journal of Ecumenical Studies.* He translated and introduced Ludwig Feuerbach's *Philosophy of the Future.* Since 1966 he has actively participated in the Jewish-Christian dialogue.

Index of Names and Subjects

187

Rubenstein, Richard 147, 158, 179
Ruether, Rosemary R. 177

S

Saadia, ben Joseph Gaon 97, 106n, 119f, 123, 132n
Sabbath 23, 24, 28, 45
Salvation 4, 41, 83n, 85n
Schechter, Solomon 180n
Sforno, Obaya 89f, 106n
Shakespeare, William 137
Shemah Yisrael 29
Shoah, see Holocaust
Sin 69, 84n, 135
Sinai 5, 27, 54, 93, 141
Social Change 169f
  disorientation and 170
  geopolitics and 169
Solzhenitsyn, Aleksandr 168, 180n
Soviet Jews 8, 171
Spero, Schubert 6, 9n
Spinoza, Baruch 53, 55
Suffering 48, 57
Suffering Servant 48
Survival 140, 146, 171
Synagogue 23

T

Talmud 4, 103, 137
Tanakh 7, 62, 84n
Teitelbaum, Joel 159, 179
Temple 19
Theology
  liberation 177, 180n
  Judaism and 5
Thoma, Clemens 84n

Thomas Aquinas 36n, 128, 130n
Tillich, Paul 83n
Tolerance 101
Torah 18, 93, 122
Trinity 47

U

Universalism 7, 39, 42, 74
Unetane Tokef 122
Untermeyer, Louis 179n

V

Vatican Council II 5, 101, 102, 107
Vogel, Manfred 7, 82n, 85

W

Walters, Harry 180n
Ward, Barbara 180n
Waxman, Meyer 36n
Weber, Max 82n
Weinfeld, M. 81n
Wiesel, Eli 137, 147, 155n
Wilderness Ethic 8, 162-163 passim
Witness
  biblical 89
  Christianity and 84n, 96, 101
  collective 108, 126
  conceptual 109, 115
  dialogue and 101f
  everyday life and 105
  historical 126
  personal 127
  post-rabbinic 97
  rabbinic 93
  universalism of 96, 149

STIMULUS BOOKS are developed by Stimulus Foundation, a not-for-profit organization, and are published by Paulist Press. The Foundation wishes to further the publication of scholarly books on Jewish and Christian topics that are of importance to Judaism and Christianity.

Stimulus Foundation was established by an erstwhile refugee from Nazi Germany who intends to contribute with these publications to the improvement of communication between Jews and Christians.

Books for publication in this Series will be selected by a committee of the Foundation, and offers of manuscripts and works in progress should be addressed to:

Stimulus Foundation
785 West End Ave.
New York, N.Y. 10025